Urban Undesirables

Urban Undesirables presents urban transition experiences over nearly three decades in Bangalore based on the narratives of the city's street-based sex workers. Sex workers – female, male and transgender – have been omnipresent in Bangalore's streets for decades. However, despite being blacklisted as 'undesirable' and hazards to the 'ideal public', they have their own unique imaginaries and narratives of the city and its mutations.

In mapping out their spatial and social ecosystems and experiences with technology, this book redraws, rewrites and relooks at a city and its transformations from their perspectives. The analysis of their experience is anchored to concepts around neoliberal urbanism, gender, labour informality and the politics of technology. The authors take an unconventional journey through their spaces, comrades and battles, through their toil to announce and affirm their individuality and agency, through their empowerment strategies, and through their struggles to reclaim their spaces and assert their identities as informal workers and legitimate citizens of the city.

Neethi P. is with the Indian Institute for Human Settlements, Bangalore. She works on urban labour informality and focuses on women informal workers. She has published in the areas of garments, electronics, ports, home-based work, street vending, sanitation, mill work and sex work. She is the author of *Globalization Lived Locally: A Labour Geography Perspective* (2016).

Anant Kamath is with the National Institute of Advanced Studies, Bangalore. He works on technology and the subaltern in India. Concerns on inequality, urban transition, social mobility, spatiality, gender and caste undergird his published research on technological experiences and outcomes. He is the author of *The Social Context of Technological Experiences* (2020) and *Industrial Innovation, Networks, and Economic Development* (2015).

Urban Undesirables

City Transition and Street-Based Sex Work in Bangalore

Neethi P.
Anant Kamath

CAMBRIDGE
UNIVERSITY PRESS

University Printing House, Cambridge CB2 8BS, United Kingdom

One Liberty Plaza, 20th Floor, New York, NY 10006, USA

477 Williamstown Road, Port Melbourne, vic 3207, Australia

314 to 321, 3rd Floor, Plot No.3, Splendor Forum, Jasola District Centre, New Delhi 110025, India

103 Penang Road, #05–06/07, Visioncrest Commercial, Singapore 238467

Cambridge University Press is part of the University of Cambridge.

It furthers the University's mission by disseminating knowledge in the pursuit of education, learning and research at the highest international levels of excellence.

www.cambridge.org
Information on this title: www.cambridge.org/9781009180214

First published 2022

Printed in India by Thomson Press India Ltd.

A catalogue record for this publication is available from the British Library

ISBN 978-1-009-18021-4 Hardback

To our dearest Madhavi

Contents

Maps

Acknowledgements

No amount of heartfelt thanks will be sufficient for all the voices, hearts and minds that built this work; their narrations echo the lives and accounts of the faceless thousands who survive in the margins, labelled as immoral people and undesired workers. We sincerely hope this book does at least a small measure of justice to immortalise their words, sentiments and experiences.

Thanks are due, paramount, to the organisation Sangama and their head, Rajesh, who has been our guide through the entire process logistically, motivationally and, to a great extent, intellectually too. Equal is our deep gratitude to Prabhavati, who greatly facilitated the rapport building and conversations with the street-based sex workers. Thanks are due to Azim Premji University, which funded the entire fieldwork.

While there are nearly sixty individuals who have narrated stories and anecdotes from their life, most of whom cannot be named here, there are a number of other people and organisations whose inputs must be acknowledged. These include the Alternative Law Forum (ALF), Aneka, Solidarity Foundation, Sadhana Mahila Sangha, Bhorukha Charitable Trust, Samara, the National Network of Sex Workers, and the Karnataka Sex Workers' Union. We must mention Gowthaman, Vinay Sreenivasa, Lekha and Mohammed Afeef of ALF; Shubha Chacko; Prof. Rajendran of the People's Union for Civil Liberties (PUCL); Adv. Venkatesh of Reach Law; Shakun; Bhagyalakshmi of Society for People's Action for Development (SPAD); Nisha Gulur, Shivani and Ashwini of Sangama; Kumar of Payana; and the incomparable Chamundi at Kolar.

Besides them, we would like to thank Anant Maringanti, Solomon Benjamin and J. Devika; the anonymous reviewers of *City*, *Globalizations* and *Gender, Technology, Development*; Supriya Roy Chowdhury and the reading group on 'labour and the city'; Mathew Idiculla and the Critical Cities Circle; Vinay Kumar; and Simran Arora. We have also benefited from interacting with our fellow participants at the Indian Institute for Human Settlements (IIHS) Urban Arc 2020; the Society for the Social Studies of Science at Toronto; the IIHS Urban Lens 2021; the Online Workshop conducted by WIEGO (Women in Informal Employment: Globalizing and Organizing); and 'Sensing the City' by the Urban Studies Institute of the University of Antwerp, Belgium.

Our respective institutions – the Indian Institute for Human Settlements (IIHS) and the National Institute of Advanced Studies (NIAS) – deserve many thanks for providing a congenial, stimulating and accommodating environment to write out, revise and complete this work. We must mention Benson Isaac, Chetan Choithani and Aleena Sebastian for taking the time to painstakingly read portions of the manuscript with a critical and compassionate eye. Of course, we also thank the anonymous reviewers of this book manuscript, the staff at Cambridge University Press and especially Anwesha Rana for guiding us all through.

A big thanks to Raji for helping us peacefully devote our minds to this work, to our parents who have encouraged us and, finally, to our dearest Madhavi, to whom we dedicate this book about her fellow Bangaloreans.

1

Libidinal City, Outcast Workers

India's Silicon Valley, a garden city, a modern metropolis, a global city, the future city, a pensioners' paradise – but a *sex workers'* city? While the list of sobriquets for Bangalore city is endless, the last one may seem the least likely and might even raise shudders of revulsion. In one of the earliest conversations that we had when gathering the material for this book, a retired street-based sex worker, the moment she heard what we were exploring, remarked with eyes tightly shut and arms stretched over her head:

> Oh Bangalore? Just sex, sex, sex everywhere!

While this could have easily been passed off as just brash mockery from a woman whose body and spirit, like tens of thousands of others in her guild, has borne first-hand the grit and lechery of the streets of this metropolis for decades, little did we realise that she was quite accurate in her feisty statement. It slowly unfolded to us that her pronouncement applied to Bangalore's streets and public spaces so much more than it did to so many other cities in India, because while sex workers in cities such as Mumbai or Kolkata are associated mostly with 'red-light areas', the whole of Bangalore city is one.

Cities like Bangalore are reminiscent of a hackneyed Dickensian condition: the best of places, the worst of places, bringing hope, bringing despair, capable of liberating, capable of overwhelming, offering solace, offering turbulence, a heaven, a hell, where one can gain everything, and where one can be left with nothing. City spaces are the stage upon which street-based sex workers encounter these clashing conditions, perhaps all of them within the course of a single day. All of us claim our romance with the city spaces we regularly traverse, along with the bus stops we wait in, the traffic signals we cross, the benches we occasionally sit on, the eateries we enjoy and the businesses we engage in. When elbowing through the rabble of KR Market, or while stumbling upon countless faces in Majestic, or even while strolling by the shimmering emporia of MG Road, the 'decent' people who claim Bangalore as rightfully only theirs would not be able to (or would not choose to) see street-based sex workers. However, the truth is that street-based sex workers are actually *everywhere* in Bangalore, sadly unacknowledged as integral actors among the dramatis personae of a city that desperately exerts to glitter on the world stage.

The purpose of this book is not to document a linear chronicle of their life and times, if such a thing were at all possible. This is an account of the experience of the street-based sex workers of Bangalore – male, female and transgender – with respect to the city's sweeping changes over the last three decades. During this period, that is, from the early 1990s, city spaces in Bangalore have steadily been forced to transition from being collages of urban commons to parcels of urban commerce. Street-based sex workers have for long been an integral part of the city's human tapestry as a subaltern informal workforce, countless in number, probably numbering more than software engineers in this 'IT Capital' or pensioners in this 'pensioner paradise'. But they have been consistently denied their place in the city and have been systematically losing their tracts of life and livelihood due to the spectre of urban transition that has haunted and sprawled through the public spaces of Bangalore. Street-based sex workers claim the city to be as much theirs as do software engineers, factory workers, shopkeepers, food vendors, teachers, lawmakers, the police and other 'decent' people. However, multi-layered and perpetually tormenting vulnerabilities in their operations, even threatening their very existence, have not only dispossessed them of their positions in the city landscape they have dotted for decades but also disregarded even the *existence* of a story of city change from their viewpoint. Their image and experience of the city have been muted.

The aim of this book is exactly to present this story. It is about a people who seem invisible in a city but are omnipresent and have experienced the city's metamorphosis in their own distinctive way, which needs to be proclaimed for all to see and understand. We trace the locus of spaces and the menagerie of actors around street-based sex work that construct their material and social experiences. We bring out the ordeals of Bangalore's overwhelming transition through textured accounts provided by the voices of female, male and transgender street-based sex workers themselves. Five dozen street-based sex workers in Bangalore, in eighteen months of conversations, provided torrents of narratives of the theatre that *their* Bangalore is and of the actors in that theatre who frame the human cartography around street-based sex work.

Abstaining from generalisation, this book focuses on the particular places, the lived experiences, structures, relationships and the many ecosystems around street-based sex work. We redraw, rewrite and relook a city from their eyes, their feet and their minds. For the last three decades or so, the meaning of 'public space' has undergone a dramatic change, alongside the very definition of who ought to constitute the 'public' in a city like Bangalore. Public spaces have been recast as accessible only to those legitimate individuals and social groups who fit into the imagined city and do not pollute its image. Street-based sex workers, who have been a ubiquitous and integral part of the human landscape of Bangalore, are seen as unpleasant eyesores in a city conjured up as 'sleek' and 'modern', a setting which only certain kinds of people can claim the right to. In the revanchist construction of the vista that is Bangalore, these serious immoral blots are to be conveniently pushed away and their existence is to be denied altogether. The saga of struggle continues for street-based sex workers in this city, not only with regard to their traditional crusades of identity, individuality, citizenship and continuing health hazards but also in their battle to claim their right to their city.

We chart out the experience of urban transition in Bangalore from their standpoint, which is quite a contrast with what generally constitutes mainstream conversations around city change in Bangalore. Often – conveniently, lethargically or deliberately – Bangalore is misunderstood as an IT city at its heart, while in reality this is but only one layer of a metropolis that is a miscellany of multiple layers of work- and spatial ecologies. We draw out the loci of the city's transition by plotting the expected and unconventional elements in their cityscape and trace the rivulets of narratives of their tempestuous experiences in getting to grips with the dramatic and jagged transformation of Bangalore city. We bring out the dismal intersections that undergird their life and work and introduce the roles of the myriad actors and agents that both facilitate and scorn their existence in the process of envisioning and unravelling the realisation of a city. We also present their strategies of empowerment and response to all these, their migration to digital platforms and the vagaries within those new spaces, and the struggles to reclaim their city.

Through this book, we take an unconventional journey through their spaces, comrades and battles, through the rugged drama that their working lives are, through their toil to announce and affirm their agency and through their struggles to claim their spaces and their identities as informal workers. Chapter by chapter, we voyage through these. This first chapter, aimed at laying out a sturdy foundational framework of understanding, is quite distinct in content and timbre with the chapters that follow in this book, which are based almost entirely on material from the ground – narratives, places, experiences and responses. This chapter presents the conceptual cores of this book: around urban transition, demographic inclusion, labour marginalisation and the narratives of street-based sex work; it is within these frameworks that we present the sex workers' story of city transition. Wantonly, in this chapter (or in this book as such), we have avoided either promising the reader any new concepts or overcomplicating the dominant theories, concepts and frameworks that support us. This is to ensure that we are held up by a theoretical scaffolding that is sturdy but which does not end up stonewalling us within; this would also allow the narratives from the workers themselves to guide us all the way through. Chapter 1 hence provides a dense study of the imaginary of a city, of who may constitute and work in that imagined city and of where the place of street-based sex workers is in that imagination of the city, its people and its workforce. Chapter 2 lays out why we inclined towards narratives and oral histories, the narrators we sought and the places that form our stage. After these two chapters, we pause academic voices and begin the uninterrupted flow of their narratives.

In Chapter 3, we familiarise ourselves with the full collection of characters who frame the human medley around street-based sex work in Bangalore city, understand taxonomy and nomenclature in this occupation, visit issues of caste and class, explore entry into and exit from sex work, reflect on families and aspirations, assess client spectrum, solicitation and negotiation and reveal the intensity of violence. Chapter 4 details and unravels the assemblage that makes up their workspaces, weaving out the spatial cartography of street-based sex work, including expected and surprising places and artefacts, territories and solidarities, commons and issues of inclusion and fragments of the ambience in these spaces. Chapter 5 then charts out, from their own narratives, the upheavals in their city and among those who were their ancillary actors, and the central human actor in their occupation – the police; in this chapter, we draw from nearly three decades of archival material on sex work in the city and also provide maps depicting the loss of spaces in the major focus areas. Our work therefore might be one of the first attempts to use archival material to document urban transition from the point of view of street-based sex workers in Bangalore. One of the reactions to their traumatic experiences in the loss of city spaces and supporting actors has been the migration to digital platforms, which brings along with it the intense organisation, reorganisation and engagement with technology through mobile phones, the media and increased surveillance. This is the concern of Chapter 6, where we look at technological experiences in their lives and livelihoods as an intersection with body politics and their negotiations therein; this chapter introduces a few conceptual insights that enrich the interpretation of the narrated account around technological experiences. Finally, in Chapter 7, we conclude on a buoyant chord, understanding their collective mobilisation and responses on the ground to reclaim their city and fight for their civil rights.

To begin this expedition, we first understand how 'decent' people imagine a 'city' and its 'workforce'. Who are the 'desired' in the human ecology of the fabricated urban imaginary? Who are preferred as workers within urban spaces? Who are, therefore, pushed to the edges in the human-spatial and the commercial-spatial spectra in the city? We engage with these questions in this first chapter – first, by understanding the imagined city, its desired human zoo and who in that assemblage is a 'proper' worker and a 'proper' citizen.

Building an Imaginary

Few other cities have captured the idea of 'modern' in the Indian imagination the way Bangalore has. With a long history of over a century and more in defining the frontiers of education, research and production in the domains of science and engineering, Bangalore proudly maintained itself as a beacon in those spheres. It was, after all, the first city in India to be electrified. From the late nineteenth century onwards, institutions of national importance were installed in Bangalore with full patronage from state and society, and soon after independence, a number of high-technology and engineering industries began to be instituted here. By the 1980s and especially in the 1990s, Bangalore claimed to be the epicentre of India's information technology-enabled services (ITES) sector and its several ancillary industries, soon awarding itself the title of 'Silicon Valley of India'.

What it actually resembles in reality and lived experience, however, is a typical fast-growing second-tier classic industrial city in Latin America or South East Asia, hosting a hub for low-paid garment production, countless small workshops catering to localised economies, a burgeoning informal sector and an electronics industry with only a minority of its firms actually specialising in computer systems.[1] Bangalore is an incongruity, where some people live in a 'highly advanced information society' while the others rely on informal, insecure, low-paid, low-quality economic activities, inequalities nakedly visible both within the city and right outside of city limits.[2] The city's ITES sector built itself on existing class and caste divisions in Indian society rather than absorbing, either directly or downstream, a broader cross-section of the population into the technical–professional workforce; this created a stark urban dualism with polarised labour markets.[3] As a 'Silicon Valley', Bangalore began to resemble less its alleged sister district in California with respect to innovativeness and more in terms of a showpiece of socio-economic inequality (especially at its peri-urban fringes), mass displacement and dispossession, social tensions, incomparable traffic crises and severe water and sewage issues – more like a world-city nightmare.[4] City-planning, too, seemed to have little regard to relevant and everyday informal activities on the streets, for that matter urban informality as such.[5] Bangalore has always tried to be something else – a Singapore, Silicon Valley, futuristic city, pensioner's paradise – than what it actually is.

But, turning a blind eye towards these dazzling contradictory realities, anyone living and working around Bangalore, or migrating into it, soon attained a status of being fortunate enough to live in a 'sleek' and 'modern' city, with only a few stray crumbs left over from either the ruins of the British era or the burdens of regressive Indian traditions (or both), which were deep in the character of other cities such as Delhi, Mumbai or Kolkata. Jawaharlal Nehru himself had presided over the metaphorical investiture of Bangalore as the city of the future because

[1] Heitzman (2004); Nair (2005).
[2] Ibid.
[3] Upadhya and Vasavi (2006); Upadhya (2007).
[4] Goldman (2008, 2010).
[5] Roy (2009); Keswani (2019); Keswani and Bhagavatula (2020).

it did not carry the burden of history.[6] Bangalore continues to occupy a special position in the imagination of those seeking a 'modern and resurgent' India,[7] its linguistic and cultural hyper-heterogeneity crucial to this modern imaginary and the perennially congenial weather serving as its unfailing trump card. Here was a city which supposedly did not care about chief ministers usually lasting half their terms and their cronies squabbling to gain and regain power, and which did not allow sluggish bureaucratic machinery to obstruct its futuristic trajectory – instead, it spring-boarded on the industrial and economic policy shifts of the 1990s and pinned itself on the sociocultural map of India as a shining futuristic beacon. In this polis of modernity, supposedly, skill mattered more than caste, the urgent quest for upward economic mobility mattered more than archaic hankerings for political loot and immediate issues of 'development' mattered much more than bloodied divisive issues around constructing a temple thousands of miles away. This was a space where spreading gardens and avenues harmoniously fitted with peaking glass and concrete towers and where white-collared urbane software engineers traversed earthy groundnut festivals and muggy flower markets. Here was where the twain – the traditional and the contemporary, the unhurried retiree and the whizzing youngster – crossed paths, not hurling their encumbrances at one another but amalgamating their virtues fruitfully. Bangalore was not just a 'modern Indian city' but an 'international' one.

Such chimeras are not unusual, as urban imaginaries are generally inclined to be 'international' in character, shaping lived experiences for people and producing an urban scape around them.[8] The tenor of these urban imaginaries not only mould how people perceive their city but also what materialises around them in terms of the city's planning, how people work, how they involve in recreation, how they perceive the role of government, what flavours of development come about, and so on.[9] These imaginaries have been influenced greatly by the urban middle (and upper) classes by the intensified circulation of images of 'global' cities through media, popular culture and metropolitan planning.[10] The attractions of life (real or fantasised) under Anglo-American capitalism pushed urban visions of 'modern' infrastructure that meant high-technology imports and new service industries, giving its more privileged citizens their right to unhindered access to public spaces and a clean and healthy urban environment.[11] As a result, the realities of how the city is *actually* lived out was cast aside for a more fantasised view of how a 'global city' functions.[12] And as the case generally is with 'global

[6] Nair (2005).

[7] Benjamin (2010).

[8] Anjaria and McFarlane (2011).

[9] Ibid.

[10] Borrowed from Partha Chatterjee (2004).

[11] Ibid.

[12] Anjaria and McFarlane (2011).

cities', high-income jobs that harmonised with the high-priced urban space whipped up a gold-rush that attracted gargantuan swarms of workers to low-wage jobs that for them did not translate into high-opportunity or sustained upward mobility but instead legitimised their disempowerment.[13] This sort of urban imaginary became the 'common-sense' vision of 'our city', culturised, conditioned and ingrained the public imagination, with the normalisation of the status quo and valorisation of extreme inequality (casting it as inevitable, even beneficial).[14]

At the nucleus of all this has been the reorientation of the state in affairs of political economy. Neoliberal capitalism has percolated through all layers of economy and society, and the nation has been recast as an attractive 'investment destination brand'.[15] Contrary to popular belief, the state has not withdrawn across the board for the benefit of everyone's material prosperity but has retracted for some while facilitating others, recklessly applying market principles in all aspects of economic life for the benefit of big capital.[16] The state – which was supposed to be working for everyone, for whom it was supposed to assure economic prosperity alongside social justice – eventually reoriented itself to being a hesitant (and increasingly shrinking) provider of welfare services while moving in more proactively to patronise and facilitate big capital (local, regional or global) and consumerism.[17] Gradually, the well-to-do were able to create their own exclusive experiences such as shopping malls, gated residential spaces and corporate enclaves, while the urban poor and working classes were gravely affected and their opportunities to create such experiences for themselves systematically left out.[18] Urban life, therefore, has become a divergent and uneven experience; it has become more disconnected for many, with empowerment and redistribution being put on the retreat and economic growth strengthening as a priority.[19] Urban transition wanes as an organic or democratic process and instead transmutes towards greater privatisation, gentrification and exclusion.[20] In this view, the city warmed up as a 'safe' haven for market-oriented development and elite consumption practices, where semi-public, semi-private spaces are generated and urban public spaces are gradually commodified, modifying citizens into consumers

---

[13] Sassen (2002).

[14] Adapted from Gramscian thought, borrowing from Crehan (2016), as well as Gupta (2000), Robotham (2005) and Natrajan (2012).

[15] Kaur (2020).

[16] Büdenbender and Zupan (2017).

[17] Nair (2012).

[18] Desai and Sanyal (2012).

[19] Brenner and Theodore (2002); Short (2014).

[20] Nagendra (2016).

and marginalising select social groups.[21] Sites of consumption are planned in accordance with Anglo-American silhouettes, as if from a catalogue and with no relation or local history and culture, attracting citizens-turned-consumers to immerse into them.[22] Ground-level processes – such as local governance and neighbourhood politics, civic life and the moulding of spatial histories – are also not spared of neoliberal values.[23] Selective inclusion and exclusion, and gendered injustices, get imprinted into the urban experience, and the city turns into a battleground for a micro-politics of urban life, wherein access, control and representation become battle-points, with routine clashes between spatial rights and spatial claims.[24] Urban freedoms and urban control fight head-on, emerging as deep contradictions of urbanity.[25] Direct or indirect violence, physical or non-physical, and in forms ranging from structural, direct or personal, and cultural, becomes a routine experience.[26] All this is, quite simply, *neoliberal urbanism* in thought and in practice, in life and in livelihood, manifesting in restructuring, rescaling, reconstitution and mutation.[27]

However, what we must bear in mind at all times is that the direction of the relationship is not simply 'neoliberal urbanism shaping urban transition', but that both reproduce one another in sombre harmony. Cities have served as ideal settings for the reproduction, mutation and reconstitution of neoliberal urbanism themselves.[28] They have become the sites of the most acute articulation of neoliberalism, such that the placating of corporate interest and its involvement in urban governance and planning has become 'common sense' to public administration and the popular press, and to the extent that inner cities have emerged as indicative spaces through which to evaluate the march of neoliberalism.[29] While images associated with neoliberal urbanism[30] were traditionally associated with the character and transition of megacities such as New York or London or fin-de-siècle Paris in the West, we now know that the present neoliberal variety of urban transition has diffused globally, and its presence has steadily percolated through Asia and South America. In fact, Neil Smith's work, and the scholarly literature on the subject that bloomed following his thought, has shown that the developing world is actually a leading frontier at which the

---

[21] Brenner and Theodore (2002); Short (2014).

[22] Bender (2007).

[23] Brenner and Theodore (2002); Ranganathan (2011).

[24] Hubbard (2004a, 2004b); Tonkiss (2005); Mohan (2017).

[25] Tonkiss (2005).

[26] Galtung (1969).

[27] Peck and Tickell (2002); Hubbard (2004a, 2004b); Banerjee-Guha (2010).

[28] Brenner and Theodore (2002); Banerjee-Guha (2010).

[29] Hackworth (2011).

[30] For more robust accounts and analyses of neoliberal urbanism, see Harvey (1989); Weber (2002); Walks (2006); Leitner et al. (2007); Büdenbender and Zupan (2017).

process is unfolding, in its regional variations.[31] Its unfurl and spread are glaringly visible in India too, particularly in metropolitan cities and emerging towns. One such city in India that has been offered extensive attention is Mumbai, where real-estate price inflation as well as intricate connections with global financial markets has shaped it into an archetypical neoliberal city and has attracted analyses on urban neoliberalism, spatial governmentality and exclusion.[32] There has also been academic attention on Delhi, Kolkata and Bangalore.[33]

Associated with urban neoliberalism is the process of *revanchism*, which we also adopt as one of the foundational pillars of this book. 'Revanchism' (from the French *revanche* relating to revenge) was first offered a serious treatment by Neil Smith in the 1990s, based on the spatial and economic processes and exclusions observed in New York City at the end of the twentieth century. Smith employed this term to indicate a 'vengeful' reclamation of city spaces from specified groups such as minorities, the working class, women, the homeless, sexual minorities, immigrants and others.[34] This vengeance, stoking and riding on aggressive public sentiment and its endorsement for forceful action, is directed against progressive movements, multiculturalism and immigration, and lays the ground for violence against these aforesaid groups. Stripped of its veneer of reclaiming morality and gentrified-correctness in urban space, revanchism simply operationalises into 'purifying the neighbourhood', market-oriented development and eradicating 'undesirables' in the human composition to portray a positive image of that city.[35] Portrayals of such an image include cosmetic refurbishing and privatisation of public spaces such as streets, parks, public toilets, recreational areas, and so on, which results in systematically excluding and physically displacing certain targeted communities and values.[36] City spaces, especially around their centre, become a corporate landscape of leisure and playgrounds of consumerism catering to the affluent to attract global capital that feeds itself.[37]

---

[31] Ferguson and Gupta (2002); Ghertner (2014); Yang and Zhou (2018); Hudalah and Adharina (2019).

[32] Whitehead and More (2007); Davidson (2007); Banerjee-Guha (2010); Ghertner (2014).

[33] See Ghertner (2014), Goldman (2008), Holst (2015), and Rao (2016) for Delhi; and Bose (2015) and Doshi (2015) for Kolkata. For Bangalore, see Nair (2005), Goldman (2008, 2010), Vanka (2014), Damodaran and Haldar (2016), D'Souza and Nagendra (2011), Kaliyanda (2016), Derkzen et al. (2017), and Chava, Newman and Tiwari (2018).

[34] Smith (1996). An important study in this regard has been Murphy and Venkatesh (2006) in the context of policing, reclamation of the city and its impact on sex work.

[35] Smith (1996, 2002); Tani (2002); Johnsen and Fitzpatrick (2010); Swanson (2007).

[36] Duncan (1996); Mitchell (1997, 2003); Allen (1999); Shapiro (2000); Amster (2003); Atkinson (2003); Macki, Bromley and Brown (2014).

[37] Hubbard (2004a, 2004b); Swanson (2007).

The idea of the 'revanchist city' has proved to be highly influential[38] in recent years, especially in building the discourse around marginalised urban communities. Whatever may be its type or local variation, aesthetics politics that is performed within urban space – encapsulated in the simple but treacherous term *image* – remains at the heart of revanchism and urban gentrification.[39] In the process of building and maintaining an 'image', a new genre of culture and power dominates, social relationships are reconfigured and spaces are appropriated by forces of privatisation, commercialisation and aestheticisation.[40] While places were traditionally politically fluid, their informally and organically constructed constitution and their heterogeneity weakens with gentrification and neoliberal urbanism.[41] Urban space appears to 'forget' its time-honoured character of unrestricted and universal access, where economies were constructed informally but not haphazardly or neutrally, and where complexities delightfully abounded in the city's objects, spaces, persons and practices.[42] 'Redevelopment' and infrastructure projects, accompanied by exceptionalising certain unpleasant aspects of cities and institutionally displacing unpleasant people from these newly remade spaces, begin to produce new dramas of social and spatial relations.[43]

---

[38] Academic studies such as Johnsen and Fitzpatrick (2010) expanded on this concept, exploring its mechanisms and the articulation and impact of enforcement initiatives arising out of it. They even categorised it into various types, including legislative (such as the criminalisation of street lifestyles), physical (manipulation of urban space to exclude undesirable groups or activities), surveillant (in the form of increased surveillance and policing of public or quasi-public spaces) and discursive (in the portrayal of homeless people as dirty, dangerous or culpable for their own plight). Other studies such as Atkinson (2003) outlined different strands of the revanchist – such as, a mode of governance to control the public realm and to dictate recognised or approved uses for such space, a set of programmes designed to secure public space (Davis 1990) or the behaviour of users of such space, a prophetic and dystopian conception in which public spaces and the city are seen, in themselves, to represent a form of urban malaise and distress from which vengeful policies may act as an ameliorative, and a reference to economic objectives in the connection between urban economic development and the need to secure capital investment. He unravels how conformity becomes an increasingly essential prerequisite to utilise and enjoy a public space, with deviant individuals and groups systematically penalised in the process. Urban gentrification is, in general, a feminist issue too, as shown recently by Kern (2020). See also Fyfe (1991) and Fyfe and Bannister (1996).

[39] Swanson (2007); Büdenbender and Zupan (2017).

[40] Duncan (1996); De Neeve and Donner (2006).

[41] Duncan (1996); Simone (2004); De Neve and Donner (2006); Massey, Allen and Pile (1999); Keswani and Bhagavatula (2015); Keswani (2019).

[42] Hubbard (2004a, 2004b); Sanders (2004); Simone (2004).

[43] Hubbard (2004a, 2004b); Burte and Kamath (2017).

All this gradually dissolves the idea of the city as a space of open flow, human interaction and proximate reflexivity,[44] with Lefebvrian rhythms orchestrating the consonant and dissonant harmonies of daily urban life. Instead, what we have is neoliberal urbanism reworking urban space (for that matter, urbanity) as purified, decontaminated, reclaimed and made respectable.[45] Urban space becomes the principal theatre whose social, economic, political, architectural and commercial components become gentrified. The full choreography of all this is only glaringly evident in Bangalore.

Urban Pseudo-Invisibles

Over time, Bangalore has ceased to be a city for all and has begun to look like a brand for the few, where inequalities are produced, reproduced and contested.[46] These imaginaries were not provided by any singular overarching authority but by a collective reverie of a few dominant groups. This brand of urbanism holds social exclusion as one of its cornerstones, where admission is offered to those who choose to define themselves (and only those like themselves) as 'the city' while the rest immediately become outcasts and ugly sights that not only scar the visual image of this great city but need to be eventually cleaned out by employing tactics ranging from quiet disdain right up to brute force. The remodelling and restyling of urban spaces redefine *who* the public is, drawing out new boundaries for everyday spatial citizenship.[47] Regulation of permissibility and visibility of disorderly bodies dovetails seamlessly with neoliberal urbanism, gentrification and revanchism, as these bodies are perceived as threats to the 'urban renaissance' who commit 'quality of life' crimes.[48]

Completely brushed aside is the fact that a city cannot be simplistically conceived as having a monolithic geography, a selective and linear history and a singular future, where people who wholesomely participate in the urban economy move around unnoticed and unseen.[49] In the new imaginary of the public space spawned by corporate-led urban design, even 'sitting outside' can generate uneasiness and anxiety among the marginalised, who are then deliberately 'othered' and displaced or forced to isolate or separate, and routinely disciplined violently, often proactively, by policy.[50] By marking the 'undesirable

---

[44] Amin and Thrift (2002).
[45] Brenner and Theodore (2002).
[46] Mohan (2017).
[47] Massey (2011); Tonkiss (2005).
[48] Hubbard (2004a, 2004b).
[49] Massey, Allen and Pile (1999).
[50] Galtung (1990); Sanders (2004); Kunkel (2016); Rishbeth and Rogaly (2018). See also Rogaly (2016).

element', strategies for exclusion (and hence close surveillance) are created.[51] Other strategies include self-imposed spatial segregation among the middle and upper classes to remove themselves from the city's 'dangerous' quarters and to retreat to fortified enclaves and high-security gated and walled communities that are socially homogenous and therefore considered 'safe'.[52] Spatial segregation produces social segregation, which changes the nature of urban space, city life and social interaction.[53]

Those on the drawing board drafting blueprints of the imagined city informally create the 'ideal public', classifying 'strangers' in terms of how they can be recognised as being roughly equal to themselves, different or inferior.[54] And too often, these strangers find themselves in the eye of a storm where tensions are drawn between the aesthetics of the city and the aesthetics of the body.[55] These strangers lend disfigurement to the urban human composition and include those who visually and behaviourally fit the grotesqueness bill (such as transgender individuals), those who hold revolting amorous preferences (such as homosexuals) or those who dirty the lanes and boulevards with their immoral activities (such as street-based sex workers). The last group, particularly, carries multiple layers of aversive attributes, which range from insulting nomenclatures around their livelihood to the visual unpleasantness of their stance and gait and to the utter immorality at the core of their livelihood.[56] Particularly with women sex workers and transgender sex workers, the state and 'decent' citizenry have colluded to cast them as pathological to the vision and spirit of the city. To these workers, the promises of scintillating metropolitan visions are meaningless and inedible, while the modus operandi set forth by 'decent' people towards attaining these glittering goals are fraught with danger and threaten their very existence. For street-based sex workers, who have been neatly docketed as threats, the realisation of the Bangalore imaginary has been a living nightmare. To be marginal in such a city is to be a threat to the rest of the city.[57] Modernity, for them, has been nothing but the modernisation of misery.[58]

There are innumerable accounts of communities such as street vendors or slum dwellers who have lost their livelihoods and spaces due to such exclusionary imaginaries and practices. These are indeed despairing tales, but they are still at least heard. Given their physical visibility, open self-identification, solidarity, and

---

[51] Prasad-Aleyamma (2018).
[52] Kelly (2008).
[53] Ibid.
[54] Froystad (2006).
[55] Swanson (2007).
[56] See the work of Hubbard (1998, 1999, 2004a, 2004b) and Kerkin (2003).
[57] Short (2014).
[58] Wacquant (2008).

so on, it is relatively less complicated[59] a task to document their urban experiences. With street-based sex workers, however, the task is fraught with thorny obstacles in even trying to identify them. The situation of these communities in an urban human landscape is particularly precarious in terms of life and livelihood, where terms such as 'exclusion' underestimate the problem.

At this point, let us visit the work of Partha Chatterjee, [60] which helps us demarcate the difference between Citizens and Populations.[61] While Populations are administrative categories that have designated or attributed social and economic features and are useful for drawing out boundaries of inclusion for targeting of welfare, Citizens are those advantaged individuals and groups who have the biggest stake in the share of state sovereignty and therefore have a greater say in claiming rights for themselves and those like them. Populations are, drawing from Chatterjee, subject to simple classifications and usually do not attract the immediate and concerned attention of authorities. Citizens, however, constitute the fabled 'civil society' in a city that have constitutionally protected rights both as individuals and associations and are more legitimate in the eyes of the state. However, Citizens and Populations are *visible* creatures when we chart out who the city is. How does one classify a group of individuals who do not have the privilege to view themselves as Citizens (first-class inhabitants, essentially the *bhadralok*, even if not highly genteel) but at the same time do not accurately fit into the Populations (second-class inhabitants) as well? How do you go about bearing the weight of neoliberal urban transition when you are, in the first place, denied a tangible presence in the human ecology of the city? How are those who are subaltern even to the Populations to be labelled?

It turns out that they are not entirely invisible but are, adapting from Fran Tonkiss,[62] *pseudo-invisibles*. That is, they sink in and out of the Populations. Street-based sex workers, though neatly falling into the category of invisibles in the meta-narrative, are not bodily inconspicuous in the physical spaces of the city. In the pre-neoliberal city, they were castigated the moment their stance, gait, profession, and so forth were visible but were otherwise left to their own immoral and unsanitary sanctums, whether in lodges or alleys or groves. In the neoliberal city, however, they are deliberately hunted down. This is why, even though they have been, for the most part, unseen and to their own, they are routinely hounded. We propose that while the demarcation between Citizens and Populations is more comprehendible (though certainly not a stark non-porous binary), the boundaries between Populations and pseudo-invisibles is

---

[59] We say 'less complicated' with the full understanding of the risk of oversimplification it connotes.

[60] Chatterjee (2004).

[61] The capitalisation in these terms is ours.

[62] Tonkiss (2005).

not only blurry but intermittently morphing too. Individuals and groups bob in and out of invisibility, with some in the Populations occasionally becoming pseudo-invisibles and vice versa. They sink into invisibility when popular and policy imaginaries are churned out but instantly become undesirable visibles when popular and policy imaginaries and media-gentrification operations are bulldozing both buildings and humans out of the way.

To help us further build the idea of the pseudo-invisible, let us also visit another classification of the urban human menagerie that has been elegantly schemed out by Peter Marcuse.[63] Along material lines, the city hosts the *excluded* (at the margins and without the protections won by the working class for labour), the *working class* (including the euphemistic middle class, white- as well as blue-collar workers, skilled as well as unskilled, service as well as manufacturing workers, but underpaid and producing profit for others), *small business people* (individual proprietors, small entrepreneurs, craftsmen), the *gentry* (the more successful small businesspeople, professionals, highly paid workers of multinational firms), *capitalists* (owners and decision-making managers of large business enterprises), the *establishment intelligentsia* (the media, academics, artists and others active in the ideological aspect of the production processes), and the *politically powerful* (including aspirants to high public office). The working class and the excluded may be combined as the *deprived*. Along cultural lines, there are the *directly oppressed* (along sociological and cultural aspects but could even be included in the economic sense), the *alienated* (of any economic class, artists, a significant part of the intelligentsia, in resistance to the dominant system), the *insecure* (a shifting group, varying with conjunctural changes, including much of the working class and periodically some of the gentry), the *hapless lackeys of power* (including some of the gentry and some of the intelligentsia) and the *underwriters and beneficiaries* of the established cultural and ideological hegemonic attitudes and beliefs.

While the usual practice in scholarly work is to seek more granularity in social classification, here, we actually move in the opposite direction and conflate a few of Marcuse's categories, assimilating them into Tonkiss' 'pseudo-invisibles' because the categories of street-based sex workers that are of interest to this book fall into multiple brackets in the Marcuse categorisation – that is, the excluded, some of the working class, some of the directly oppressed, some of the alienated and some of the insecure.

Street-based sex workers are hence *pseudo-invisibles*, getting ensnared in the merciless jaws of neoliberal urban transition through exposure, policing and other regulatory strategies.

As a simple example to help understand Citizens/Populations/pseudo-invisibles, let us take Cubbon Park, Bangalore's largest continuous green space.

---

[63] Marcuse (2009).

The Cubbon Park Walkers' Association are certainly Citizens of the park, food vendors in the park become its Populations, but sex workers and transgender individuals for whom these spaces have traditionally been sites of informal work are pseudo-invisibles. They cannot be identified by the Citizenry of Cubbon Park upon immediate sight, but they are familiar to its Populations and are immediately disowned by the latter and subject to condescension by the former whenever unearthed or exposed. Harini Nagendra[64] has pointed out that all over the world, civic movements around parks have actually been quite elitist while the subaltern (here, pseudo-invisibles) have systematically been left out (here, dispelled of), due to which 'saving of parks' has in reality been their gentrification, and urban green spaces have been made to look like semi-private property. However, green spaces have, globally, been as much sex zones as recreational areas for Citizens or sites of commerce for Populations. Sex workers have cast these places for themselves as sites of both commerce and recreation, with sex work even emerging as the dominant industry in these spaces at certain times of the day. In Cubbon Park, Citizens and Populations have eagerly endorsed exclusion upon these pseudo-invisibles using a palette of strategies. As Janaki Nair[65] has revealed, campaigns in 1998 to 'save and protect' Cubbon Park heralded the processes of shifting the users and uses of the Park from more plebeian and inclusive to more recreational and elite, framed within concerns of 'threats' to the environment and 'character' of employment among the lower classes in the Park, with full backing from the state and media. The agitations from the middle- and upper-middle classes resulted in a reclamation and transformation of the Park from being honestly public to a more 'aesthetically pleasing' space that suddenly saw locked gates and chain-fences installed, keeping everyone out except joggers, walkers and only the very necessary commercial activities serving those joggers and walkers.[66] The unacceptable conversion of recreational and (morally upright) commercial spaces into libidinal spaces by these workers is why these spaces were to be policed and why these pseudo-invisibles needed to be eradicated.[67]

In the process of demarcating the neoliberal city, strategies to erase pseudo-invisibles such as street-based sex workers become an implicitly stated, if not explicitly documented agenda. It begins with questioning the presence of individuals such as transgender people, or unescorted or consort-less women of lower-middle or lower economic classes. In any case, the voices and bodies of women (very particularly transgender individuals) as such have conventionally been largely disregarded in the design of cities, with women of the underclasses (and transgender individuals in general), when emerging into urban public

---

[64] Nagendra (2016).
[65] Nair (2005).
[66] Ibid.
[67] Short (2014).

spaces, seen as bearing the potential for problematic behaviour, which threatens purity, class status and mainstream heteronormative gender expressions.[68] The 'loose' woman on the street (or, for that matter, even the transgender individual 'loitering' in a public space) becomes discernible in the human ecology of the street as a dubious and confronting presence who needs to be swept away to clear the streets of immorality. The public woman carries and displays sexual licence and commerce, smacking of contagion, with the potential of danger and harm to the citizenry and image of the city.[69] In certain urban spaces, she needs to legitimise her presence by bringing along a consort to quell any uncertainty about her visibility there; the presence or absence of a legitimate and morally sanctioned companion clarifies whether she frequents a public space as a moral oppressor or if she is the one who is oppressed and requiring protection. That is, she has to prove herself a member of the Populations, even if not the Citizenry, but certainly must not be caught red-handed as a pseudo-invisible.

Hence, while some people are welcome on the streets (since they are Citizens) and while some other types are necessary and tolerated (since they are Populations), others, such as street-based sex workers, are unwelcome. They remain invisible to Citizens and are acquainted with Populations but become suddenly visible when cleansing operations are called for. They associate with Populations routinely, but these historic bonds are called into question during gentrification processes (ironically even by the Populations who themselves have to fight for survival). Informal policing begins whereby unwanted people (particularly pseudo-invisibles) are monitored and managed in urban space, and where ordinary social actors (namely Populations, fuelled by Citizens' advocacy in these directions) enforce spatial consensus by ensuring visibility of all actors and behaviours in public space; the space takes on different meanings for each person present in it, with some types of individuals emerging as more equal than others.[70] In fact, in Bangalore, the building of flyovers, cutting of trees in public spaces, regulation of 'behaviour' and 'loitering' in public parks, restrictions around the use of public toilets and similar erosion and modification of other worksites have heavily corroded the workspaces of sex workers, in addition to criminalising them (in ascending order of degree across men, women and transgender individuals), in the backdrop of redefined urban aesthetics and efforts to push Bangalore as a 'world class city'.[71]

This was not the case in Bangalore city across the centuries of its existence. In so many such cities, urban spaces have been traditionally sites of sexual commerce, where the sexual and the spatial constituted one another, and

---

[68] Kern (2020).

[69] Tonkiss (2005).

[70] Jacobs (1964); Anderson (1990, 2013); Tonkiss (2005).

[71] Vijayakumar, Chacko and Panchanadeswaran (2015).

where individuals experienced, negotiated, manipulated, reinterpreted and reconstructed sexualised spaces, perhaps immoral or unsafe spaces, but certainly as *meaningful* spaces for these workers.[72] Where brothel-based sex work has been minimal (like in Bangalore city), commercial sex scattered across city spaces and occupied mainstream structures in these public spaces.[73] City spaces have therefore had an existence, as Denise Brennan reveals, as 'sexscapes' or spaces that are inextricably tied to commercial sex.[74] City spaces emerged as not just geographical spaces but also ecologies of workspaces that individuals reworked (by maximising business from customers and minimising detection and violence from other actors) in order to sell sex, and spaces where sexual identities were inscribed on the landscape as much as they were on the body.[75] But Citizens and Populations in Bangalore and elsewhere have accused sex workers of 'dangerously blurring' territories in urban public space, when actually they were only working through spatial and sociological negotiations like all other informal workers in these workspace ecologies. The sex worker softens the private (intimate) sphere and the public (civil, formal, rational) sphere by intruding body and sex into public space and converting it in this space into instrumental and commercial entities.[76] Naturally, Citizens and Populations react with shock to this interpretation of public space, and they begin to distrust these pseudo-invisibles and view them menacingly. One strategy has been to respond to the strong feelings of vulnerability by deliberately weakening the bonds of territorial community among these groups in public spaces, alongside retreating into one's respective private spheres such as the household.[77] However, the strategy usually unapologetically employed against pseudo-invisibles, such as street-based sex workers, is that of force. The visible aspects of public sex are forcibly zoned out of existence (sometimes demarcated by class and sociological identity) in the imaginary of the public space or are bodily forced out by revanchist interest.[78]

More Unequal than Other Unequals

Street-based sex workers hence suffer the highest and most multi-layered precarity, given their status as pseudo-invisibles. These individuals suffer from what Loïc Wacquant has termed as 'advanced marginality'.[79] Individuals trapped in advanced marginality do not experience merely economical backwardness

---

72 Bell and Valentine (1995); Tani (2002); Sanders (2004).
73 Sahni and Shankar (2008).
74 Lowthers (2015). See also Browne, Lim and Brown (2009).
75 McQuiller Williams (2014); Bell and Valentine (1995).
76 Tonkiss (2005).
77 Wacquant (2008).
78 Binnie (2000); Williams (2014).
79 We draw from Wacquant (1996, 1999, 2008) in what follows in this section.

but a bouquet of intersecting vulnerabilities and oppressions. Advanced urban marginality arises from the womb of urban inequality wherein disparities yawn wider over time and space, due to which extremes – 'opulence and indigence, luxury and penury, copiousness and impecuniousness'[80] – proliferate alongside one another. For the advanced marginal, a number of realities materialise.

Street-based sex workers suffer from advanced marginality not only within the general demographic population of Bangalore but also along the strata of informal workers that populate the working class of this city. While globalised cities routinely demand more informal women workers[81] (as is at the heart of neoliberal capitalism), only those who fit into the Populations gain legitimacy, therefore, not pseudo-invisibles such as street-based sex workers. Street vendors, security guards outside glass towers and residential enclaves, lift operators and janitors in new malls, food and snack vendors in crowded shopping areas and transport terminuses – all these are comfortably included in the imaginaries we laid out in the opening line of this book. But street-based sex workers in Bangalore, too, are as much an informal labour workforce as the aforementioned workers. They cannot be simply oversimplified as trafficked or oppressed individuals who await to be rescued from the pimps and madams of a brothel and yearn to return to 'homes' and 'families'. Tens of thousands of street-based sex workers in Bangalore leave their homes for sex work and return each day to children, spouses, parents and siblings. So many of them have extended family interactions and regular neighbourly relationships with those inhabiting around them, just like the rest of us do, and participate in community religious events and local politics. They are workers too, like the rest of us 'decent' workers. However, their working lives and their very existence are far removed from what 'decent' people endure. They are far more unequal than the many other unequals, who may suffer the tribulations of neoliberal urbanism, but are not even 'decent unequals' like other informal workers. This is because there exists a spectrum of moral acceptability and legitimacy even within informal work, and street-based sex workers lie around the negative end of this scale, which aggravates their marginality, precarity, vulnerability and pseudo-invisibility.[82] Their variety of labour does not match with the informal work associated with urban modernity,

---

[80] Wacquant (1999: 1641).

[81] Sassen (2002).

[82] The advanced marginality of their status as unrecognised informal workers aggravated during the COVID-19 pandemic in India – a country that stood as a top achiever globally in highest daily infections and deaths in 2021. As Tripathi and Das (2020) recognised in the middle of the first wave of infections in India, since sex workers often have no savings and the lockdown blocked their source of income, they become unable to pay rent and are left practically starving. Their study predicted, correctly, that even when lockdowns are lifted gradually, this occupation may not entirely be sustainable for thousands of people since physical distancing emerged as the new normal.

such as taxi drivers or 'food delivery executives'. It is not even that their kind of work is considered archaic and traditional. The attitude is that, quite simply, *it should not exist.* When they are visible, these creatures need to be stamped out aggressively due to the immoral nature of their activities, which remain viewed as personalised shameless deeds, never 'work'. They are not permitted to participate in constructing the Bangalore imaginary, and the city is not shared with them.

Sex as Work

The denial of the city to these workers begins not with an outright expulsion from urban spaces, but from apprehensions about their very existence and misbeliefs about their capability to exercise a sense of agency for themselves. Their experience of urban transition, the ensuing responses they have developed and the interventions that have assisted these responses, are all rooted in how state, judiciary, citizenry and intelligentsia have understood what they actually are, what their work actually is, what their needs actually seek and what they are actually capable of. Sex workers' agency over their own bodies, and their sexuality, has always been seen as problematic and dangerous for the city.[83] They are regularly labelled as dispossessed damsels in economic distress who are devoid of agency over their bodies, lives, families and work.

But street-based sex workers have as much an effective role as public individuals as anyone else does, which exhorts them to reclaim their civil rights, corporeal rights, labour rights, health rights, family rights, their right to be free from harassment from the police and 'decent' citizenry and rights over the custody of their children – that is, their rights as individuals, workers and parents, which are on far more perilous ground than those of other more privileged individuals, workers and parents whose rights are readily entitled.[84] As a sex worker, one is, therefore, actually a political subject aspiring towards greater citizenship, as well as an empirical subject coping up with the extreme subaltern position that one is relegated to.[85] These individuals demand a more carefully crafted civil rights package detailing a series of 'freedom-from's' as well as 'freedom-to's'[86] on account of their very special conditions that range from existential concerns of individuals right up to their importance as a worker cohort in the larger citizenry and economy.

The discourse around these workers all over India and in many other parts of the world is now far from the archaic position that sex work is exclusively induced by poverty or human trafficking, or that these individuals need rescue,

---

[83] Kern (2020).

[84] Duncan (1996); Kapur (2005); Kotiswaran (2011, 2012).

[85] Ghosh (2008).

[86] Sutherland (2004).

rehabilitation or HIV/AIDS intervention; the discourse is now steadily moving towards acknowledging them as informal workers in the unorganised sector of an urban economy.[87] But a major barrier Indian sex workers still face is their legal status because sex work is not really illegal in the country, but they are viewed as 'abused' individuals (women, by default) around which a whole range of criminal activity revolves.[88] Organisations constituted by and working for sex workers all over India – from the Durbar Mahila Samanwaya Committee (DMSC) in Kolkata to the Karnataka Sex Workers' Union – have repeatedly sought legal clarification over their status, ambiguities within which have led to avenues for harassment and grievous misunderstanding from a full variety of people and institutions.[89]

Ambivalence in their status arises not only from careless homogenisation[90] and unclear legal definitions but also from divided intellectual camps which state and judicial systems are intricately connected with and are informed by. These systems compartmentalise sex workers into sweepingly broad positions that are quite simply reckless generalisations that rob every sense of agency among these workers.

One faction insists that they are 'deviant and immoral individuals', engaging in a service that is 'beyond the bounds of respectability' and which needs to be 'corrected', while the other camp typecasts them as 'victims suffering from false consciousness' who need to be pulled away from their 'oppression'.[91] Sex work (widely labelled 'prostitution') has been condemned by these blocs for its legitimisation and objectification of sex, the commodification of women's bodies and romanticisation of an experience that is actually exploitation and (economic, physical, sexual, emotional and social) alienation.[92] Sex workers have been conventionally assumed as irresponsible towards themselves and their families.[93] This 'bad women' camp reinforced the already entrenched stigma and called for legal and morally corrective consequences of their 'transgressions', while the 'victims' camp belittled their sense of choice and agency, which again requested legal intervention to 'protect' them.[94] The 'oppression theorists' (in either camp) cherry-picked the worst of sex work and treated that as representative.[95] In the Indian context, sex work undertaken voluntarily was perceived as being

---

[87] Kotiswaran (2011, 2012); Lowthers (2015).

[88] Kotiswaran (2011); Vijayakumar, Chacko and Panchanadeswaran (2015).

[89] Gooptu (2000, 2002); Gooptu and Bandyopadhyay (2007); Kotiswaran (2011).

[90] Tambe (2008).

[91] Duncan (1996); see Kotiswaran (2019) for a thorough engagement on these issues in the Indian context.

[92] D'Cunha (1991). See also Boris, Gilmore and Parrenas (2010).

[93] Sutherland (2004).

[94] Ibid.

[95] Weitzer (2009).

seriously dishonourable and an extension of 'western' practices around sexuality and immorality that masquerade as libertarianism that are antithetical to 'Indian culture'; by the same token, organisations advocating sex workers' rights were viewed as funded from 'western' sources.[96] Superficial and convenient conclusions by the state also revolved around regulation of sex work, by either calling for its abolition (bringing with it the criminalisation of actors besides the workers themselves) or decriminalisation (bringing with it 'welfare' to the workers), on the one hand, or criminalisation of female activity (bringing with it greater surveillance of individuals), on the other hand, which are both radical and contradictory positions.[97]

These divisions – that is, the 'victims' camp and the 'bad women' camp, or a combination of both – were in combat with one another for very long, in fact for decades. The positions that these camps steadfastly held were actually derived from their definitions of 'work' as material, economic and modern, and 'sex' as shameless or violent.[98] An oversimplified understanding of criminal law and sex markets led to comprehending sex work as a venue for violence, which consequently called for repressing sex markets and enforcing criminal law; to add to this, an oversimplified understanding of their suffering called for rescue and rehabilitation (with its own counterproductive effects) that assumed a state of poverty or migrating to other low-wage occupations as superior to sex work.[99] As mentioned earlier, even in academic literature, for long, writings on the sociology of sex work have been inclined towards discourses of morality, sexuality, gender and power, and analyses of solicitation dynamics, client intimacy and regulation of street prostitution, mostly around *women* who sell sex.[100] 'Victim' identities in scholarly work also overlooked male and transgender work[101] or relegated focus on them to the margins of sex work analysis. Another form of simplification in academic literature on sex work has been in terms of how much it considered the role of other actors as not just incidental characters but as integral parts of the setting of sex work.[102] From the part of state bodies (such as the National Commission for Women in India in the 1990s), sex work was simply a collective violation of human rights and equality, as a form of exploitation and as irreparable harm, which led to their conflating of all sex work as servitude and slavery and as the ultimate embodiment of male patriarchal coercion and a lack of consent against these

---

[96] D'Cunha (1991); Kotiswaran (2011).
[97] Rajan (2003).
[98] Sutherland (2004).
[99] Kotiswaran (2008, 2011, 2012); Pai, Seshu and Murthy (2018).
[100] McQuiller Williams (2014).
[101] Agustin (1988).
[102] Fey (2017); Brown (1992).

structures, which provided for no sensitivity or acknowledgement of male prostitution, child prostitution and chosen informal work.[103]

To make matters worse, while the abolitionist feminist[104] standpoint that informed the state's stance viewed the need for sex work as stemming from an 'urgent male sexual need' that crosses legitimate marital boundaries, which then called for reining in 'men's behaviour', the standpoint that begged for enhanced surveillance also viewed these workers as 'public health threats' as principal diffusers of HIV/AIDS.[105] While, formerly, medico-legal concerns were an item within the sex work discourse, for several years now, sex work has been placed too casually within the HIV/AIDS discourse, placing them as prime suspects in the HIV/AIDS problem; in fact, sex workers began to gain greater visibility with the expanding global discourse on HIV/AIDS in its early decades. While the issue formerly was taking the disease out of them for the safety of their clients and themselves, in the neoliberal city, fed by this brand of abolitionist feminism, *they* are now the disease to be expunged.

The bloc that viewed sex work as purely 'female bodily exploitation driven by economic need of poor women' called to rectify a restricted view of female poverty, a comprehension that sprung from a construct of sex work that acknowledged only male domination and patriarchal structures.[106] While sex workers all over the world struggled to assert the need for human rights, many radical feminist camps remained mired in such confusions (even questioning whether these workers' needs were 'feminist' enough) due to their staunch abolitionist stand.[107]

---

[103] Scoular (2004); Kotiswaran (2011).

[104] Jeffreys (2009) explains in detail how radical feminists, such as Andrea Dworkin, Catherine MacKinnon or Kathleen Barry, exceedingly held a violence-centric point of view, which evolved from their scholarship on the construction of sexuality, prostitution and pornography, and body-image politics. They assert that the body (the primary territory that many women have though not entirely under their control) is the commencing point for women's experience of the world. Their bodies are turned into instruments that men may enter at will or through payment, which results in women having to disassociate from their own bodies for their own survival. These have been termed 'sex-negative' feminists. Kotiswaran (2011) alleges that this problem was not confined to white western radical feminists alone and that Indian feminist theorists too mirrored them, though with a slight tilt towards a socialist feminism and with it a critique of cultural nationalism.

[105] Rajan (2003); Jeffreys (2009).

[106] Jeffreys (2009).

[107] See Jeffreys et al. (2011). Kissil and Davey (2010) succinctly present the debate: radical feminists versus sex radicals (Scoular 2004), sex positive feminists versus anti-sex work or abolitionists (Lerum 1998; Wahab 2006), prostitutes' rights versus feminists-against-systems-of-prostitution (Simmons 1998), social versus radical feminists (Monroe 2005), and sexual-equality-first versus free-choice-first (Jolin 1994). The main dividing lines, according to Simmons (1998), were around: (*a*) whether these individuals were coerced victims or entrepreneurs and empowered whores, or (*b*) whether the solution should be decriminalisation, legalisation or abolition of prostitution.

In fact, radical feminists continued to use the term 'prostitute', instead of 'sex work', to convey the exploitation and coercion found in commercial sex.[108] If all this were not enough, popular culture has also been misleading in the representation of sex workers as either those who wear provocative clothing and stand on dingy pavements and alleys helplessly working for rugged pimps or as more elegant women with full personalities who are eventually saved by either a prince or a hero figure (such as the male hero figures in the films *Pretty Woman* or *Taxi Driver*), crafting an image that sex work is a temporary course of action that is concluded with a dignified ending.[109]

Saviours were not necessarily wealthy or heroic men alone. Historically, the middle class, even in Europe (not only stay-at-home women but also social and religious workers), was known to view themselves as important figures suited to help, control, advise and discipline the sexual conduct of the poor.[110] In France, and soon followed by Britain, legislation was passed to control poor women and eventually rescue and rehabilitate them by placing them in hospitals, penitentiaries and refuges where they could be watched, corrected and persuaded to behave more 'respectably'.[111] And, finally, to add to this all, female sex workers from developing countries had the extraordinary responsibility of throwing off the burden of imperialist representation that they were imprisoned into by white feminist (usually abolitionist) agendas and state policies of advanced western governments, which emerged from Victorian feminist campaigns that bracketed women within western categories, subjects and experiences, and called (once again) for middle-class feminist 'saviours' to 'rescue' them into 'honourable work'.[112]

In reality, selling sex is complex and contradictory across space and time, and depends heavily on the structuring roles of culture and class.[113] The binaries of sex work in its Anglo-American conceptualisation – victim–agency,

---

[108] Kelly (2008).

[109] See Dalla (2000). Though Voicu (2018) in her analysis of Ruti (2016) provides a more generous account of the interpretation of such films, even arguing that *Pretty Woman* might have softened or deconstructed gender binaries and might even have anticipated third-wave feminism that emerged a short while after the film's release in 1990.

[110] Agustin (1988).

[111] Ibid.

[112] See Walkowitz (1980); Burton (1994); Scoular (2004); Kapur (2005); Jeffreys et al. (2011). Lowthers (2015), drawing from Kempadoo (1999), explains how there was minimal historicisation among such intellectuals from the west, which followed into negligible geo-political contextualisation and universalisation of the subject from bounded locations and experiences. The 'non-western' woman's experience was lent little ear, and for nearly a century, western categories dominated the international discourse on sex work.

[113] Scoular (2004).

danger–pleasure, Third World–West, modern–postmodern, poverty-stricken streetwalker–high-priced call girl, and so on – are too oversimplified.[114] These trends commonly shared two outcomes – first, they silenced workers; and, second, they dismissed their consciousness and operationalisation of their agency. The principal casualty here was, squarely, sex workers' *agency*.

The opening that began rectifying this was to first embrace them as fellow workers. Sex worker movements around the world recognised that the circumstances that they were driven by were not only facilitated by mainstream patriarchal society but were also derived from the failure of the radical feminists (reprising their familiar attitude in other movements too) to listen attentively to what these workers really wanted or to see who constituted them, and their attempts to speak 'on their behalf' instead.[115] The 'victims' position also needed to be distanced from, based on the argument that a victim, technically, is overwhelmed with so much bewilderment and trauma that she loses instrumentality over herself and suffers from some kind of Stockholm Syndrome (as what a few rehabilitation programmes allege), which entirely glosses over the fact that sex work is an occupational choice, albeit a heavily constrained one, for many workers, and is an option among a limited rational choice set that allows one to provide for oneself and family.[116] Sex work was always only understood as being about sex and money and never about consensual sharing, survival, livelihood and real work, which required dignity and recognition as an economic engagement.[117] But when it was realised that sex often becomes work and work often demands sex, the need to move significantly away from the fetishising of sex and the dignifying of work became more and more pertinent, which compelled a redefinition of sex work.[118]

Third-wave feminism that emerged from the 1990s welcomed the reasoning that supported sexual liberation and agency, allowing the individual to decide for oneself how to negotiate desires of gender equality and sexual freedom, and persuading a deeper respect for pluralism and self-determination; these were on the premise that individuals (across gender and not only women) interpret similar experiences (such as sex work) differently based on their positions and cultural perspectives, and that therefore the 'right to work' and the meaning of 'prostitution' differed across culture and geography.[119] This new wave allowed for context-specific sexual subjects, which enabled and visibilised the full

---

[114] Law (2000); Sutherland (2004); Weitzer (2010).
[115] Jeffreys et al. (2011).
[116] Richter (2012).
[117] Tambe (2008).
[118] Kotiswaran (2011).
[119] Scoular (2004); Martin (2007); Snyder-Hall (2010).

texture and complexity of sex work.[120] A 'polymorphous paradigm' began to emerge, acknowledging the constellation of occupational arrangements, power relations and worker experiences.[121] From an institutional capacity, the World Health Organization (WHO), in 1988, articulated sex work as an occupation by defining a clear customer–seller relationship of a sexual service, as a strong contrast to definitions and nuances that revolved around immorality or victimisation.[122] Such a materialist analysis of sex work began developing not only alongside a more refined feminist vocabulary around the occupation but also from the proliferation of more fine-grained and grounded studies of the sociology of sex markets that recorded and analysed interactions between the stakeholders involved, and which took a relook at labour and sex work.[123] Sex workers, on their part, worked tirelessly through collectivisation and movements (as seen most explicitly in Kolkata but also in other cities and towns) to reinvent the worldview and self-perception not as socially alienated victims but as actors endowed with a sense of collective rights and capacity.[124]

It emerged that the 'work' part of 'sex work' should not have been so carelessly dropped, rendering this occupation as only 'sex', which was perceived to be inherently abusive to women as it led to rape, harassment, abuse and pornography; both sides of the hyphen in 'sex-work' needed to be read with equal weight to grasp its essence.[125] True, sex work compels individuals – particularly women and transgender people – to alienate from their real selves by forcing them to change names and identities, distancing them from family and mainstream society and, of course, pushing them into a brutal experience that may break the person and indoctrinate new values.[126] Many sex workers indeed have little control over the choice of entry into this occupation, while others have greater agency than women in restricted married-housewife roles; sex work operates across a full spectrum of unequal privilege, as all other forms of labour do.[127] Sex work certainly involves significant amounts of bodily, psychological and emotional degradation and brings with it, almost inescapably, strong waves of stigmatisation and demonisation for many workers.[128] But it is, still, a form of work.

---

[120] See Sutherland (2004). The empirical work of Weatherall and Priestly (2001) shows how it is possible for a single individual sex worker to display contradictory descriptions of power that parallel both radical-feminist and liberal-feminist explanations. Respondents in their study reported how sex work was free choice but it also meant being passive and powerless. They made the rules but were exploited too.

[121] Weitzer (2009).

[122] WHO (1988); Kissil and Davey (2010).

[123] Kotiswaran (2008).

[124] Gooptu and Bandyopadhyay (2007).

[125] Sutherland (2004).

[126] D'Cunha (1991).

[127] Kong (2006).

[128] Kinnell (2002).

Rajeswari Sunder Rajan[129] vividly explains how denying sex work as work implies either its abolition or its reform, or, in other words, that there is an inherent contradiction between fighting for women's sexual rights and fighting to exterminate the system of sex work. Her writing urges us to determine what kind of work this is and underlines that we must understand how legitimising it would include sex work within socially useful and productive work in an economy, dissociating its default connotations of crime, health hazard and deviance. She correctly interprets abolitionist feminists as those who look at sex work as a *system*, while more progressive sex-radical or sex-positive feminists advocate it as *practice*, which pays greater attention to the voices of workers, researches into their experiences, inculcates a culture of dialogue between feminists and workers and improves feminist support of identification with sex worker movements. Once again, Rajan argues, this would prod us to rethink notions around agency, sexuality and work, which are distinct yet overlapping such that a position on one automatically entails an associated stand on the others. The more nuanced understanding of these, which, as we have seen earlier, emerged with third-wave feminism, understood sex work as an *occupational choice* with sexual self-determination, which commercialised one's sexual skills (as much as individuals sell their mental and manual skills), did not permit for offering one's body without consent (as in the case of marriage) permitted for unionisation and the strive for welfare (as in all other forms of labour), and which would eliminate the stigma that arose from notions of immorality and criminality.[130]

We must also be aware that though the sexual economy relies disproportionately on the most disadvantaged among the working poor, members of other social classes also make their entry into the job.[131] The entry into the occupation as a 'choice' is assuredly from within a severely constrained choice set for most workers and is usually placed within exploitative systems and tough institutionalised structures (such as the valorisation of sexual servitude to one man – a husband at home).[132] For example, Nalini Jameela revealed in her 2007 autobiography how, especially for female workers, when finding a job becomes urgently critical, the choice set becomes so stiflingly restricted that economic support to the family becomes a greater priority than 'faithfulness' within it. Upon deeper introspection, it ought to become clear how *everyone* chooses their occupations within such constraints – economic and social liabilities, family and community concerns, religious beliefs, personal psychology – and very few people can honestly claim completely free choice in opting for livelihood strategies.[133] As seen in J. Devika's ruminative

---

[129] Rajan (2003).
[130] D'Cunha (1991).
[131] Bernstein (2007).
[132] Duncan (1996); Kotiswaran (2011).
[133] Kinnell (2002).

exposition[134] that thoroughly spells out this position, the 'ordinariness' of sex work in their lives, especially for poor women, is unmissable, implying how their choice to engage in this profession need not be driven purely out of poverty or purely due to trafficking.

Christine Overall[135] argues in a spectrum of angles – since most workers under capitalism sell their labour for a fraction of its value for their and their dependents' subsistence, why should sex work be seen any differently? Why must we look only at those elements of sex work that highlight danger, disease, mistreatment, indignity, abuse and emotional pain, when these are not unique to sex work? How far do women 'choose' other occupations that also invariably harbour these elements? How different are the conditions of sex workers from heavily exploited (particularly women) workers in other occupations that offer little control over one's body and labour? Does sex work also not thrive on the cultural construction of gender roles in terms of dominance and submission? Sex workers surely have a far more constrained choice set than other workers, and sex work significantly brings much greater job risks than many other jobs, but the direct and default mapping from poverty to sex work is erroneous, and sex work is indubitably an economic activity even where explicitly illegal.[136] Sex work is across a continuum that could include sex work proper (in its conventional understanding of agreed fees paid for sexual services) and transactional sex (a financial arrangement within relationships characterised by friendship, affection or romance), not just survival sex (sex work as prompted by utter poverty).[137] Also, unless they are moved by means of coercion for the express purpose of being sexually exploited, sex workers are not always trafficked individuals.[138] And, in addition, sex workers are not restricted to sex work full-time, as they may include it in a set of income-earning strategies that simultaneously include activities such as domestic and construction work, or are undertaken seasonally or intermittently.[139] Sex workers come with an array of economic, cultural and bodily resources that provide them with access to various types of local and global men, straddling across porous boundaries of work, intimacy and personal life.[140] Commercial sexuality is experienced in diverse ways by diverse individuals through space and time.[141] Multiple social, political, cultural and economic factors coil around one another, and ethnic and cultural histories emerge as crucial to sex work.[142]

---

[134] In the foreword of Nalini Jameela's biography.
[135] Overall (1992).
[136] Kinnell (2002).
[137] Busza (2006).
[138] Richter (2012).
[139] Schultz (2006); Sahni and Shankar (2008); Shah (2014).
[140] Hoang (2011).
[141] Ibid.
[142] Kelly (2008).

Hence, sex work is undoubtedly *work*, and sex workers are like countless other legitimate workers who are able to choose and provide for themselves through this occupation, within which they indeed encounter marginalisation, sexism, exploitation and violence.[143] Sexual commerce is part of a range of informal labour practices.[144] It ought to be de-stigmatised simply for its sexual aspect and should be regulated, by which both 'sex' and 'work' in 'sex work' are proportionately weighted to understand how both are intertwined and bring with them pleasure, danger and agency.[145] Elements of gender and sexuality play decisive roles in sex work, but this occupation cannot be reduced to simply gender or sexuality.[146] The call for stimulating worker agency is not about satiating any urgent male sexual needs but more about improving the lives of sex workers themselves.[147] In fact, what many scholars and activists now increasingly argue is not to abolish sex work per se but the *poor conditions* therein, which draws from the demand that what sex workers actually want is to change their circumstances without changing their trade.[148] Sex workers are social and political actors who have a sense of collective rights and capacity, and – as they have made it plain to see in Mumbai, Kolkata, Delhi and so many other cities and towns in India – they have been at the forefront of a range of ongoing movements for collective self-representation and expression of community identity, to interrogate established norms of social hierarchy and distribution.[149]

Therefore, what is required for any sort of progressive advancement in the state and society towards these workers is, as Ratna Kapur explains,[150] to adopt three major shifts. First, to recognise subjectivities among workers instead of simplistic assumptions about realities and subject positions; second, to foreground the peripheral subject in order to facilitate normative shifts; and third, to understand the resistance of these workers as not just a claim for rights but also a means to ensure the production of a narrative that moves beyond 'victimisation' or stigmatisation. And it is precisely these shifts that this book champions.

Acknowledging the presence of sex workers in the public sphere and listening to their voices would add to more informed streams joining in the discourse around sex work, choice, consent, autonomy, exploitation, consciousness, power, structures and understanding.[151] A lived-experience approach – which we

---

[143] Tambe (2008); Jeffreys (2009).
[144] Shah (2014).
[145] Sutherland (2004).
[146] Zatz (1997).
[147] Kinnell (2002).
[148] Pheterson (1996); Kong (2006).
[149] Gooptu (2000, 2002); Gooptu and Bandyopadhyay (2007).
[150] And we expand Kapur's (2005) suggestions to include all sex workers, not only female.
[151] Duncan (1996).

unfailingly follow here in this book – would fill the void between the bipolar images of 'slavery' and 'radical' in the feminist debate over sex work, which would set everyday experiences of these workers within micro-concerns of moral and criminal surveillance and macro-conditions of larger society.[152] Visibilising them, not by representing them or speaking on their behalf, would firmly secure their proactive presence, image and voice in the discourse of urban space and life. Their occupation would become recognised and acknowledged as just another alternative circuit of survival in cities that are pressurising themselves to become 'globalised'.[153] It would crescendo their demand for labour rights and improvement in work conditions like so many other occupations in the urban economy are also crying out for.[154] As McQuiller Williams has strongly argued,[155] the importance of place and space in the livelihood strategies of these workers, and how they rework and adapt existing spaces for themselves, as opposed to those who are simply chased from place to place by the police and others, would be given due highlight if such a spatial approach is pursued. These marginal figures would then be constitutive of the public sphere, even if they are considered 'improper'.[156] It would critique the hypocrisy among those Citizens who champion sexual 'liberation' for themselves in urban space but who deny it for sex workers around those same spaces. Recognising their consciousness and their agency would alleviate them from their advanced marginalised position and would appreciate their legitimate participation in urban economy and society.

Summing Up

Urban transition in Bangalore has entrenched the advanced marginality of these pseudo-invisibles. The nature of this transition has been unabashedly elitist and neoliberal, with little regard for the historical legacy of the human landscape of Bangalore. While Populations assuredly face the heat of this transition, and some factions of Citizens in its penumbra may suffer accidental nicks and cuts, it is the pseudo-invisibles that face the full fury of this cyclone, which is why we perceive them as the archetypical advanced marginal in a city like Bangalore where neoliberal-fed inequality is laid bare on the streets and in urban spaces for all to see and experience. Street-based sex workers in Bangalore have faced a hostility like few other cohorts of informal workers in this city, with their claims

---

[152] See Kong (2006), who also directs us to developments in the sex work literature that emerged from the late 1990s onwards (for example, Wendy Chapkis and Kari Kesler) which bring out the voices of workers themselves, from writers among whom some have claimed to have been former sex workers themselves.

[153] Sassen (2002).

[154] Tambe (2008).

[155] McQuiller Williams (2004).

[156] Mokkil (2013).

to city spaces being systematically denied in a most brutish manner, violating not only their rights and liberties to occupy city spaces but also corroding the sources of their livelihood and ravaging their very bodies. They are blacklisted on two fronts. First, they are undesired in the humanscape of the urban imaginary as they are viewed as serious immoral blemishes in the creation of the neoliberal fabrication that is Bangalore, so much so that they are considered a hazard to the ideal public. Second, they are cast and rendered as structurally worthless workers within the greater project of neoliberal capitalism and associated urban transition. As blemishes and undesirables who are seen as worthless, unchaste and hazardous, street-based sex workers are repudiated from existing as citizens, workers and sometimes even as humans. Because of this, they are systematically ostracised in city spaces, which have always been sites for establishing identity, sustaining livelihoods and building solidarity. They are denied their positions as workers in the informal labour force within sites of commerce in urban spaces. In both these spectra – the human–spatial and the commercial–spatial – they are banished to the very margins. It is as a result of both dismissals that they live and work as pseudo-invisibles and that their presence and their narratives become entirely unacknowledged.

However, they too very much define the city through their eyes, quite apart from how 'decent' people do. Therefore, it becomes a compelling task that these pseudo-invisibles also need to have their narratives identified and chronicled, to reveal a fresh viewpoint of neoliberal urban transition. This book is a beginning towards this pressing task.[157] A general descriptive account of sex work in Bangalore city across economic class and privilege is in want, but it is a subject matter that deserves a separate dedicated volume. In this book, we reinforce sex work as a theme in urban studies (that is, how neoliberal urban transition attacks spaces of sexual commerce) and reinforce the urban space as a theme in sex work scholarship (that is, how urban spatiality and everyday artefacts and sites are critical to sex work), with implications of gender and labour informality underlying the entire presentation and analysis in this book. We place this interweave of urban transition and street-based sex work within the larger political economy of contemporary neoliberal capitalism in this region, anchoring on *urban transition* as the core process, but with themes and concerns of gender (in terms of feminist perspectives, policy attitude and the ideal public), labour (the geography of urban informal work, the agency and advanced marginalisation of labour and illegitimacy or immorality of labour practice) and technology (body politics and politics of technology) tightly tethered to this anchor.

---

[157] Earlier versions of some parts of this book have appeared in the journals *City* (Neethi 2020), *Gender, Technology and Development* (Kamath and Neethi 2021a) and *Globalizations* (Kamath and Neethi 2021b).

We need to accept that urban spaces are also 'sexscapes' (planes of sexual commerce) – that is, one of the planes in Bangalore's metaphorical counter-maps is a 'sexscape' that is as integral as its many other layers. We need to understand that sex work is an integral commerce within urban space ecologies. We need to understand that certain elements, artefacts and spaces within the city, and the experiences of urban transition, need to be seen not from a representative set of eyes but from their own. Such a perspective would redefine what a 'modern' city is, who the 'public' ought to be in such a city and finally, of course, what a 'city' itself is. After all, *their* city can only be seen through *their* eyes.

2

Narrators and Settings

Narratives are central to building the imaginary of a city, as well as the character of its transition. Narratives and imaginaries tell the story of a city more than objective cartographic maps.[1] However, urban imaginaries – including policy plans, popular or journalistic chronicles and academic or policy analyses of urban transition – are usually founded on narratives of mostly Citizens and Populations. Communities of pseudo-invisibles that suffer the wariness of urban transition are invisible – not as physically obscure but as absent in the popular and policy meta-narrative of *who* the city is.

The dominant nature of both urban imaginaries and urban transition processes are deeply imbricated with a literate, codified and, therefore, homogenised social cohort, that is, the privileged. We say 'homogenised' with caution: indeed, there are varying shades among the privileged, as they are certainly not monolithic, but they are homogenised with respect to their convergence towards a narrow, limited spectrum of urban imaginary and transition, which is usually in neat concordance with an Anglo-American catalogue of options. On the other hand, sections such as our street-based sex workers are non-literate for the most part, do not have documented histories and are highly heterogenised across gender, age, caste and clientele, with their imaginaries and transition experiences hinging upon their collective memory. Their narratives are almost entirely oral (and not codified), swirling with subjectivity (as opposed to uniform and objective) and have been marginalised. Therefore, we can visualise a direct link between (*a*) the literate, codified, objective, uniform and, therefore, dominant urban imaginary and construction of urban modernity and (*b*) the non-literate, oral, subjective, scrambled and, therefore, marginalised experience of production of urban imaginary and trajectory of urban transition. The latter mapping corresponds perfectly with our street-based sex workers in terms of their status as pseudo-invisibles, their condition of advanced marginality and their experience of urban transition.

For our purpose here, among street-based sex workers, subjectivity and a scrambled sense of visualising the city are not obstacles but complications to be cherished. As knotty as the task was, collecting their stories and experiences – occasionally gauzy, every now and then exaggerated and usually overrun with emotion – was

---

[1] Cinar and Bender (2007).

the very point for us. Individual oral accounts and an unpolished but articulate barrage of information were precisely what we sought while putting this book together. In general, too, despite a gigantic body of work on sex work and promising progress in sex worker rights movements, everyday concerns of sex workers remain scanty – especially with regard to street-based sex work, their relationship with the city they live and work in and furthermore for Bangalore city – due to the sparseness of documented narratives.[2] The material in their stories have the potential to build the spatial and historical associations between people and places, to uncover tensions of the city produced by spatially constituted social relations, to bring out the politics of the spatial and local (in the production of power, differences and inequality) and, above all, to shed new light on urban life in India.[3] Their oral accounts and portraits of the city and its people, and of turbulent change in both, help appreciate the centrality of city space in their lives and livelihood and acknowledge the various sexualised places that are almost always missing from urban narratives.[4]

The privileged, who are the seen and the heard in the daily life of cities, generally superimpose their narratives on the rest, deciding who the 'appropriate' and who the 'out of place' are.[5] Those who possess this capacity to be seen and heard brandish their power to ensure that their narratives and outlook become the written word as well. Written sources are said to be preferred by default due to ascriptions of purity attributed to them, while oral information is treated not only as subpar but as something 'to put up with' as they are 'second best histories about communities with poor sources'.[6] However, this is undoubtedly a prejudiced view of the oral source, an attitude that stems from the cynicism that is cast around communities who possess the verbal narrative. While it is mostly the case that these communities have limited access to the written word, this lack of access is least because of functional or scholastic illiteracy and much more due to the effects of systematic historical subjugation and social marginalisation. However, oral sources of qualitative information are of immense advantage and are far from being either second-best or suboptimal. While they may not be able to put up a facade of authoritarian credibility that documented sources with numerical data often notoriously do, oral sources are powerful in that they offer a first-hand view of lived experience in history.[7] Quite unlike archival records and mainstream codified information, oral sources are bountiful wellsprings that bring out subjugated voices, which have been for long disenfranchised

---

[2] Ditmore, Levy and Willman (2010).

[3] De Neve and Donner (2006); Massey, Allen and Pile (1999).

[4] Gothoskar and Kaiwar (2014).

[5] Allen (1999).

[6] Prins (2001: 121).

[7] Janesick (2014).

and corroded of agency due to the sociopolitical and cultural affiliations of these voices.[8]

To construct this book, we needed a social research methodology that is not only an effective information collection tool but also matched in spirit with the very endeavour of this book to construct an alternative historical geography in the form of a 'metaphorical counter-map' of Bangalore's urban transition. In other words, what we needed was an approach not simply to elicit oral data, which could be achieved with simple interviews, but which has as its spiritual core the task of contravening a homogenised and privileged urban narrative. All this was satisfied by embracing the oral histories method. The principal task of oral histories is to collect memory.[9] Assembling, aggregating, collating and reconstructing recollections and personal commentaries – about experiences, people, artefacts, spaces and other entities – and drawing out a pattern of these experiences while simultaneously celebrating subjectivity and heterogeneity in experience are central. While collecting and recording histories, we seek not confirmation or rejection of hypotheses but instead harvest explanatory accounts. This is a virtue that few quantitative methods, or even mainstream methods within qualitative methodologies, can boast of. While in mainstream approaches, 'sturdy' sources such as personal documents, interviews with experts, biographical materials and surveys are sought, in the oral histories method, we seek the individual actor, personal experiences and large portions of life and experience; this method is interactive for the most part, with the enquirer and narrator engaging in what appears as a conversation about these experiences and facets of life.[10] The oral histories method congregates stories, statements and reminiscences from individuals or groups who relate these as first-hand narrations of what *they* think is important, rather than what the scholar thinks is consequential to satisfy the 'research objective'.[11] The oral histories method also holds the potential to reveal intersectional experiences. Adapting from the thought of Eric Hobsbawm on the historical method, the oral histories method is not employed to merely corroborate the reliability of casual verbal sources of colloquially shared reminiscences by laypeople.[12] But it must be noted that we did not employ the oral histories method in all its glory; instead, we collected *micro* life histories, that is, oral accounts of twenty to

---

[8] Bosi and Reiter (2014).

[9] The conceptual material in this section on the operationalisation of the oral histories method is adapted from works such as Mandelbaum (1973), Allen (1999), Ritchie (2003), Janesick (2014), Porta (2014) and Bosi and Reiter (2014). In addition to these sources, we must also acknowledge with due gratitude the inputs of Prof. Anil Sethi during our initial discussions on the oral histories method with him, back in 2015.

[10] Porta (2014).

[11] Ritche (2003); Janesick (2014).

[12] Prins (2001).

thirty years – much shorter than an entire lifetime.[13] A close cousin of the oral histories method, which also forms an integral part of it and shares many core inclinations, is what is termed 'narrative enquiry' or 'narrative analysis'.[14] Quite simply, narrative enquiry is a way to gather and understand human experience through stories lived and told by narrators. As a method, narrative enquiry collects autobiographical descriptions from individuals that are built through the detailing of their experiences and how meaning was attached to the socio-economic and political contexts in which these experiences were embedded.

However, we anticipated, and were warned by other informed scholars, that relying too much on oral histories and narratives from them might slide us down either slope of reminiscing an idyllic past or bitterly evoking one that was entirely nasty and brutish. There are indeed tendencies among narrators, when recollecting the past, to be biased towards either extreme – either casting a golden glow or painting it too dark. Hence, we decided to rely upon secondary archival material for longitudinal information. The more expected sources of secondary material – for example, accurate chronological everyday accounts, first information reports (FIRs) by the police, academic work on street-based sex work in Bangalore city or even literary and artistic treasures such as songs, sayings, letters and correspondence, reminiscences or writings (which are aplenty in Bengal[15] or Kerala[16]) – were either inaccessible, deficient, sketchy, scarce or given just a passing mention. This prodded us to follow Sirpa Tani[17] to turn to newspaper reports and media narratives, elicited from the archives of the Bangalore edition of English newspapers such as the *Times of India*, *The Hindu*, the *Asian Age*, the *New Indian Express* and the *Deccan Herald*, among others, over the period 1998 to 2018. For this, we gained invaluable archival support from the organisation Sangama. One of the original purposes of Sangama was to serve as a resource centre on sexuality with a focus on the rights of sexual minorities and sex workers. To achieve their aim to enlarge social, cultural and political space for sexual minorities and sex workers, Sangama documented information in Kannada and English within newspaper clippings, journals, newsletters, books, reports, conference papers and films and documentaries. In this research, it was principally Sangama's vast and well-ordered archival collection of newspapers that served as a treasure trove in excavating a two-decade-long journalistic narrative around sex work in the city. Besides newspaper archives, reports pertaining to sexual minorities and sex workers across Karnataka were also preserved at Sangama.[18] Our work, therefore,

---

[13] Following Kamath (2018, 2020).

[14] For which we have sought inputs from Clandinin and Connelly (2000) and Prakash (2015).

[15] As Banerjee (1998) has vividly shown.

[16] As seen in Nalini Jameela's (2007) autobiography.

[17] Tani (2002).

[18] However, for this study, we selected only those articles concerning the outlook towards these individuals, police atrocities and policy analysis pertaining to sex workers within Bangalore city.

might be one of the first attempts to use archival material to document urban transition from the point of view of street-based sex workers in Bangalore.

Hence, the oral histories method (along with narrative analysis and supplemented by archival material) is cardinal in its purpose in providing a historical presence to those who cannot participate in the writing of the 'history from above'; therefore, as an instrument to build and collate the narratives of those who are in need of strengthening their personhood and self-identity and of reclaiming their position in the human landscape, it is, no doubt, a *social justice project* in its own right.[19]

Collecting Memories

Narrators

Over eighteen months of conversations, we collected the nature of life and work among male, female and transgender sex workers and collated artefacts and spaces to build what 'their' city and its transition looks like, what kind of shifts in relationships they faced with their ancillary agents and the police, and how they responded either by migrating to operating within the digital space or by mobilisation and collective movements or through the recourse of law and justice. We freely allowed narrations, opinions and accounts from the participants in the social and economic organisation of street-based sex work on how they related, behaved, perceived and interpreted their own experience of the labour force that they were supporting. We included in our collection of oral histories those who identified themselves as male, female or transgender street-based sex worker, who depend on this informal work as a full-time, part-time or occasional occupation, but confirmedly as an occupational activity to earn or supplement income. There are innumerable categories of who would constitute a 'sex worker', and to provide an exhaustive list of categories to abide by while marking boundaries for sampling would be impossible. Commendable contributions in laying out the full spectrum of typologies can be seen in the scholarly literature.[20]

For example, Kimberley Kay Hoang[21] accurately classified sex work on the basis of capital, intimacy and duration. Within the context of Ho Chi Minh City, Hoang classifies female street-based sex workers in terms of class as low-end, mid-tier and high-end. Low-end sex workers transact only sex and money for a short one-time meeting, consist of poor urban or rural migrant

---

[19] Eriksen (2014); Janesick (2014). See the Appendix for more on methods used.

[20] See Harcourt and Donovan (2005) for a rich list of typologies on direct and indirect sex work and risk categories. See also Buzdugan et al. (2010), who classify based on the main place of solicitation and on place of sexual service.

[21] Hoang (2011) is a valuable study that examines the sides of both the sex worker and the client, and goes beyond the transactional nature of sex work in Ho Chi Minh City.

women and can barely afford expensive makeup; these women are considered crude, dirty, uncultured and are said to speak in an uncouth tone of language. Mid-tier workers are those whose transactions may be short- or long-term, can morph into gauzy relationships and may also involve the exchange of gifts along with the usual sex and money transactions; workers in this strata are usually urban poor, adorn some form of hair extensions, invest in a bit of plastic surgery and have a basic functionality with the English language. High-end workers, however, are those whose transactions can go well beyond sex, gifts and money, involving even intimacy which turns into short-term relationships devoid of marital intent; they have usually benefited up until higher education, can afford designer clothing and plastic surgeries and can navigate upmarket restaurants and bars while spending time with clients. Customers can also be clearly demarcated with this typology, according to the ruggedness or polish that characterise the transaction from one end of the spectrum to the other.

While this is an effective taxonomy for Ho Chi Minh City, evolving such a classification for street-based sex workers in Bangalore is challenging. To stratify them neatly in terms of relationship and experience with a customer was nearly impossible. While indeed there are sex workers catering to a higher economic strata, who resemble the high-end workers of Ho Chi Minh City, they do not solicit customers in the open streets and city spaces in Bangalore. They are sourced either online or through pimps or well-guarded cliques. The street-based sex workers of Bangalore city lie in the grey areas of what Hoang classifies as low-end and mid-tier (with the distribution skewed towards the former). *These* are the pseudo-invisibles in urban spaces, who are targeted during gentrification drives (not the high-end ones who are possibly even 'necessary' workers and whose presence need not be scrubbed away from the city). The workers who swarm the streets of Bangalore city are those who cannot possibly adorn excessive makeup or sport hair extensions or invest in plastic surgery, not simply because of impediments in affordability but also simply because that would make them glaringly visible – something they cannot risk. Even if they can afford to invest in bodily capital[22] – investment in corporeal enhancements that give short- or long-term dividends – they cannot allow themselves to be seen tangibly as street-based sex workers. Besides, it is also not expected of street-based workers to polish up their enunciation or vocabulary in English (or even Kannada or Telugu or Tamil) because it is not required by most of their customers in Bangalore; in fact, it might even intimidate potential customers since a street-based worker with glossy etiquette and articulation might signal an unaffordable price, rendering a lose–lose outcome for both the worker and a potential client. Much like low-end workers in Southeast Asia or South Asia, female and male street-based sex workers in Bangalore are unapologetically plain-clothed and might look like

---

[22] Bernstein (2007); Hoang (2011).

the family members that both the customer and the client left back at home; both parties need to adorn this sartorial and cosmetic shade to match class dispositions with one another.[23] Transgender workers, however, are the diametric opposite, loudly announcing their presence and furiously attracting their visibility to everyone around because they are *already* identified, ex-ante, as impure beings who would anyway do this work. They invest heavily in bodily capital, may learn a few extra languages to grab a bit more of market share in this multilingual city, and have nothing to lose except possibly their lives.

We did not seek sex workers who (*a*) operated exclusively via information and communication technologies (ICTs), (*b*) operated as escorts through agents or privately, (*c*) worked covertly within closed spaces in various forms such as brothels, private homes, massage parlours, pubs, clubs, bars, hotels, (*d*) were involved in pornographic productions, (*e*) were involved in sex work for drugs, or (*f*) undertook sex work as a ritual occupation. Similarly, we avoided those who undertook sex work under bonded labour conditions, or by being exploited in rehabilitation homes or refugee centres, as travelling entertainers, or anyone who undertook sex work sporadically for rewards in kind rather than sex work for earning cash.

Following this initial process of elimination, we then drew from Prabha Kotiswaran[24] in identifying *who* to speak to. We adapted Kotiswaran's boundaries and restricted the research to sex workers who perform in the institutional setting of the street economy, soliciting their customers at public venues, bus stands, railway stations, cinema halls and highways *without* third-party mediation (such as pimps). These workers may, after gaining clients, move to secluded public places or private enclosed spaces for providing the service. We expanded liberally within this category, even including sex workers operating in unusual sites and elderly female street-based sex workers who have withdrawn from this profession due to old age or other reasons, but who are still part of the sorority of female sex workers in the city. However, here, too, there was some elimination: we avoided commercial street-based sex work involving minors, as well as those who were trafficked into the city exclusively for street-based sex work (while acknowledging the existence of a blur, however negligible as our narrators claim, between trafficking and sex work). Class identity and class conflict among the sex workers was one of the recurrent themes during discussions with our narrators. Hence, we had to also eliminate 'high-class'[25] street-based sex workers. This was an especially important choice. If we chose street-based sex workers of an economically more privileged strata, we would be going against the grain of everything we have argued for thus far – such as street-based sex workers who

---

[23] Hoang (2011).

[24] Kotiswaran (2012).

[25] We use the term 'high-class' here, reproducing our narrators' own terminology.

solicit outside of pubs and higher-end locations in more elite parts of the city still count as Citizens, do not risk being advanced-marginalised, are not aggressively blacklisted and have not really lost their spaces (they might have even gained some with gentrification!). The narrators we sought hail from lower socio-economic classes and mostly from historically deprived castes, fit into all dimensions of disadvantage listed here and are among the most unequal of unequals. They had several socio-economic attributes in common, but we had to acknowledge[26] and include, even within this restricted and targeted cohort, the wide diversity of practices, gender expressions and sexual identities that play a distinct role in the livelihood strategies of these workers – male, female and transgender.

In the end, we collected narratives from five dozen street-based sex workers in Bangalore city, spending eighteen months visiting and revising them. Our research assistant Prabhavati was invaluable in allowing us to build rapport with the workers themselves; serving as our icebreaker ship in the understandably hostile, justifiably hesitant and impenetrable landscape of the street-based sex work sector in Bangalore. Most interviews were conducted in Kannada with Prabhavati's support, as well as with timely help from Vinay, who stepped in on two or three occasions, the latter helping us in translating longer oral histories more effectively. Many workers were visited more than once and were spoken to in groups of about half a dozen. We located our narrators through organisations such as the Alternative Law Forum (ALF), Sangama, Aneka, Solidarity Foundation, Payana, and others, who then led us to associations such as Sadhana Mahila Sangha (SMS),[27] the Bhorukha Charitable Trust, Society for People's Action for Development (SPAD), Samara, the National Network of Sex Workers and the Karnataka Sex Workers Union. While these last two associations are unabashedly explicit in title and purpose – therefore directly affronting cultural and moral connotations of sex work from the state, society and media – other associations, which have been no less proactive in this struggle, are more concealed and operate under the shelter of livelihood improvement organisations, community-based organisations or women's welfare organisations across the city. Due to fears of extreme hostility that they potentially face in their local regions and communities, such organisations cannot be named here. We also identified and included other actors associated with street-based sex workers, who are auxiliary to them in some form, at times as accomplices or adversaries.

---

[26] Following Chacko, Panchanadeswaran and Vijayakumar (2016).

[27] A community-based organisation led by sex workers and engaging with sex workers, the SMS has been engaged with street-based sex workers in Bangalore for over fifteen years and has addressed issues of health, safety and violence. Today, this organisation works as an agent of social change and supports all struggles against human trafficking, sex workers' rights over the city and violence against women. One leading lady of this organisation has even been awarded the President's Medal.

Apart from the organisations mentioned earlier, we gained invaluable insights from Reach Law and People's Union for Civil Liberties (PUCL). Equally important were our interactions with street vendors, shopkeepers, lodge managers, autorickshaw drivers, bus staff, hospital staff, lawyers and activists providing legal and other moral support, and the jewel in the thorny crown – the police. During this entire process, the organisation Sangama[28] stood as our leading light – logistically, motivationally and intellectually.

Our narrators could not always be spoken to in open and exposed urban spaces, either individually or in groups (which would especially attract unwarranted attention). Some of our more defiant narrators were willing to talk to us while we sat on pavements, steps of shops and cinema theatres, restaurants, bus stands and bus stops, railway stations, parks, street corners and alleys. But many others offered to speak to us only inside the secure spaces of the organisations we mentioned earlier, since they either did not want to be viewed narrating their experiences on the streets for fear of being identified by passers-by or feared being intimidated by the police or other agents for even *speaking* to 'decent and legitimate' Citizens such as us researchers. Some of them spoke to us in spaces that were neither enclosed nor open, such as in the backyards of Victoria Hospital and a gated recreational area on the fringes of the city. Others, especially transgender sex workers, were accessible only in their traditional habitations known as *hamam*s (which we shall elaborate on in the next chapter), which are often dozens of kilometres outside of the city on highways and other desolate areas.

Sites

Street-based sex work has made its imprint all over Bangalore, literally in every neighbourhood, commercial area and open or un-gated urban space. Since it was impractical to cover all of Bangalore city, even if we restricted to city corporation limits, we chose locations that were not only geographically central within the city but also focal for street-based sex work. These locations included the Majestic area, the KR Market area and the MG Road area in the centre of Bangalore (with a brief foray into the areas of Peenya and Yeshwantpur). The first two areas have been traditionally the hotbeds of street-based sex work in Bangalore, with a greater than average density of sex workers.[29] The centrality of these areas was informed to us by our respondents and the organisations working for them. What we have provided here in this chapter is only a keyhole introduction to these areas. Our narrators will walk us through them in much greater detail in the upcoming chapters.

---

[28] Sangama is a Bangalore-based organisation working for the rights of sexual minorities (homosexuals, bisexuals and others who are discriminated due to their sexuality), sex workers and people living with HIV.

[29] This is impossible to verify statistically, as was informed to us verbally, and easy to confirm visually.

'Majestic' is the colloquial and more widely used name for Kempegowda Bus Station, the central bus terminus of Bangalore city, but is popularly used to refer to the entire area around the southern part of Gandhi Nagar, northern Upparpet and the winding streets around KG Circle. The name 'Majestic' was based on a cinema theatre built in the 1920s that was pulled down in the 1990s,[30] but the name stuck on to the central bus terminus[31] and is what any kind of transportation towards this area announces as its destination. The Majestic area boasts countless lodges and hotels across a wide price range. Restaurants with air conditioning and 'family rooms' and waiters in crumpled white livery thrive alongside small eateries where one would have to serve oneself a budget meal and eat it standing. There are also legions of street vendors selling snacks and meals, 'export-rejected' clothes, footwear of all possible designs copied accurately off high-end brands, travel agencies in alleys struggling to make ends meet, small peepul groves affiliated to tiny decrepit but thriving temples, beggars galore, shopkeepers selling practically everything from bulbs to musical instruments and liquor and half a dozen brand new sleek malls and shopping areas with thousands of lights glittering inside. There is no count of how many millions of people throng across these streets and bus stations each day. Majestic hosts mostly a floating population that appears like a swarming beehive, which belongs to no one, but from which everyone can claim their little part. Only very few permanent residences can be spotted in the area, which are either above shops or are crumbling heritage houses where people have rented out a good part of their estate to warehouses and other companies. People jostle and bump into one another from the early hours of the day right up until late night, but the area is kept away from by most residents of the city during the night hours because during that period emerges a population of what are popularly called 'anti-social elements', which include criminals of all flavours, drunken pavement dwellers, rough sleepers, shadier factions of the working classes and, of course, street-based sex workers.

Our second area is KR Market, a kilometre south of Majestic. This is the central wholesale market for horticultural products, flowers and a few other agricultural commodities, from where most street vendors and shops across the city source their perishable stock. Like Majestic, 'Market' (as it is announced on public transport) colloquially includes the entire area of Kalasipalayam around the 1928-built market named after the then Maharaja of Mysore Krishnaraja Wodeyar alongside the road leading to Mysore city 100 kilometres away. The market area operates on a twenty-four-hour basis, and it is not only a

---

[30] Majestic Theatre was demolished much like many other theatres in the area – a topic that is crucial for our sex workers, and for which we provide a detailed treatment in the chapters ahead.

[31] Which, again, was built after erasing the Dharmabudhi Lake – once again, a topic that is important in the context of our sex workers.

regular hunting ground for those with trade and commercial interest around the market but is also an exotica for photographers, journalists, writers, and other artistes. KR Market is a thriving centre for street-based sex work catering to lower-income groups among the working classes and the economic classes below even them (that is, pseudo-invisible workers serving pseudo-invisible customers), who operate within the crammed streets around the main indoor market building. This overloaded and choked area is also home to interstate bus services run by private operators. Occasionally, street dentists and other mendicants pitch camp here. The northern fringes of the KR Market bus station leak out into Avenue Road and the serpentine lanes of Chickpet area –which hosts shops for wholesale of an endless list of commodities ranging from saris to schoolbags to firecrackers. A large mosque graces the area, as do little temples, which are circumambulated by street vendors and shopkeepers in the thousands. Bordering the southern fringe of the market or *pété* area is the old fort of Bangalore, which was inhabited from the sixteenth century and passed on from ruler to ruler, finally to the British East India Company who breached its walls in 1791, a moment of significant historical importance to the creation of the British stronghold on southern India. KR Market is where Citizens would never really visit, because, as they would say, they do not really have much to do there except to visit the fort and Tipu Sultan's summer palace just across it, or to shop for electrical wiring by the 100-feet, or to take a private interstate bus. 'Decent' people and tourists would have to have their eyes everywhere in this area, for pickpockets, chain-snatchers, gropers, sex workers and, worst of all, they would have to wedge through a more-than-tolerable density of transgender individuals who call the area home.

Our third site is the MG Road area, which is just a few kilometres eastward in geographical distance from KR Market and Majestic but continents apart in cultural distance. However, street-based sex workers of a lower-income group still haunt the area, especially during the late hours. MG Road is very popular among middle- and upper-middle classes, with rows of practically empty high-end shops alongside pavements overflowing with strollers. Though locals do not merge all the streets in the area and call it 'MG Road', as they do for 'Majestic' or 'Market', for this study, we conflate MG Road with its sister streets Brigade Road, Church Street, Brunton Road and Primrose Road – everything from Anil Kumble Circle through Mayo Hall and right up to Trinity Circle. Though there are indeed street vendors selling t-shirts or inexpensive, deliberately misspelt Ray-Ban sunglasses, here is where one could step out of a posh showroom and look to the westward skyline to behold a crass imitation of a Manhattan skyscraper called UB City, India's first luxury mall. The MG Road area is the first choice by the city corporation for any manicured infrastructure development in Bangalore city, the first place that Citizens would take their relatives from out of town to show what an urban imaginary ought to be, and where our street-based sex workers solicit a different species of clientele.

We also spoke to street-based sex workers based in Peenya and Yeshwantpur, located in the north-western area of the city. Peenya is essentially an industrial area comprised of informal and semi-formal blue-collar factory workers and gigantic public sector units. Alongside Peenya is Yeshwantpur, which hosts not only a bus terminus and a major railway station but also another principal agricultural market (the APMC Yard) in Bangalore where a great deal of sex work is offered. Street-based sex work here is similar in character to that of KR Market in terms of clientele, as well as the architectural and infrastructural landscape.

Our fieldwork not only constituted speaking to street-based sex workers and other individuals and organisations, but also involved long bouts of observation for weeks within these areas to study the humanscape, to observe the soliciting of commercial sex and to record the disappeared spaces and architectures and their gentrified replacements in order to build maps of the disappearing sex work landscape. This exercise of observation was to identify and relate to artefacts and spaces associated with our narrators – in essence, to strive to undo our own visual associations about them and to take a clean-slated relook at these urban spaces through the eyes of street-based sex workers. After all, our purpose was not to 'represent' them but rather to keep aside our usual privileged orbit around these areas and instead walk their footsteps, and to shed our mental images of these sites and see them afresh through their eyes. This was a mentally gruelling and mystifying but immensely rewarding task.

Ethics and Contradictions

Throughout the enquiry, we addressed our respondents as informal workers with self-declared identity and agency, constantly bearing in mind the risk of paternalising them. We bore in mind from the beginning of the study, and even as we write this, that we were engaging with *sex workers as narrators* of the city, and not 'a few narrators among sex workers', which was an important stance to pivot our oral history elicitation and narrative analysis. This is because what we sought to establish was that street-based sex workers had *their own city* that needed to be metaphorically counter-mapped through their narratives, as opposed to rounding up a 'sample' of articulate sex workers to understand their problems and generalise them. To reiterate from the previous chapter, ours was a task to lay out and build the city's sexscape and chart its transition experience through their eyes and feet, which is why we engaged with them in the capacity of being *narrators of the city*. We had to make a concerted effort not to construct an exoticised adventure drama or to attempt any voyeuristic cowboy ethnography,[32] and not to tease out thrilling and rhetorical stories of hardship in the manner of tragedy porn that is characteristic of 'rescue-' feminists and activists. We were aware that in the traditional radical feminist representation of ethnographic or empirical

---

[32] Hoang (2015).

material about sex work, there has been cherry-picking of gruesome stories or exposition of exclusively the brutality of their experience.[33] We wished to follow literature that moved beyond the usual tropes around sex work (of sex-tourism, HIV/AIDS, trafficking or aspirations of 'escape' to a better occupation),[34] such as the outstanding work of Nalini Jameela, Svati Shah, Gowri Vijayakumar, Salla Sariola,[35] Kaveri Kaliyanda,[36] Nandini Gooptu or Prabha Kotiswaran. Like what Sumanta Banerjee[37] unveiled in the case of Bengal, we too saw during our conversations an intense evocation of drama and storm, sometimes even mockery and wrangling amongst themselves, but rarely self-pity, guilt, repentance, false modesty or woefulness we usually see in mainstream cultural representations that make these workers appear like vamps or victims.

Across the rest of this book, we reproduce dozens of their narrations. These are not a few individual stories cut up and patchworked across the chapters, but instead pieced together from thousands of lines of narrations by dozens of people, which we have deliberately kept nameless before each quote. Suspicions may arise in the reader's mind about the authenticity or the interpretation of the narrations we present here, due to the appearance and semantics of the text in this book, but we wish to clarify that the intention was to not only retain every ounce of the spiritual essence of these narrations (adapting the original Kannada and Tamil narrations and sarcasms, and attempting to reproduce idiomatic expressions in English) but to also steer clear of tragedy porn at the same time. At this juncture, we recall their determined and assertive voices:

> Do not assume anything about the sex workers you are meeting in advocacy situations. Do not assume anything about the sex workers you meet on Facebook, who you see in the media, who you see doing advocacy. Do not assume we have not been victims of assault, discrimination, family breakdown, abuse, violence, bad work conditions, domestic violence, poverty, police corruption or crime. We are people, just like you, who have faced everything in a life that any human being faces. We have a right to privacy about trauma we have experienced in our lives. But as sex workers we also face deep-seeded stigmas which mean that if we don't disclose to you our stories of tragedy and the demeaning experiences we have faced, we run the risk of not being believed by you.... When we don't tell [you], we face the accusation that we are covering up the 'truth' about sex work. For example, when we speak about the low prevalence of incidents of trafficking in the sex industry, we are accused of being in denial about migrant sex workers' lives.

---

[33] Sutherland (2004).

[34] Law (2000); Lowthers (2015).

[35] Sariola (2010).

[36] We must mention Kaliyanda (2016) as especially noteworthy and significant for us, since it studies neoliberal urbanism and gentrification in Bangalore, and its impact on street-based workers such as sex workers in the city; we consider this work as the precursor of this book.

[37] Banerjee (1998).

When we present actual statistics about drug use in the sex industry, we are told that we are ignoring or lying about drug use in sex work. We are expected to perform stereotypical narratives of tragedy porn for feminist audiences and when we don't, we are disbelieved. Sex workers don't want to be only believed when we perform these normative stereotypes about sex work. Why do you only believe a sex worker when they are telling you about a bad day at work, but have trouble believing a sex worker who tells you that decriminalisation and human rights will improve our workplaces and increased regulation will not?[38]

Many other concerns also arose. These were considerations mainly about the interaction between a privileged set (around whom city imaginaries are built and urban transitions are chalked out, and who are very visible as more than equals even among the Citizenry in the city's human composition) and an advanced-marginalised cohort (a group that is not weak but is forcibly invisibilised, stands towards the bottom of the social hierarchy and is considered a smudge on the city) – namely the interactions between us researchers and our narrators, the street-based sex workers. We, too, realised[39] soon that, even during the conversations, we were part of the very inequities and inequalities that we wanted to dismantle. As earnest as our intentions were to not 'represent' them or 'lend them a voice' (both of which are tendencies that would end up viewing them as voiceless, disempowered, devoid of agency or a sense of self), we knew at every stage, including as we write this now, that documenting urban transition through their eyes or walking their paths or deconstructing the dominant urban imaginary were all Sisyphean tasks. They would really never be fulfilled to the extent we aimed at, with thorough success and with complete justice to this set of informal workers, because the power inequities between us visibly lingered and swirled around the room during our interactions with them and during the narrations. To even pretend that we were perfectly neutral beings who were merely conducting enquiries would be self-deceiving. Even when we requested Prabhavati to conduct the interaction all by herself – in order to narrow the cultural distance and gap of privilege between the enquirer and the narrator – her enquiries still ended up carrying our vicarious presence and its embedded inequalities. We quickly realised[40] that since we could never (and did not wish to) hide our identities and socio-economic advantage, that glaring inequalities of privilege at the interactional level were to be accepted as inevitable, and that we would never be able to guess how they interpreted our enquiries and explanations. Our positions based on our identities (by class, caste and gender) clashed at every single moment of our fieldwork. The different spheres of advantage that our

---

[38] Jeffreys et al. (2011: 278–279).

[39] Inspired by Clandinin and Connelly (2000), Murray (2003) and Neethi (2016), which provide expositions of such concerns.

[40] As also forewarned by Clandinin and Connelly (2000), Sparke (1996) and Murray (2003).

narrators and we separately lived and worked in, our different purposes in life and work and differing ways in which we accounted for ourselves, were unconcealed and laid bare at all times. However, what pushed all of us through – sex worker (advanced-marginalised, mostly non-literate, male, female, transgender, mostly Dalit caste), social scientists (cisgender, upper caste, metropolitan, researchers, who were hitched) and research assistant (working class, literate, subaltern caste, urban, female) – was that our concerns about redrawing the city and re-chronicling its change were indubitably identical. We went back each day to our siloed and severely unequal worlds but regularly returned together on common motivational ground.

3

People

Implanted within the knotted lanes and on the grey, dusty streets of this city is an entire workforce of a guesstimated hundred thousand who are unseen in plain sight, except by two kinds of people – those who ardently demand their services and those who avowedly want them out. Millions of people who call this city their own and boast about having lived here for decades may either be in denial of their existence or would have simply not noticed the armies of women and men who wait for customers to sell their service – sex. Practically every corner of Bangalore is frequented by street-based sex workers, but one reason for the obliviousness towards this huge and omnipresent workforce may not always be due to the denial that is usually varnished by concerns of morality or intentions of revanchism. It may simply be because most of them do not stand out in appearance in any way as *sex* workers.

Street-based sex workers in several parts of Southeast Asia or in the West and, of course, in the red-light areas of Delhi, Calcutta or Bombay, would find some similarities with stereotypical images of female sex workers, but in Bangalore city these workers[1] barely fit such a typecast even by an inch. They are, for the most part, not sharply recognisable because they look like *anyone*. They are the vendors who sell you mint and coriander on the street, the domestic workers who come home, those who would be on their way to garment factories and small manufacturing cottage units, those who sweep the streets and collect garbage, those who work in small shops and hotels, those whom we see standing on the front end of the everyday bus trip; *anyone*. Only their customers and the police would know them for sure, for contrasting reasons. The rest of us, especially Citizens, would recognise them if and only if they stood in street corners well after dark and a car, which appeared incongruously expensive for a woman like that, swooped by and picked them up. Only then would we be aghast at what is happening on the streets of our beloved city. One can only imagine the cold horror that would creep up the spines of our Citizens if they realised that they crossed a dozen street-based sex workers every day on their way to the market, that the lady who helps out in cleaning the *puja* room and kitchen on an

---

[1] Henceforth, throughout this book, we employ the term 'sex worker' or just 'worker' interchangeably with 'street-based sex worker' for the purpose of brevity and in the context of the subject matter of this book, and not to casually conflate the dozens of varieties of sex work.

auspicious day might be a part-time sex worker, that the same voices who bargain about onion prices also bargain with clients about a condom-free experience. Bangalore's Populations would be more knowledgeable about these double lives, but Bangalore's Citizens probably do not even fathom that street-based sex work is happening at an arm's distance.

However, some street-based sex workers are only too visible. Transgender sex workers are the most identifiable not because they carry a placard announcing their services, but because they are immediately equalised with sex work and its associated disease, deviance and depravity. Most people approach transgender individuals to seek their ascribed sorcery but would like to see less of them in the city if possible. Female workers are, with some discernment after long observation, identifiable because no woman would just stand there on a street for hours on end unless she were up to something immoral or illegal.[2] Why would that lady stand there with that handbag visibly doing nothing but also not really fitting the 'homeless' appearance? Why would that woman spend the entire day on the step in front of the medical shop and not buy a single pill or syrup? Why is she speaking over the phone and then appearing and disappearing intermittently, each and every day? Where is her husband?

While female street-based sex workers are not specially dressed for the workplace or the job, emitting only the most subtle visual and behavioural signals to announce their availability, male workers are, conveniently and quite simply, invisible. Male workers simply fade into the teeming crowds since people do not look for such markers in men. Why can a man not just stand there on the street for hours on end? Why should he not just sit in front of the medical store all day? Why can he not speak over the phone and then disappear – perhaps he is doing errands? Why bother what his wife is up to, whether he has one at all? After all, who would suspect a man on a street of being up to impure activities when urban space is generally constructed around masculinity? Barring transgender individuals and their special dismal status, women and male street-based sex workers cannot be immediately ascertained as part of this occupation in the same manner as brothel-based sex workers or high-priced escorts.

The imperceptibility of street-based sex workers was a challenge to us too, when walking through the streets undertaking this study. It was unimaginable, and would smack of visual typecasting, to assume an individual on the street as a sex worker and approach him or her; even if we did strike right, their immediate reaction would convey intimidation. They are visible at once only to those who require their services, or to social workers targeting them for medical outreach or to the local police constable. They appear to shuffle through three

---

[2] This is very similar to being 'seen' in San Francisco, where streetwalkers could be discerned not only because of their distinctive dress but because no other women would wander the sparsely populated and dim streets (Bernstein 2007).

personae – being demanded, being helped or being outcasted, with little else in terms of identity as public individuals. The throngs of people around them can rarely be co-citizens or indifferent passers-by; they are either customers, ancillaries or adversaries. This forces street-based sex workers in Bangalore to constantly jostle between all of these compartments, unlike other people who can roam the streets and stand under a tree passing the time or simply smoking a cigarette or thumbing through one's mobile-phone screen. While most 'decent' people would have certainly heard of female street-based sex workers, even if in denial of their operation under one's nose, it is not improbable that they are unaware of the existence of male street-based sex workers. This is not our assumption but evidenced from some of our first meetings with civil society organisations where we were asked quite bluntly, '... you know there are male sex workers on the streets too, right?' which at first appeared offensive to our sensibilities but on hindsight revealed the large-scale ignorance, willing or naive, harboured by our 'decent' society. The yawning ignorance reveals itself when we realise that, let alone identifying a street-based sex worker, it is virtually impossible for the untrained eye to spot designations, genres and styles among them. Would a regular passer-by in KR Market, a loiterer on MG Road or a commuter at Majestic be able to identify a street-based sex worker, let alone discerning the nuances between a *kothi* and a 'double-decker' or a 'pant-shirt'?

The Chief Protagonists

There are male workers who offer services for homosexual men, for women, for bisexual men, for men who like men in feminine attire, for men who like men in male attire but radiating feminine coyness, for men who like only oral services, for men who are exploring their homosexuality, for homosexual men trapped in heterosexual marriages, for male customers who reciprocate such pleasure that no payment is required – the categories are practically endless. Services range on a continuum from solely economic transactions to intimate-erotic encounters.[3] Among male sex workers, besides the conventional MSM (male sex worker catering to men), and MSW (male sex worker catering to women), there are other categories that also have assigned nomenclature. MSMW are male workers who cater to both men and women. *Kothi*s are born male but are effeminate in behaviour and may cross-dress and offer receptive services mostly to men. *Panthi*s are males who prefer anal penetration more than reception. 'Double-deckers' are male by birth and in demeanour but are internally feminine and offer services to both men and women and are both receptive and insertive (hence the name). 'Pant-shirts' are an interesting cohort, who are male by birth and exaggeratedly display femininity while dressing conventionally male, which attract several male

---

[3] See also Lorway, Reza-Paul and Pasha (2009) on Mysore.

clients who desire a masculine body with 'feminine' attributes. What about female customers? When we enquired about this, the common response, exhibiting both banality in articulation and profundity in insight, was that if women were allowed to freely roam on the streets as men could, they would want such services too.

Female workers are also not monochrome, and they offer services to cis-men, to bisexual men, to men who wish to only touch at various spots but not have penetrative sex, to men who yearn to explore a woman's body devoid of sexual intercourse, to men who want only oral sex, to men who wish to have a female companion in physical proximity with no touch at all, to men who want to gain some 'training' before an impending marriage, and so on. Transgender workers share a very different experience in the services they offer – in fact, their service portfolio spans all these and expands much beyond this spectrum.

The element of caste is integral to street-based sex work. Caste and sex work share an intricate bond in India. While traditionally, some castes were compelled to engage in sex work as a ritual requirement either in Hindu temples or in fiefdoms both in rural and urban areas, gradually, sex work became an option in cities and smaller towns, and began to be populated by those who have little avenue for upward mobility either socially or economically – hence, invariably those of lower caste. Male and female workers in Bangalore belong mostly to subaltern classes and castes that have historically lived and worked in systematically imposed penury. Street-based sex workers usually hail from Dalit communities that are historically deprived and formerly untouchable castes, who have traditionally been placed at the very bottom of the Indian caste system and for centuries have been subject to severe deprivation and often even intimidation and violence; they are also termed politically as 'scheduled castes' in the official vocabulary of the colonial and post-colonial state.[4]

While a caste census of these workers is impossible to obtain (or conduct), it was reported to us by both civil society organisations, who associated with these workers, and by the workers themselves, that sex workers (male and especially female) are overwhelmingly of the Dalit caste or lower caste. Naturally, not all Dalit women end up as sex workers, but the vast majority of sex workers across gender are invariably Dalit. This should not be surprising. When we understand that most workers choose this occupation in utter economic desperation, a condition that for these individuals is not seasonal or cyclical but historically and prospectively a permanent economic state of being, we immediately realise that the social groups that fall into this dystopic long-term economic damnation are inevitably of Dalit (or other deprived) caste. Workers that participate in this occupation who belong to a more privileged lot in terms of caste or class usually do not solicit on the streets but are high-end online sex workers, both male and female.

---

4 Prakash (2015); Kamath (2018).

Those who are on the streets are usually working-class or economically poor Dalits who rarely have any other option. They end up in this profession early on, at the age of sixteen or eighteen, supported by other sex workers who recognise the abject circumstances from their own lives.[5]

Resources are meagre for those who wish to get quality education – a luxury for most – or even some form of industrial or vocational training. It is commonplace for employers at small hotels to discriminate against Dalits and not to employ them to avoid food being ritually contaminated, as food, second only to procreation, is obese with norms and practices around purity and pollution. They might appoint young Dalit men and women to do tasks that are relegated historically to these castes, such as unclogging drains or sewers in their establishment or sweeping after working hours of these hotels, but *never* cooking and serving. Many other occupations, such as a shop assistant, a petrol pump worker, delivery boy, and so on, require at least a minimal level of quality education that is out of reach for most Dalits, which is also a reflection of the general state of affairs of public education in reaching out to the vast majority of Dalits for whom the state must obligatorily facilitate basic entitlements such as literacy and education. They gain a rudimentary functional grasp on reading and writing as they age but are rarely beneficiaries of quality formal education or skill training. Almost all of them, who had seen the inside of a school, drop out as easily as they walked in. In the end, most Dalits have very few options in front of them except to proceed into occupations such as domestic work, construction work, garbage collection, sewer cleaning, human and animal carcass removal, cleaning of human waste, caretaking or other highly precarious and humiliating jobs that do not sustain families enough for even a hand-to-mouth existence. Economic frustrations, among those who cannot fathom even in their imaginations the opportunities enjoyed by thousands of people around them, simmer in the mind and heart. Prohibitively high medical costs, a range of requirements of dependents at home, such as the aged and young children, abandonment by husbands and parents and bleak possibilities of any sort of upward economic mobility (in addition to negligible possibilities of upward social mobility) bring their condition to a steady-state equilibrium of perennial desperation for subsistence day in and day out.

---

[5] All our narrators, all civil society organisations and several others we had spoken to during the course of our fieldwork had insisted that the landscape of sex work in Bangalore is dominated by street-based workers and that there were minimal chances of these individuals being trafficked, and hence they entered the profession 'by choice'. However, we were advised a note of caution by these organisations that while street-based sex workers may not entirely be stereotypically trafficked or coerced by violence, there surely are individuals in pockets and within closed quarters who enter the occupation in highly violent and coercive circumstances.

Many sex workers enter this profession in their late adolescence[6]; several others enter the profession in their twenties, having already worked (or still working) as domestic maids or factory or construction workers who are even more hard-pressed with dependents at home. The large body of workers in Bangalore, however, are in their twenties to their forties, with participation dwindling as they age. 'Retirement' from this profession differs across individuals, with some workers holding on until late middle age, while others move out of sex work in their late thirties if income options improve.

Stories of hunger, despair and abuse abounded in our conversations with women sex workers when they recounted how they entered the occupation.

Hungry for days, having just drunk hot water and tea, I did not know what to do. No one would employ me even for the most menial of tasks, which I was prepared to do. I was prepared to do anything – *anything* then included offering sexual services. After the very first service, I was paid with a *masala dosa*. That was the end of my hunger for that one time, but hunger would surely strike again. The next time onwards, it wasn't a *dosa*, it was cash.

I worked as a domestic help, cleaning house after house. Yet, it just wasn't enough. Cleaning all the houses in the world didn't seem to satisfy the money I needed for my family. Once, when I was crouched swabbing the floor, my employer took a fifty rupee note and delicately inserted it into my blouse. I could have said no, or just run away, but I realised I needed the fifty. In those days, I could eat for a whole day with that fifty. At that moment, I entered this world!

At sixteen, I was gang-raped by a bunch of unknown men on a street. I couldn't face myself, my family, my friends.... I just ran away from everything I knew and fled to Bangalore city, where I realised that at that age, I didn't know anything or have any skills to even approach someone for a job. I got into a conversation with some women who happened to be sex workers and realised that was one way ahead to survive.

Do you know how many mills in Bangalore closed down during the 1990s? They fell like large trees, one by one. That's where a small supply of sex workers came from. I was one of them. The mills were doing quite well, and I enjoyed my job there, even if it was for sweeping and for a low pay. I don't know why they had to close down, but a couple of us couldn't get any other sweeping job and moved to

---

[6] While we are sure they exist perhaps as a minuscule minority, it was related to us by sex workers themselves during fieldwork that there are 'quite assuredly' no underage (younger than age fourteen) street-based sex workers in Bangalore. In fact, sex workers whom we had spoken to say that they are, in fact, instrumental agents in fighting the trafficking of young children for sex work in this city, something which brothels in other Indian cities cannot do as effectively. This is also in great contrast to young children being even presented in glaring public view on the streets of Southeast Asian cities as sex workers.

sex work. Of course, we couldn't solicit in our old mill colonies, so we came to KR Market and Majestic.

Guess who pushed me into this? The person I was supposed to be faithful to. Many of you need to hide this job from your husbands, but in my case, I was forced into this by him. At first, he invited his friends and allowed them on me, and he made sure I never get pregnant. Then, he started charging them for it. I had no other meaning or purpose in life for two or three years. So, I finally thought, why should *he* make cash out of *my* body? I ran away from him one night when he was very drunk and began sex work in Majestic. After that, no one else got paid for my body.

My supervisor at the garment factory was constantly hinting that he wanted free sex. My friends there said he keeps doing that and that the hopeless fellow finally doesn't get any sex. But it was getting very difficult. So then I went to another job as an office cleaner where the boss even offered me money for it, but then I knew that this would repeat over and over again. In another job after that, the hotel owner kept rubbing against me while walking around and gestured, enquiring whether I liked it. Finally, in a fourth job, the supervisor actually jumped on me one day. Luckily, nothing adverse happened because I ran away at that moment. I was exhausted finding jobs and these escapades were getting tiring. I had little other choice after that apart from sex work but realised that, here, I could at least say no to a customer.

Oh, my mother was a sex worker back in Belgaum. So what else did I know? And she didn't say anything either when I began.

Stories of entry into sex work among male workers shared the element of abuse but were, however, a world apart on other matters.

I was regularly abused by my father at home. His three brothers used to laugh and make fun of me when he touched me in front of them, asking where it tickled. Maybe I was the only opening for him to do this, and I was the easiest target too. They never touched my sisters, though. But my mother turned a blind eye to all this. Over time, he even brought two of his friends over, who forced themselves on me. It became ingrained into me that this was all I was existing for. For sex. I don't belong to a very poor family. We even had a black and white TV when I was a kid. But I didn't know what else to do except sex work, since I was anyway being touched for free during my childhood.

I didn't do well in high school, but I learnt something quite important – I was attracted to boys, and I followed some of them into the bathroom to catch a glimpse. I used to watch them bathe too. Sometimes the older boys teased me, suggesting I was gay, but that embarrassment didn't stop me from discovering my sexuality. You know how young boys experiment with their bodies. When I went ahead after school to PUC [pre-university college], I found some like-minded boys

... we actually discovered each other through conversations, and then it was the green signal! I decided this was something I could even earn money with.

I am married and have two daughters. I work at an office next to the Vidhana Soudha and have a steady job. However, when my wife visits her parents, taking the kids with her, it allowed me enough time to begin this, which gives me good money and immense satisfaction that I am able to love the way I really want to, not with women.

As we have already mentioned earlier, in urban spaces abound with masculinity at every layer and crevice, men, whose sexuality and engagement with sex work cannot be discerned except by their aficionados, are able to freely walk the streets and sit in front of that medical shop all day. They are able to secure work and cheaper accommodation and are able to travel in public transport at all times of the day even when off-duty from sex work – something that women workers cannot. They are able to lead lives as Citizens and Populations and undertake sex work too. Of course, this is not to suggest that for male sex workers this is entirely some kind of a hobby or pastime to earn some extra cash, but they do benefit from being able to operate in a flux where earning and sexual pleasure meet, with some encounters entirely for earning and some purely for pleasure, but all in the context of *work*. Many men are full-time sex workers and continue for decades, even if it means abandoning families and living rough off the streets. Many are harassed by the police since they are male street-based sex workers and not 'gays' – a typology ascribed by low-rung street-based workers to higher-end English-speaking male homosexual sex workers. However, on a spectrum of entry into sex work, male workers score much lower on the economic vulnerability factor than do women workers and are, hence, relatively 'better off'.

A large proportion of homosexual male workers are forced into heterosexual marriages, in which it is not uncommon for them to beget children, adhering to social and familial requirements. Those whom we had spoken to, who were not married or did not want to marry at all, usually ran away from home during adolescence when they began discovering their sexual orientation as deviant from the mainstream. Those of an effeminate personality, *kothis*, were teased all through adolescence and young adulthood, which left an indelible imprint of rancour on their minds. *Kothis,* as was told to us, face the highest stigma right from their immediate families and are often thrown out of their homes and left to fend for themselves on the streets, where they begin sex work. Cross-dressers are ridiculed, being forced to adorn female attire for the purpose of amusement and jeering among male friends. In most instances, all this does not stop male workers from engaging in sex work, even if it is right under the noses of their families. This is simply because they would rarely be suspected of any sort of non-heterosexual activity in the first place, unless it is conspicuous as in the case of cross-dressers. Many men discover their non-heterosexuality with no knowledge that such an orientation is even possible, relating to us during conversations that they found themselves 'strange' during adolescence, least interested in either gaping at girls in school or in the neighbourhood (when that is mostly what the other boys would talk about) and, instead, shrinking into themselves wondering what might be wrong. Several of our narrators recalled how they finally managed to discover other boys with a similar wavelength and opinions during higher education or among friend circles with whom they not only discovered their sexuality but even gained opportunities to realise their desires. If the pressure to get married was unbearable, they would run away to the city (or if they lived in the city, to a faraway neighbourhood within that city); if due to financial helplessness they could not just run away and live rough, they would proceed with that marriage and consummate it with as much intimacy as could be pretended. The recourse for thousands of such men lay in sex work. A man could leave the house and not require to report to his wife or parents where he was going; he could take a trip with male friends without arousing an ounce of suspicion, especially if it was proxied as 'work-related' and as long as one could say that with a straight face; if unemployed (in the sense of a mainstream job), he could spend hours on end hanging around in KR Market or at the Majestic bus stand on a certain platform number, and no questions would be asked even if he encountered relatives or acquaintances; he could stand outside a public toilet, with no eyebrows raised. He was free. In fact, it was even possible to gaslight the rest of the family when necessary if uneasy questions were asked on those rare occasions.

> What do you think I am, some local tramp or vagabond roaming the streets? See how much money I bring home?

We slowly learned that sex work was an avenue for sexual liberation for many non-cis men, who were trapped in marriages and families and did not wish to be indifferent to their desires. One of our elderly male narrators even said that he loved coming to Bangalore from Chittoor town in neighbouring Andhra Pradesh so he could meet his male friends and clients and have a joyous time even for an hour if possible during the job. We had the good fortune to meet him when he was in Bangalore on one of those trips.

> I love coming here; I have my regular room in my regular lodge ... even the bell boy doesn't suspect anything [chuckling]. My regular friends come over that room and sometimes bring paying customers too ... my age radiates my experience! And through my trips here, I go back home to Chittoor with my pockets filled with money from my normal work and sex work and my heart filled with joy.

Another narrator told us about how he could take a few minutes off from his journey from work (in an office) to home to meet some of his regular customers or friends.

Oh, who's going to ask at home if I am around ten to twenty minutes late? Being stuck in traffic isn't even something that you need to mention in this city … it's quite understood. I don't need to 'report' home at exactly some time, so I sometimes used to stop by, in the good old days in that area where Majestic metro station now stands, meet some regulars and go back home … they knew where to find me so my customers were assured. When mobile phones arrived, it became even easier.

While neoliberal urban transition and city gentrification has indeed hit male sex workers (as we shall see in the later chapters), their vulnerability on the streets is far lower than that of women, for the same reasons that they are able to escape monitoring by family members. Their relationships at home continue for decades in complete separation from sex work, rarely clashing except very accidentally. Sex work for men, as many of our narrators told us, lay on a continuum of pleasure, discovery and commerce. It was not smooth sailing at all times, especially when you were caught by those who knew exactly what you were doing outside that public toilet and those in uniform who left cane-baton marks on your body to remind you not to dirty the city with your activities.

Female workers also take great care in keeping strict silos between family and sex work but are usually unsuccessful. Female street-based sex workers, for the most part, offer services to men who are solicited on the street, which cannot be kept entirely clandestine or couched within any 'work-related trip' or 'job' or 'business,' though sex work does technically fall into all of these. Many female sex workers straddle the worlds of domestic work, garment factory work and sex work. We name exactly these three occupations more than, say, street-vending or nanny services, because this has been reported in several instances. Neither of these occupations can singularly provide for the material needs of their families, and, especially when Dalit, other occupations are hard to secure. It would be hard to say whether sex workers engage in domestic work or whether domestic helps engage in sex work – and we do not find the need to configure this chicken-and-egg puzzle – but the fact remains that all female sex workers, like a large proportion of male sex workers, are not full-time 'career' sex workers. While a number of workers we spoke to have spent a major portion of their lives as sex workers alone, the greater majority have juggled other occupations, particularly domestic work, along with sex work. Spanning across multiple worlds of work, each with their own grading on the morality scale, provides the perfect shield for many female sex workers, who report to their families that they are actually engaging in the other job while undertaking sex work too. Many women leave their dependent parents, children and spouses (often dependent too) early in the morning, travelling several kilometres away to begin their day with domestic work, which rarely crosses noon in most households, and then move on to their selected streets for sex work. We stress the distance for the simple reason that the inconspicuous nature of street-based sex work would prohibit them from conducting this in their neighbourhoods around familiar people. On the other hand, the teeming crowds at Majestic or KR Market provide the perfect camouflage to seamlessly blend in and continue their occupation. Our narrators provided a number of instances where they spotted acquaintances at Majestic or KR Market and had to quickly hide, or if they accidentally bumped into them, had to draw from a quiver full of reasons why they were there at that time of the day. Conversations on what they were doing in Majestic on an odd day and time were never in the form of a warranted justification from the part of these acquaintances and were more of a simple and easy 'how come here?' which would then flow into a casual chat. However, encounters were not all plain sailing, and sex workers have related to us about how they were sometimes caught red-handed in the act of soliciting or speaking to a man who was evidently anonymous or even through hearsay. In such cases, as we heard, there would naturally be colossal confrontations in the household and always around morality and fidelity. If separation or attempted murder did not result, settlements were made based on various arguments.

> When he began beating me, I asked him where he thinks the money to run this house comes from! He demands cash every evening, of course, for alcohol, and I told him *this* is where his drinks' money comes from. He still continued beating me that day, but from the next day, neither did the alcohol money demand stop nor did my sex work. He needed to beat me that evening, to satisfy his rage, but after that he never beat me about this issue.

Naturally, this instance does not imply that the husband either condoned the occupation or realised his folly. It just meant that business had to be as usual since this was how the household escaped poverty.

> A couple of my customers wanted to only rub themselves on me. No penetration. Some wanted me to only use my hands, and they never would touch a single part of my body. The good thing about this was that it was the cleanest and safest thing for me, and I didn't need a lodge room. I could offer this in an autorickshaw or even behind some big trees. At first, it was surprising to me, but on asking one of my customers, he gave me the strangest answer. He said that he really wanted to have someone engage in oral sex, which his wife would not do, but he didn't want to cheat on his wife by 'sleeping' with another woman. So this was the best of all worlds. No 'cheating', but fun too.

> One fellow had full penetrative sex with me, but he didn't touch his mouth on me. I tried to offer, but he just turned his face away. After everything, I asked him what happened, and he said that he was married and didn't want to 'love' me and only wanted sex, hence no kissing. Very faithful fellow [laughing].

Narrations about the responses of workers' children, who were young adults in high school or college, were noteworthy.

My daughter didn't say anything at first and didn't speak a word the whole afternoon after she found out from her friend who saw me at KR Market every day. I found her crying a little later on, but what do I tell her? How could I explain that this was my job? She's too young and innocent to understand such things, which even I took a while to understand at that age, moreover, only much after I entered the job. But I was wrong. I guess she understood that her mother does sex work and that this was how we got by. No word was spoken of it after that, but at the same time there was no approval either. We had to continue in this manner.

My son was teased in school by his seniors that his mother is a prostitute. He just retaliated with a few fistfights and kicking up some dust, knowing that there was no way he could either justify it or deny it.

My daughter told me that some 'aunty' in the neighbourhood told her that I was up to some dirty job. I asked her gingerly about what the aunty had exactly said. She shuffled around a few words, possibly because it was more embarrassing for her to say the words 'you are a sex worker' than to cope with the actual fact. But what surprised me was how she thought about it. She ended the conversation shrugging and telling me nonchalantly, 'That is your fate, Amma, so you have to do it.'

My children knew very well I was doing this, but how else could I fund my younger sister's wedding? How else could I fund that heavy loan that left us practically starving?

During one interesting narration, a worker turned the tables in the argument, challenging the accuser almost biblically that they may cast a stone if they have not sinned themselves.

My husband heard about my sex work. He once even passed by my cruising spot to confirm what he had heard. He had a helmet on to make sure I didn't see him. When I got back home that day after being spotted by his own eyes, he was waiting near the door like some warrior ready for battle ... the only thing he didn't do then is to take a knife and kill me. I had to hear all sorts of screaming: 'Do your parents know you're a prostitute ... how this family has been contaminated ... how *I* have become impure too by touching you ... is this how faithful you are to me, to my children?' ... blah blah ... But then you know what I did? Risking everything, I asked him to answer with a straight face: 'Haven't you hired a sex worker too! I've seen you!' And then ... just like that ... all the heat of that argument just vanished to zero, and he plainly went out to smoke a cigarette as though nothing had happened. I laughed so hard inside myself when I went back into the kitchen to wipe my face off the sweat of that fight. I didn't know he actually *had* hired sex workers! Honestly, it was a daring shot! It was surely some divine spirit that made that incisive dialogue exit my mouth!

Unlike brothel-based workers, and much like escorts, street-based sex workers live with families and very often in 'regular' homes with children, neighbours and others. Festivals are celebrated on the streets together with acquaintances, trips back to the village are as common, people invite one another for weddings, puberty ceremonies, funerals, cradling ceremonies and other events in the family – like *anyone* else, just that sex work also happens alongside their other jobs. Very similar to male sex workers, female workers also dodge families and relatives about their occupation. However, very unlike male workers, for female workers, the risks are far higher and consequences far more dangerous within the family if discovered. Pressures to keep the family afloat are far more biased against women, as they are everywhere else, and these demands wax and wane according to illnesses or debts or other reasons, urging them to engage in more than one occupation, invariably ending up in sex work. In so many cases narrated to us, families, whether agreeable or disagreeable to the job, had to understand that the end goal of this occupation was neither sex for pleasure nor was this committing promiscuity, but for supplementing income in an increasingly harsh world, in an increasingly gentrifying city, with material aspirations only exponentially increasing in lower-strata families and with medical or other contingencies that rear their ugly head only too often among this strata. There were several cases among our narrators and, in general, of workers living rough on the streets as homeless individuals. Across gender, street-based sex workers are often thrown out of their families out of stigma for undertaking this occupation and end up on the streets and in bus stands with their precarity heightened manifold, now not only in work but in their everyday existence too.

Transgender workers redefine what a home and family is. Violence and discrimination against them often define their home environment, where they are put under persistent pressure to allude to 'normal' gender expressions in the wide spectrum of settings they visit (schools, extended families, religious congregations, workplaces, and so forth), naturally pushing them away to the streets and seeking the patronage of other transgender individuals. Some of them live off the streets where one needs to sleep with an eye open and be vigil day and night for harassment and expulsion. A tiny proportion of them lives in homes in poor neighbourhoods and slums, which allow them to co-reside. However, the great majority of them in Bangalore live in *hamam*s, a space that draws its name from old bathhouses where one could bathe, now used as a label for the living quarters within which a small group of transgender individuals sleep, bathe, communally cook and eat and realise their selves and awaken their sexualities. *Hamam*s are found all over the outskirts of the city, as single-structure buildings with one or two rooms and a common kitchen and bath area. Not all of them have running water and continuously supplied electricity, and toilets are usually outside the main home and communal, but this is the place where they can live with a much greater sense of security and community. *Hamam*s are generally headed by an older transgender individual called a 'guru' (who may be in one's thirties or older, if one at all survives into middle age) from whom an aspirant needs permission to enter and join as the disciple. Aspirants need to serve allegiance to the guru for the period of time that they live in that *hamam*, which can be either just weeks or months, or sometimes several years. Changing *hamam*s upon shifting allegiance to another guru is not uncommon and can occur when there is either a spat with one's guru or with other members, or when one needs to move away for earning better. Along with all the other members of the *hamam* family, all of whom may not be sex workers and may be restricted to begging or ritualistic performances, one has to bring in income and submit it to the family, which is then shared for everyday living. Though most transgender workers we spoke to referred to their gurus and *hamam*s as literally 'mothers' and 'families', they were very clear of the hierarchy and informal disciplinary system put in place in *hamam*s, which were highly necessary given the hellish world outside and the protective hearths they needed. *Hamam*s, many narrators said, were where they trained themselves in various skills, and the only fifty square feet in the city where they were safe and secure and could be themselves emotionally, spiritually and sexually.

Accomplices, Scoundrels and Lovers

Clients, customers, regulars, lovers – the sexscape of Bangalore teems with these. While it is not possible to strictly classify customers aligned to workers in the manner that Kimberly Kay Hoang has done for Ho Chi Minh City, there is a blurry cross-section of clients that we can attempt to demarcate, aligned to location. In fact, as narrated to us by the workers in vivid detail, it is the location that classifies workers as well as customers. Let us visit our major locations once again.

The lowest economic stratum of workers and customers is in KR Market. By virtue of the nature of the place – a wholesale market for horticultural and floral commodities, a bus stand, shops and vendors slotted alongside one another, relatively uncontaminated by gentrification – the economic purchasing power of the general populace is relatively low, and it is also characterised, unlike the other two major locations, by a floating community who enter and exit the area on a daily basis in connection with commerce and employment. Trucks blaring their air-horns and dusty buses enter the area every day all through a twenty-four-hour period, offloading fresh sooty green vegetables, fruits and tubers sporting a layer of fine sod, bright flowers by the ton floodlighting the area with their natural, joyful colours – all these manned by those from the villages around Mandya, Dharwad, Hubbali and nearby Magadi and Kolar for whom Bangalore is no IT city or start-up hotspot, but the final destination for agrarian commerce, for tiny and recurrently rickety businesses, for political rallies when paid and invited and, of course, for easy-to-access sex. A large workforce travels to the area for day jobs, ranging from the manual work of heaving and hauling grimy sacks, to work that involves digging through black, slushy ground around the streets or even construction work. Many travel through KR Market as a stopover to access other parts of the city, delivering cloth, hardware, machine spare parts, plastic, small electronics, foodstuff and a full range of everything that makes up a city's commerce and services. Seated inconspicuously in the middle of these small and tiny businesses and deliveries are transactions of sex and erotica too. Many customers demanded sex before dawn, right after delivering their produce to the market at around 1:30 a.m. and just before they left the area at about 5 a.m. to return to their villages and towns. Among the areas we studied, the range of prices of these transactions is the lowest in the KR Market area. While in MG Road, a female sex worker aged under thirty can command a good 2,000 rupees[7] for a single session, at the very other end of the scale, in KR Market, a female worker aged over forty years deals with transactions of even 50 rupees or 100 rupees, depending on the depth of the client's pockets and the urgency of his demand. Our narrators said that those who 'wanted urgent' are charged less since they took up less time, finished the matter off in minutes and did not care much about the diversity of services during the session. The logic, our narrators said, was simple: '… what can clients afford in an area like KR Market?' Understandably, therefore, the population of street-based sex workers around this area are those who are older, more desperate for everyday livelihood and who generally grew up in dire poverty. Many of them take up sex work, as narrated to us, even for a single meal or to buy alcohol. As much as the customers 'wanted urgent', many of the workers in KR Market also need customers urgently to get by for that day. Negotiations with customers are quick and to the point and rarely involve long sessions or more conversational interactions. Transgender workers abound the area, as they told us, felt least threatened in this locale, and hence they constitute a good proportion of workers here; in fact, they are visibly freer and seen fluidly moving around or sitting or sleeping on the streets comfortably in this area than in other areas of Bangalore.

Sex workers in the KR Market area cater to clients who are also, as illustrated, equivalently poorer, more rural or urban working class, often homeless, and who can cough up a very maximum of about 200 rupees for services. Rates are usually communicated to one another by word of mouth, and there is a general understanding that one cannot command more than a limit as customers simply cannot afford more than a limit. Condoms or other forms of protection against diseases were reported to us as a rarity in these areas, as very often the price

---

[7] We had little 'proof' of these figures except for triangulating with civil society organisations or former sex workers who now work for the empowerment of their colleagues. While some space has to be granted for exaggeration at both ends of the price spectrum, since many of these figures were independently reported during narrations, and since one cohort at one area attested to these rates about the other cohort in another area, we present them here verbatim.

of a purchased condom emerges as some proportion of the price of the service itself, and the content of the negotiating conversation while agreeing to offer the service is also devoid of this item. As a few organisations working for the health of sex workers in this area told us, the only way to ensure health and safety was to distribute condoms freely, a task that was relatively easier in the past than it is now since the streets are being cleared of these workers and they are now harder to source. Hence, in terms of price, safety, economic strata and even the ambience, KR Market is certainly the underclass of the sex work industry of Bangalore. Interestingly, in the context of urban transition, this stratum is the one that has been relatively less affected by the neoliberal gentrification of Bangalore.

The clogged lanes of the Majestic area were different, we were told, as workers and customers here were not only of a slightly 'higher' pedigree, lower than middle class (in the self-proclaimed middle class's definition of the middle class) but also did not slip into the derelict underclasses that inhabit the areas around KR Market. However, we find this hierarchy of classification, as presented to us by our narrators, to be problematic as there are indeed scores of homeless and poor people who live around the Majestic area, many of whom demand cheap sex, and many who offer it at inexpensive rates too. Street-based sex workers in Majestic serve a clientele who are mostly local and hence urban, unlike customers in KR Market who are a mix of both city dwellers and rural migrants. The workers themselves are also mostly of a middle-age range of thirty to forty-five, with a small scattering of those above forty-five or fifty years of age. They were noticed, in our observation, to be dressed in more expensive attire compared to workers at KR Market; this fact must not be viewed as incidental or trivial, but instead must be read alongside the concept of bodily capital discussed earlier. Workers, especially female, at Majestic may deliberately adorn saris or handbags that appear more expensive than those one would buy off the streets or those that appear cast away or used second-hand and may take a little more effort in enhancing their appearance. Time stretched for a little longer here for negotiation and final service. Unlike the crowds at KR Market who had a tight time frame that concurred with the amount of time they spent there during the pre-dawn hours or who could just about afford fifty or 100 rupees, here were shoppers who could be negotiated with for that extra 100, sometimes even convinced to pay up nearly 500 rupees for a session, if one is under thirty years of age, of a lighter complexion and dressed well. Mid-age-range workers could also command around 300 rupees for a session in Majestic, while older workers could earn up to 200 rupees for a single session of even non-penetrative sex. The negotiation in this area was more complicated than in KR Market. While rooms in lodges (a theme we take up in greater detail in the next chapter) were utilised in KR Market for providing services, the presence of lodges as a perennial and standard stage for sex work was much more in Majestic, so much so that one cannot think of sex work at Majestic without conjuring up the lodge room in the same breath. This meant that the negotiation for prices involved variable costs of lodge rooms also, the fixed costs of paying up the manager and staff of these lodges and maintaining cordial equations with these individuals. Hence, investment in the job in the Majestic area went much beyond just keeping up looks; it meant investment in clothes and a few accessories, investment in people and investment in one's health, too; as a worker, you did not want to look as ramshackle as the clients in KR Market, you wanted to look a little more uppity and with a little more toned body language.

Negotiation here also meant learning the tricks of the trade to get the best price. Male sex workers, positioned outside their regular cruising points such as public toilets (which, again, we take up in greater detail in the next chapter), walk right in and give quick and fleeting glances to the potential customer, signalling clearly that a service is possible. While some people who do not wish to be customers may retort with looks of condescension and irritation, and while some may pretend to not see these overtures, others wish for the next signal, which our narrators told us is usually a long stare with a light daubing of the tongue around one's lips. Now, if the last signal was not clear enough, but the blank staring continued, then, and *only* then, would the worker approach the individual who was possibly a potential customer and ask him directly, 'Oral *beka?*' ('Do you want oral sex?'). Most of the time, stage two was sufficient, but in some cases, even stage one was not necessary since informed customers would spot a male worker almost automatically, especially if he were a *kothi* or *panthi*. Female workers required almost no overtures, as was narrated to us, but did have to still rely on long stares and a light nod asking whether the individual would like to avail of her services. If it was retaliated by an even lighter nod from the customer, the next task would be to set a rate. After dusk, one could speak, but during broad daylight, it meant twitching two fingers for 200 rupees, scratching one's head with three fingers for 300 rupees and placing a full palm on the side of one's face in expectation of 500 rupees for a regular service. Once this was somewhat agreed upon, the next task was to go to the location where services would be offered. No doubt, the Majestic transaction area is a few notches higher in strata than the KR Market area, but there are always the drunkards, the vagabonds, the dregs and, of course, even the police awaiting service.

The MG Road area offers a large variety of clients, we were told, ranging from working-class men right up to those who drive by in cars or motorcycles and pick up workers to consume their services in another location. Traditionally, street-based sex work around MG Road has mostly been after dusk and up until sunrise, but there are still a few workers operating successfully in a clandestine manner during the daytime as well. Workers command a price higher than the Majestic area and, of course, higher than the KR Market area. One could say that the MG Road area is populated by workers who stand on the borderline between open street-based sex work and more high-priced indoor escorts, and that this area resembles a less explicit bare-open version of some of the street-based sex industries of the West or Southeast Asia. Around this area are the cruising spots and pubs where 'gays' (as what our lower-rung MSMs from Majestic and KR Market termed them) roam around soliciting clients outside of watering holes and feeding spots in Church Street, Brigade Road, around St.Patrick's Church, Rest House Road and all the way from St Marks' Church to Trinity Circle. This was an interesting nomenclature they employed: while we conventionally think of 'gay' individuals as male homosexuals, the term was colloquially used among street-based male workers, particularly to connote differences in economic class. They repeatedly used the term 'gay' during their narrations when talking about higher-priced MSMs and MSWs around this area, who are fluent in English, wear more expensive clothes and solicit clients with deeper pockets. According to our narrators, 'gays' around this area would never be troubled by the police or heckled by more decent citizens there since they are viewed as 'cleaner' and 'less harmful' to the moral glow of society, compared to the male workers of Majestic and KR Market. 'Gays' were said to give hard competition to the male workers in this area, as the clientele would naturally be drawn to the former. Transgender sex workers are the least visible around this area, as their presence would not be tolerated as freely as around KR Market or Majestic. They would be stigmatised for their very presence there, unlike in the other areas, and would be easily whisked away so as not to contaminate the area with their appearance.

Do workers work across areas? Can a worker generally based in Majestic work a little more on bodily capital and shift to MG Road for a few weeks to supplement earnings? Or, if a worker is unable to keep up appearances at Majestic, can she move down the ladder and operate in KR Market? While the answer to this is affirmative in principle, in practice, workers usually stick to their areas for several reasons. As will be seen in greater detail, there is an intricate negotiation that workers have to craft over time, with a whole breadth of agents around them, which is not easy if a worker lands up in a new area. Workers also develop a fraternity or sorority among themselves in an area, which is not impenetrable by newcomers, but, at the same time, not immediately gained upon arrival. Prices, services, agreements on work, relationships, equations, and so on, are agreed upon in an almost cartel-like fashion, which makes mobility across areas more difficult than imagined. Of course, gentrification tendencies from the part of the state and the public have ensured that this movement happens, and when the immigration of new workers into an area is forced, the results are very abrasive. We will see this in greater detail in Chapter 5.

While there are stark differences across areas in many respects, a few commonalities still exist, such as the possibility of actual emotional intimacy between worker and customer. Female sex workers across areas and strata occasionally offered unpaid sex to those clients with who they develop personal inclinations, though these may not be in the most rosy-romantic of settings, and which usually do not result in any sort of marital relationship. While traditionally, transactions are generally wordless, brief, to-the-point economic relationships, a few clients and workers end up beginning conversations about family, financial or other circumstances in life and work, which in some instances find resonance with one another, or which then prompts the customer to offer gifts in kind in the form of, say, clothing, small trinkets, maybe even a rudimentary mobile phone and other tangibles. Even intangible offerings, such as a shoulder to seek solace, or even an ear to listen or just quality time spent with one another, may materialise. What begins as a strictly erotic–economic transaction ends up slowly becoming cosier, with a little coquetry thrown in, perhaps opening up into a friendship and eventually moulting into something more. This could sometimes offer them a little assuage in a world of work that is otherwise ridden with the risk of violence, exploitation, dispossession and disease at every moment. Occasionally, some of these men are even designated as 'lovers', to garnish the experience with a light sheen. Naturally, these relationships wax and wane, and though intimacy is enjoyed for the moment, most workers attested that they were not naive enough to allow these fleeting intimacies to consume them and distract them from their occupation.

> So many men even offer to marry us, sometimes even after just one session! Just think about it: they're going to leave you the moment they find their next interest. Just a thrill of the moment, possibly a long spell in his sexless marriage. Don't trust any one of them; we are just their hobby....

But later in the conversation, the same narrator continued:

> Yes, of course, I've had lovers. I loved a few men during my career, and they were so gentle and nice, I could spend more than an hour speaking to them about so many things – movies, life, money, what not. What I meant earlier was that it would be advisable not to fall for every fellow who proposes to marry you or says he loves you. Better not to fall for these gifts blindly. We're here to buy sex from, but we can't be bought with gifts.

There was an additional issue – that some of these men 'befriended' multiple female sex workers at the same time, which then gets discovered by these workers, much to their chagrin, blossoming into the eventual hurling of words and flowing of tears and the roaring confusion between a man being 'my lover, your lover, our lover....'[8] Enjoyed for a fleeting while, it is at best avoided, as nearly all our narrators concurred.

---

[8] Quoted verbatim from a narrator.

Another feature that is common across all areas, which is viewed as a natural companion to sex work, is violence. The hundreds of hours of narrations that we noted down bristled and crawled at every turn with horrific stories of violence, mugging, rape and plain threats to life and limb. Lovers were rare, but rogues were aplenty. Workers, particularly female and transgender, narrated that they were always on the vigil, sometimes developing a sort of sixth sense where their antennae would shoot high up on meeting a client who appeared even the slightest bit suspicious. Being taken to eerie-looking houses and cold uninhabited rooms was part of the experience, said the workers, especially when their familiar lodges were being closed down one by one. It was a monthly affair, even weekly for some workers, and all too habitually on an almost everyday basis for transgender workers, to meet violence on the face. Men would pose as clients with the commitment of payment for services, take the workers to unfamiliar rooms or other decrepit areas and very routinely at knifepoint rob them, usually after having sex. Some would even spill out their frustrations on workers by beating them with bare hands or with a small baton or rod, to vent out personal bitterness. Rarely was such aggression personal; it was usually for the purpose of ventilating one's personal fury or simply for plunder. Male workers said they were mugged sometimes for just those 100 rupees they had from the day's earnings. Female workers said that they were attacked sometimes for their little bits of jewellery or for the macabre thrill of vandalising a female body.

I demanded, like I do for dozens of customers, that he wear a condom. You know what he did in response? He threw chilli powder on my vagina! What gave me nightmares was not only that he did such a gruesome thing, but that he was actually ready with that chilli powder carrying it around and ready to meet me with it.… Don't you think he was there ultimately not for my services but for the thrill of attacking me?

Oh, how common it is for them to slap me repeatedly after services. Sometimes even after payment, sometimes no payment. Maybe they actually want to slap their wives or someone else, maybe they were single men who were jilted by someone they were pursuing ... and my face and my body turn out to be a battlefield where he wages war against his fate.

A couple of them showed me a knife. That's it. He just kept it next to his pants after he took them off. Just a small signal, but strong enough to give me the message that this might be the last day of my life. My children's faces appear at that very moment, each and every time I see a customer with a knife. Of course, none of them knew me personally and they may not cut my body into pieces, but they just wanted it for that momentary thrill.

I have a special relationship with cigarettes. I've never smoked one, but I've encountered too many. One fellow, like in the movies, just rotated a live cigarette around my breast. Perhaps to threaten me about something, perhaps just to look like a movie rapist, perhaps for the joy of it. Another fellow kept blowing smoke into my face until he finished the cigarette, and I coughed throughout that night and the next day. Yet another one kept bringing the live end close to my face, and taking it back, over and over again. But a couple of men have seriously burnt me with one. I can show you the burn marks, but you won't sleep tonight if you see them.

All too often, sex work negotiated for a certain price ends up being unpaid rape.

Not paying for services is a weekly affair. At least one of them does it every week. It may be violent, where he brandishes a paper cutting blade and points it to my nipples, sometimes circling a line around my face with it like in the movies. Sometimes, he just leaves me on the floor of the room after the service and just runs out – in one instance, he threw the mattress of the lodge room on me to pin me down and ran out, leaving me totally shocked! Sometimes, even after the service, there are no knives or blades, but he starts punching my face until it bleeds, and while I'm recovering from the bleeding, he escapes.

He seemed like any other customer. It was daytime too, I hadn't had lunch yet. He took me to a lodge that I was familiar with. The room he took me to was unlocked from the outside – I wondered how that could be, unless … yes, there were other people inside! They were just waiting for him to bring a woman, and then it was all storm and fury, with all of them taking turns to do whatever they wanted to me. Forget about payment, I couldn't move that entire day and lay down outside that lodge near the bus stop for the rest of the day, looking and murmuring like a collapsed drunkard.

Many of them think that we are here to be raped. They don't want to understand that we are doing a job here, which we need to be paid for. It's a service, you know, like how I clean three houses in Vyalikaval in the morning and get paid for it before I come to KR Market in the late afternoon. Some of them smile so nicely and wear such good clothes, but, at the end, they rape us. When it's not paid for, it's rape. As simple as that.

However, the category of workers who were subject to the greatest violence and humiliation were transgender workers. Serving as both a visual outlandish fascination as well as a laboratory for conducting the most ignominious experiments and most innovative forms of savagery were the bodies of transgender sex workers. For many people who commissioned their services, they were never humans, a privileged designation that even female and male workers receive; they were just freaks of nature who could be toyed around with. Even if it was not blatantly violent, in the sense of bodily harm, it was sometimes just with the motive of gaining a tremendous sadistic joy in humiliating them.

It was so incredibly traumatic. I told him a good price, and he took me to an area that I was familiar with. However, there were other men there who did not care for sex or even masturbation. They were there for a little fun. They tormented me by squeezing parts of my body and asking me very insulting questions about my anatomy. They even slapped me on my face every other moment, and at the end, which was the worst, they stripped me naked, took away my clothes and locked me in a used, uncleaned toilet that was outside the building. It took a very long while for someone to come and help me out, after all that shouting for help and smelling of human waste. But then, I had to get back to sex work the very next day, as if nothing happened.

On the one hand, they call us to bless their baby boys. They look upon us as some sort of divine beings who are capable of magic. But then, once, a customer took out a kitchen knife with a small blade, the ones you cut fruits with, and kept slashing my body, calling me very vulgar names. I went home back to the *hamam* that day with marks all over my chest and buttocks, which are their usual targets to attack.

Oh, most of them come to me dead drunk. They can't stand straight, but they seem to be able to attack very precisely! They come with broken bottles still dripping with the last bits of liquor and keep jabbing the sharp end between my thighs, without causing serious damage, but enough bleeding for me to require some cloth to cover it up. It's a blood-filled mess, this job. But what else do we do to eat?

There are no rules in this business. Completely anarchic and unruly, this is a fertile venue for people, particularly men, to give free rein to their most criminal of frustrations or grisly of ambitions upon a sex worker's body. While, in many instances, the process follows the charted trajectory of monetary compensation for erotic services, it is naive to expect that the affair will always abide by this linear algebraic formula in some neoclassical economics manner. Men with putrid parlance, spine-chilling impositions from clients, tales of barbaric experiences of rape and, most of all, the combination of a cavernous nausea and utter terror after the customer announces after the service that he is HIV positive – the gruesomeness of the list is a bottomless pit. At times, there are friends and lovers but, more often than not, there are demons. Other compatriots and savages also exist in their world, though not in the form of customers but as ancillary actors.

Friends, Romans, Countrymen

The assortment of actors orbiting street-based sex work in Bangalore is staggering. Unlike brothel-based sex work, which has a long line of individuals ranging from pimps to human trafficking agents who could (and ought to) be incarcerated by law, street-based sex work is aided and buttressed by all kinds of regular people. Recalling Chapter 1, these support staff are what we termed as a city's Populations, who are accorded a second-class status in the urban human conglomerate and who are crucial in supporting the superstructure, but have to limit themselves within their sphere, for everyone's health, happiness and harmony. To run a successful city, for best results, Populations may interact with Citizens within the coordinates that the latter assign to them and are forbidden to transgress those demarcations. In this manner, there's a place for everyone, everyone knows their place and upward socio-economic mobility from among the Populations is fully welcome, as long as it is confined to the spasmodic success stories of the autorickshaw driver's son who entered the civil services or the security guard's daughter who gained a scholarship to study abroad. Concrete systemic shifts in fundamental variables such as a macroeconomic reconfiguration of structural inequalities, or a dismantling of socio-historical deprivation by greater inclusion in education or subsidy or entitlements, are not entertained by the Citizenry. These would result in great inconvenience to share the wealth of society with the Populations along with spaces of living, education and work; this would crumble the very edifice of privilege that Citizens inhabit and breed within.

However, all too routinely, when members of the Populations actually rise up the economic ladder, they begin to evolve self-propelled mutations in their sentiments and convictions, which mimic the Citizens above them. Their DNA appears to metamorphose in outlook and consumption towards the same Citizens they once despised but with whom they now seek collegiality and fellowship. High consumerism and materialism begin to colour their aspirations upon upward mobility, when once upon a time they characterised a frugality that hid desperation and instead radiated a proud moralistic varnish of 'simplicity'. We despised the lifestyles of Citizens when we were down under but slyly wished we became like them someday. The result of this mimicry, very unfortunately, is that life among the Populations becomes an everyday battle against chronic financial indebtedness. While many among the Citizens have the endowments of wealth and social capital to afford the indebtedness that escorts high consumerism in their strata, the upwardly mobile Populations simply do not have those safety nets. The other issue is that the Populations are actually Citizens when viewed from a worm's eye view. That is, from the vantage point of the advanced-marginalised or pseudo-invisibles, the Populations of the city are also in some sense an elite, that is, a sort of petite Citizenry in the urban human landscape. The advanced-marginalised and pseudo-invisibles share a relationship with the Populations in an almost identical but scaled-down version of the relationship that the Populations share with Citizens, except that the Citizens need the Populations to support their superstructure while both these groups want the pseudo-invisibles cleansed out. Citizens and Populations eventually become intolerant and nurture a moral disdain towards pseudo-invisibles, which is explicitly enacted during neoliberal urban transition (as we shall see in Chapter 5). In what follows, we track the actors within the Populations, the petite Citizenry among them and the machinery that ran all the cogwheels around the grand system of street-based sex work.[9]

Those among the Populations who are specifically associated with street-based sex work included lodge managers and staff, autorickshaw drivers, bus staff, street vendors, small shops, public-toilet watchmen, park watchmen, cinema theatre staff, security guards, staff of restaurants and eateries and, of course, health workers, social workers and the police. Importantly, sex workers across gender also become critical supporting actors to one another too.

The moment a negotiation comes through with a customer, the first place that street-based sex workers usually move towards is a familiar lodge room. This naturally calls for maintaining equations with the staff of lodges around KR Market and Majestic, which are countless in number but require careful selection. Not all lodges welcome sex work, but those that do, ensure that a fine gauzy curtain is drawn between those visitors who stay over in connection with 'decent' work and those who are brought by workers for service. Many visitors come for 'decent' work but are also involved in indecent things such as sex work; they stay over in lodges and, after returning in the late afternoon or evening, casually ask bell boys and front desk staff whether they can 'get the service'. If the lodge manager is not a sympathiser of sex work, interested customers are snubbed with either a look away or with a bloodshot stare and eyebrows high up. If favourable, like the hundreds of lodge managers, then customers were asked to wait while an errand boy waves out at a worker standing in the vicinity of the lodge. Managers maintain friendships for long, a camaraderie that is lubricated not usually with free sexual services but with hard cash that is paid up either piece rate (that is, per customer and just before booking a room) or as a lump sum, depending on the mutual agreement between the worker and the manager. Rates are usually negotiated by the hour and are a fraction of what the room would cost for a day, but they still burn a hole in the workers' pockets on aggregate. If negotiations are favourable towards the worker, it is entirely possible for the customer himself to pay up for the room or pay the manager personally to use a room for an hour or more. Once rapport is built between the worker and the lodge staff, all one needs to do is enter and pick up a key to a designated series of rooms that are carefully selected so as not to accidentally encounter families and other 'respectable' visitors or to ensure that no noise leaks across to their rooms.

> The moment I entered the lodge with my customer trailing behind me, I didn't have to say a word. A little small talk about whether the manager has had lunch or his evening tea, during which he slipped me a key to one of my usual rooms. He handed it over to me quietly but not secretly, since everyone standing around him knew what this is. Sometimes the room may change if there has been some

---

[9] The reader may benefit from revisiting this section when reading the next chapter on urban spaces and artefacts.

mass booking. But a room was always guaranteed. And in case there's some other problem, like a raid or something, I always had my other lodges.

Bell boys are equally important, as are cleaning staff within these lodges. The rules are very simple for workers – not one person in the building must protest against this abominable service going on in their rooms, and not one visitor must complain about the noises (whether buoyant or barbaric) in the next room. Lodges have been routinely raided for decades by the police to excise out any such contemptible characters and practices, attributed with the all too familiar thrill of 'busting prostitution rackets', but there are always more lodges and more rooms. After all, how many lodges can the police raid at once? And how many of the practically thousands of rooms across KR Market and Majestic can be supervised? There may be raids not because the police suddenly realise that there is sex work going on in there, but possibly because the lodge managers have failed on one or two instances to pay up the weekly or monthly protection money (*hafta*) either to the police or the local mafia. After all, the police and local mafia are also beneficiaries of these services, routinely demanded for free, and would not want such occupations entirely removed. Lodges, however, are the grounds usually covered by female workers, while male and transgender workers rarely use this space; they have other fertile pastures for sourcing clients and spaces.

Transgender sex workers need to ensure good relationships, particularly with street vendors and shopkeepers. This is not because the actual service is provided within or around their premises, but that on account of their identity, transgender individuals (even if not providing sex work for that moment) need to build rapport with 'normal', 'decent' people to even *appear* in a given area. They need to ensure to the shopkeeper or street vendor that they 'will not be a nuisance to other people' in that spot and 'will not steal'. These agents are important to male and female workers, too, since they regularly provide spaces to rest and recuperate and sometimes even bring customers. While pimps traditionally conduct the negotiation and force clients upon the worker, shopkeepers and street vendors act not as pimps but as *brokers* who set up customers for them. A street vendor, selling plastic wares who has been operating in the Majestic area for two decades, said:

Many customers are interested in getting sex but don't know how to go about it. Pimps are not easy to spot, and you can't just go up to someone and ask how much! Some customers gingerly ask me '… where can I get a woman?' I ask them to wait a moment, and see who is around. I don't have any favourites around here, so I make eye contact with anyone who is immediately in my sight, nod and then bend my head down back to pretending to arrange my wares. She then comes and takes over the negotiation with the customer. Anyone passing by might think that they are talking about buying my stuff. No one would suspect what is really going on here, except the police.

Shopkeepers are very important in providing a closed and protected space for workers to either rest, maybe even take a nap and to hide from violent customers or the police. Like other agents, free sex may not be included in what they want in payment for these favours, and they prefer either money or other services such as errands. Many of them, our narrators recalled, become good friends after a long association of a few years, and in rare cases, the need to pay up is also waived.

> All we needed to ensure to the shopkeepers was that we didn't make our presence obvious, or that our conversations and negotiations with clients were audible, or that we didn't create a scene with the police or while fighting with someone. We just stood there like mannequins and waited for customers or sat down on the steps in front of their shops, not obstructing customers. Countless customers came to that hardware shop where we usually sat and did not even *realise* I was right under their noses. That's good behaviour, and what he expected if I sat in front of his shop. No money involved, just each one minding their own business.

Another set of agents who serve as brokers is autorickshaw drivers. Their roles as intermediaries are connected with transport, in the same manner as the street vendor had described earlier. Anonymity plays a critical part here, as one autorickshaw driver said:

> Some of the customers show such familiarity with the names of the streets and areas. I can't really say whether the person is a local or not – speaking or not speaking Kannada doesn't matter in Bangalore; you can be a local for years and years and still not speak the language. That comes as a huge advantage for them as I can't make out whether they're from here. But they are very clear sometimes about what they want in KR Market. Not flowers [laughing], but women. Sometimes men ask for men too! They ask – 'Do you know any woman in this area?' Or 'Do you know any man who will come to my lodge room?' I honestly don't know men, and all that is quite nauseating, but I know many women who are around. Let me tell you the truth, I haven't paid a prostitute over the last twenty-five years, but I know all of them on the streets around Janata Bazar. Some of my other auto-driver friends get very angry when people ask such questions during auto rides. But everything is forgotten once the ride is over and payment is made.

Autorickshaw drivers are important to sex workers also in providing a closed space for relaxation or to escape, just like shopkeepers. These drivers source clients from places that are several kilometres away, or sometimes straight from the railway station if a potential customer disembarks a train, takes a ride to the hotel he is staying at and, in the process, enquires about the availability of sex workers. Often, auto-drivers and lodge staff work hand in glove, with the customers being dropped off precisely at lodges where managers can call for workers; in such cases, it is the customer, and not the worker, who pays the driver and the lodge manager.

Gatekeepers are another category of agents who play supporting roles. These include theatre ticket ushers, park watchmen, security guards and public-toilet staff. Cinema theatres, as we shall see in the next chapter, were a long favourite, especially of female sex workers in Bangalore, which would imply that those manning the doors of the halls also had to be invested in as social capital. These social investments were made again usually by payment, which then slowly morphed into a non-monetary acquaintance. After all, said many of our elderly female workers who had visited cinema halls probably more than film connoisseurs did, if clients decided that the cinema theatres were better than lodges or parks, and if we brought in more customers to these places rather than others, the theatre makes good money anyway. This was not to imply that cinema theatres around the Majestic area relied on sex work for commercial survival, but that the staff working for those theatres, right up to the manager, were well aware of these nefarious activities during oddly timed shows and tolerated them since they actually affected no one else. In most cases, it was etiquette for the customer to pick up the workers' ticket too.

> Everyone was happy at the end ... we, our customers, the theatre staff ... and [laughs] I'm sure the [film] industry also made a few extra bucks thanks to us!

> Oh, I've seen ushers come and go, and the outgoing fellow always pointed to me (and my comrades), when training the new fellow, to tell him that I'm me.

Most others watching the film (like in the case of lodges, toilets and other places) probably turn a blind eye if they realised what was going on behind them, or perhaps did not hear anything due to the blaring sounds of the dialogues, violence and music from the screen. Female workers narrated how customers who did not want penetrative sex, and hence less privacy, preferred cinema theatres, as these venues were cheaper than hotels and lodges, less visible than parks and helped avoid being seen 'walking in the vicinity of a prostitute'.

> Once [giggling], a regular customer took me into a matinee show, assuming the hall would be empty on a working day, but guess what: his neighbour's entire extended family was there, and they spotted him and waved at him unassumingly [laughing out loud]. He then calmly walked up to them, saying that he was there with a few friends, pointing to two completely unknown men in the row in front of us, who were possibly also there for the same reason as him. All of them exchanged pleasantries, and then he came right back to me. From that episode onwards, he always chose the last row, and only the morning show.

> I can tell you an even better one. There was this fellow who took me to a theatre, and as usual, I began my routine on him. But then he just stopped me. I wondered whether he just wanted to watch a movie with a woman, maybe holding hands.

But when the songs came one by one, he jumped straight on to me. I asked him what was going on, and he said he wanted my services mainly during songs so that the songs served as a romantic musical background for his fantasies.

Another variety of gatekeepers was the park watchman, after parks began posting watchmen at their gates, and after parks began even placing gates. Parks have been a haunt mostly for transgender sex workers, right from the mammoth Cubbon Park to local parks in the neighbourhoods around MG Road or Majestic. Parks, as narrated to us, provide the best of many worlds. A resting place, peace and quiet, no unnecessary police, no families needling them during the afternoons or after dark, and enough niches and pigeonholes to provide services in. Watchmen of parks were like lodge owners: they were either open to workers getting in and providing services or were simply prohibitive of them. It was sometimes easy to get into a park in the morning and not get out for hours on end without being noticed by the guard (whose attention was mostly around the gate) and much simpler to conduct business without him knowing since it was out of sight. Rarely did park watchmen report to the police, and rarely did the police get into parks. In the same manner, watchmen of construction sites or shopping centres that closed after dark (which were also spaces where sex work proliferated) were also either completely friends or completely foes.

Male workers have had a strong comradeship with those who manned public toilets, yet another type of gatekeeper. While we shall see the importance of public toilets to male street-based sex workers in Bangalore in greater detail in the next chapter, we note here how the staff who collect payments for using the toilets and guard the entrance, so as to prohibit any unwanted activity, did not include sex work within the range of unwanted activities. Vandalism, drugs, criminal transactions, sleeping, sourcing water and other such activities were usually barred by the staff of these toilets, but sex work was an activity that seemed to feel at home in this space, which the staff did not openly encourage but freely permitted after the required payments have been made. Like lodge managers and staff, public-toilet staff also did not request payment, but about five rupees per customer was paid to the person guarding the toilet.

He allowed me to freely stand around until a potential customer shows up. Once I attracted a customer, it was a matter of five or ten bucks for him, and he allowed my customer and me to enter the toilet and use it for our business for about fifteen minutes or so. After all, who would carefully notice a man standing around a public toilet? So what? And who would ever notice another man following him inside? Does anyone even care? All this was very advantageous to us, but the only person who could stop this was the guy manning the toilet. Oh, once or twice we've had these moralistic saints who shoo us away like we're rats and tell us really nasty things. But most others only cared about the money since no one was going to hold them up for this going on in there.

Here, too, like in the case of lodges, workers and customers ensured that users of public toilets who enter to actually relieve themselves or bathe must not be disturbed. While sometimes suspicions have arisen among the genuine users of the toilet, this only escalated to a quick lecture on uprightness and virtue in society, which evaporated away seconds after the offended user steps away from the toilet. What was also taken advantage of was the embarrassment that many individuals had of even uttering the accusation that two men are sexually involved in the next booth. In lodges and other spaces, it is even heroic on the part of the offended person to eavesdrop on the business of sex work and decide to bring it out into the open, because it involves a female worker and male client and because one has triumphantly exposed the moral degradation of the noble lodge. However, in the case of public toilets, while snooping on strange words and sounds from the toilet next door may be routine, complaining about it involved overcoming the difficult and uneasy stage of acknowledging what is going on and of subsequently mustering the vocabulary to complain about it. Denial was quickly adopted as the wisest strategy whilst in the toilet and talking about it afterwards would befoul one's own tongue; the easiest thing to do was to simply not use that toilet again.

While we have dealt with a sweep of agents in this chapter, we have deliberately left some central operators for later chapters. These special individuals and groups stand at the two ends of the spectrum – those who outrightly facilitate and those who outrightly oppress. Most others are placed along a continuum – some avowedly want them out, some play a binary game of full support or full opposition, some straddle a grey area warming up and cooling down but generally tolerant, and finally, some play the role entirely of benefactors, defending and crusading their right to work, to earn and to just be there. Agents such as gatekeepers or street vendors were more facilitative than those who played outrightly villainous roles in this drama, such as the police. The category of ancillary actors who were patrons were civil society agents who met sex workers regularly for legal and emotional support and offered platforms for collectivisation, the health workers who scouted around for workers to distribute condoms or to check for any other disease and to refer them to doctors and nursing homes, and other agents such as scholars, benevolent journalists and artistes. There were yet others, at this end of the spectrum, who donned the attire of their champions but worked towards displacing them from sex work altogether and 'rehabilitating them' towards other professions since all sex workers were supposedly women who were 'weak and oppressed or trafficked'.

Theirs is a crowded world. Lonely in an overpeopled world but populous as a pseudo-invisible legion, street-based sex workers inhabit a world that has little rationale and abounds with contradictions within the people who swirl around them and stream through them. We noted the presence of all these agents during the course of our long conversations with the workers, and then went about speaking to all these agents in person. There are actually many more agents such as neighbours, bus staff, pimps, local mafia, goons and many more new actors appearing on the stage such as media people, but we leave these to later chapters where we lay out the vast and the minute spaces in the urban expanse and, more critically, the tumultuous processes of neoliberal urban transition.

4

Places

The story of the blind men and the elephant is only too well known: each blind man imagines that single part of the elephant that he touches as the form of the entirety of the beast. While visualising the spaces and streets of Bangalore city, we have people who are surely not blind, but whose perspectives, on aggregate, end up delivering an outcome similar to the fable. Some, never having seen the hundreds of peepul groves dotting the main city or never having walked through labyrinthine markets of Chickpete, imagine Bangalore as entirely an 'IT city' since they draw their breaths from only the eastern and southern extremities where villages transformed overnight into apartment jungles and hypermarkets. Some would like to picture Bangalore as a wholesale loss of a pensioners' paradise since all they melancholily see are the bygones, be it the commodious and composed bungalows or bare streets in balmy neighbourhoods (not having realised that their high-privilege limb of the elephant was mainly around the Cantonment area or neighbourhoods such as Basavanagudi or Jayanagar). But there are also others who touch and feel the elephant, such as street-based sex workers. Our chief intention with this book is to bring out the narratives of street-based sex workers, as one of the millions of people who also feel the elephant, and to render a visualisation of what *their* city looks like. That is, and as we have argued in Chapter 2, we do not simply stand at a vantage position and silently observe them and their spaces. We do not trace pug marks around the city to draw out a locus using our sophisticated occidental research instruments. Instead, we tether ourselves to their feet rather than putting on our indigence-proof shoes to walk around the city; we see with their eyes what their tangibles are and listen with their ears to the harmonies and disharmonies in their ambience, attempting all the while to not succumb to affluent visions from our own privileged faculties. We attempt to build metaphorical maps of a sex workers' city with coordinates drawn from their histories which indicate worksites, watering holes, hideouts and danger zones. In this process, we realise that their footprints are practically *everywhere*, often overlapping with those imprinted by other visualisers of this city, which makes us realise how the very same spaces have for time immemorial been inhabited, walked and claimed by both the respectable and the immoral.

Tapestries of a Sex Worker's City

The workers we spoke to at length about 'city change' (a casual-sounding term we employed throughout our conversations with them to proxy the Goliath of neoliberal gentrified urban transition) first provided us with a grand treatise on the spots within our three focus areas that formed their workspaces. In fact, a large portion of their narratives were descriptions about such spots, often accompanied with a warm nostalgic smile. There were those spots that were expected, while many others were unconventional – not because the latter spaces were unheard of but because they were *everywhere*, and one would not ordinarily conceive of those as associated with sex work or for solicitation. But first, let us visit the more expected sites.

When we think of street-based sex work in areas such as Majestic, the very first image that is conjured up is that of lodge rooms. There are dozens of lodges, including what are named 'deluxe lodges' in the one square kilometre around the Majestic bus station, most of which genuinely are lodges to allow for travellers to stay and refresh in but have also been the principal sites for street-based sex work in the area, particularly for female workers. Conventionally, a sex worker and client consented and negotiated a price for the service and then moved towards a lodge that either the worker or the customer was familiar with (the former being more likely, for reasons of both safety and lower price). Lodge rooms would be hired for an hour, or less or more, depending on the prices negotiated and the familiarity with the customer. Naturally, the areas around the lodges therefore served as soliciting areas too, with women workers waiting there for customers either by self-service where the customer comes up to the worker and asks for a price, or through agents such as lodge staff or autorickshaw drivers. Lodge rooms provided the ideal ambience for effectively executed service by sex workers as well as effectively executed crimes against these workers.

> For so long, lodge rooms have been our offices [laughing]. We sometimes have rooms even reserved and ready for us. Well, they're never cleaned for us, but who cares? We are not here on some honeymoon in a resort … good and easy business was possible best here. So many clients who just want to talk to us also find lodges the best places. And for us too, with those who we become intimate with, lodges have been the best.

> I will never forget that lodge room where it first happened. I came here to the city through a man I met on a train who told me that his friend who runs a lodge needs a cleaner. Only in retrospect did I realise that the lodge manager and this man didn't actually show any familiarity with one another when we walked into that lodge. I should have gotten the hint then, but I didn't since I was quite desperate for the cleaner job. I went up with him, and it was there that a number of his friends were waiting to gang-rape me. I didn't get any cleaner job and ended up in sex work

full time a few weeks after that. Many, many years later, after getting married and having kids, I once ended up in exactly the same room with a customer! This man was a genuine customer, but I could not give him the best service since everything in that room reminded me of that fateful day when I was just about twenty years old. I'm turning forty next month, my kids have completed school, my husband has died – so much has happened in life, but that lodge room still sits in the corner of my mind all the time.

I once fought with the manager of a lodge since he wanted free sex for all these years of 'providing' the room. What nonsense! I always paid him the rate for the room without fail each time, but he treats it like some favour he did to me all these years. But so what? I didn't care. I walked out and went to the lodge on the next street. 'Super deluxe lodge', it said, so I was worried about the rates, but it turned out that only the name board was super deluxe. The rest was the same shabby stuff as the previous lodge. But the manager was nicer and provided me tea once in a while too. So for me, *he* was super deluxe, even if not his drab lodge!

There was once a nasty policeman who didn't think well of sex work, and though we heard he demanded free sex sometimes, he used to hound us. He once ran after me, and guess what I did? Run straight to the nearest lodge! I paid the manager my usual client rate for about an hour, rested there, and then went out only after it was all safe. Lodges were great for hiding too.

For us *kothi*s and for the 'shirt-pant' workers too, lodge rooms are the best. Yes, when we wear men's clothing, we look like regular men and can roam the city freely. But when our clients want us to be proper *kothi*s and when we want to behave like our real selves, do you think this is possible in the streets? Never. Lodge rooms offer enough privacy to be ourselves.

Lodge rooms hence provide the perfect ambience for service, the perfect crime setting and the perfect hideout. They have for long been synonymous with sex work in Bangalore and in other cities where street-based sex work is the norm. However, they have also been sites where pimping has flourished, even in Bangalore city, where the large majority of workers are street-based and do not operate via procurers. Our narrators told us of how they might bump into men on staircases in lodges, who screened them from top to bottom and warned them.

This fellow's body was pencil thin, and his face looked like he hadn't eaten a morsel in days. But he gave me a gritty and piercing look once, on his way to the common bathroom of the lodge, and told me, 'If you don't behave here or try to take some of my clients for yourself, I'll teach you a lesson. I'll have you under me, and then you won't see your family again.' Well, I was scared that time, and I sometimes spot him near the Anjaneya Temple area talking to some men, but I keep away from him and stopped going to that lodge for my services.

Spaces around religious sites in the area, such as the Anjaneya Temple, have been important spots for sex work, where workers narrated that they have been able to not only solicit clients, but also rest under shady peepul groves and wash their hands and faces on a hot, dry day. These included not just Hindu temples but also Islamic sites such as the Jamia Masjid, where they would not be permitted within the complex, but could freely roam outside it. In fact, as shown in research such as by Smriti Srinivas,[1] the sacred has been an integral engagement in the urban public sphere. We asked our narrators whether the Hindu temple staff did not mind them there, for which they responded quite plainly that they were in any case condemned by caste and profession in the eyes of the temple staff as well as those who frequented the temple for worship who realised that they were sex workers.

> They say we are doomed anyway. So whether we sit near the groves or wash our faces, it wouldn't elevate our status or reduce theirs. We're all set in our respective places in society, and hanging around temples won't change theirs or ours.

Groves associated with religious sites have abounded in and around Bangalore by the hundreds. They have hosted, like all other ecological commons, a variety of activities ranging from the ritualistic to the recreational. These groves, consisting of one or more peepul or banyan trees with outstretched arms embraced both the sanctified as well as the damned, and, as narrated to us by workers, harboured solicitation of sex work by day and actual sex work services by night during periods when no one would frequent a temple. The giant trees and their soothing and temperate shade did not condescend towards sex workers and quietly provided them sanctuary while, the dark stone totems at their feet silently watched workers eking out a livelihood. Largely missing in the mainstream discourse around such groves is the presence of sex workers around and within them. A novel and essential coverage of peepul groves in Bangalore by the Everyday City Lab,[2] titled *The Sacred and the Public*, brought out how these groves were exemplars of the intersection between religion, ecology and urban space. The academic literature has also briefly visited their role in livelihood. Our conversations with sex workers demonstrate how a special arm of that intersection – *clandestine* livelihoods – adds to that triple grid of religion, ecology and urban space, and elevates these groves further beyond their priceless aesthetic or ecological value.

But even outside the sacred peepul or banyan groves, large trees have had a special place in sex work in Bangalore. Our narrators celebrated these sentinel beings, after lodges, as principal areas of solicitation and relaxation, and, if the trees were gigantic, they were spots to offer even services after dusk. Bangalore was full of such trees even in prime areas such as Majestic, they related,

---

[1] S. Srinivas (2001).

[2] ECL (2019).

where workers could easily hide from the police, take shelter on a hot, dry day or during a drizzle and where they might be able to sit and eat or converse with co-workers. The trees around the mouldering Janata Bazar remain today as icons where these colossuses provided a multipurpose ambience. Thickets abounded around the city, where today new neighbourhoods or commercial buildings have risen. Not very long ago, as Harini Nagendra elaborately detailed in her 2016 book *Nature in the City*, the presence of greenery accompanied every sort of human inhabitation in Bangalore, residential or commercial or common, and at scales ranging from the lowly flowerpot on the doorstep right up to regal rain-trees; this aspect of urban life has been severely dimmed in the contemporary urban imaginary or has been reduced to manicured and gated lung spaces. The visual delight of sweeping canopies, a standard character around older public buildings and around neighbourhoods, is not the norm in present-day construction or city planning. Bamboo and eucalyptus groves in the barren outskirts of the city also served as ideal arenas for sex work in the peripheries or even in the centre of the city, such as behind the main railway station around the south of Okalipura.

Oh, the eucalyptus groves were my favourite spot. I had no money for lodge rooms and no acquaintances to help me find a spot around the Annammadevi temple. So what did I do? Stand near the railway station, get a customer, and take him on a walk all the way to the [Angala Parameshwari] temple where there were a bunch of trees. I felt those trees knew me, and that they allowed me to earn something.

Sometimes, the customer didn't want to be seen around the Majestic area. No problem! I told him he had to pay the bus fare, take me all the way to Jalahalli where there were abundant eucalyptus groves, so I could provide services. Most of them didn't mind as a bus ticket was cheaper than a lodge.

A really long time ago, there were many bamboo groves around lakes. I used to take my clients there. There, you didn't have to worry about the police, only snakes!

The inviting frame of a grove extended to even parthenium bushes that had grown thick enough. This was a shrub that was as synonymous to Bangalore city as its celebrated weather and flourished all over the city in open plots or vacant areas. One worker recalled:

Ah, my favourite place was where no one else, except maybe some stray dogs, would come – the parthenium bushes where today the Kempegowda metro station stands. But then some of my clients were allergic to the plant, and I lost them the moment I took them there. Yet, so many of them didn't have such issues. I was quite sad to see all of that go.

Ecological commons, including erstwhile lakes, were an accomplice to sex work in Bangalore. Long before a few handful of lakes began being rejuvenated from their existence as dust bowls or as open septic tanks, these water bodies were sprinkled all over the city by the hundreds. In fact, the main bus stand at Majestic was also formerly the Dharmambudhi Lake, covered up during the decades when hundreds of other lakes were also put to their end for the purpose of building a city. The outer bounds of lakes were a favourite among male sex workers, who faced a lower risk in providing services more visibly, and who were capable of darting away at top speed in case they were threatened. Some male workers among our narrators even commented how dried up lakes were 'less convenient' since boys arrived to play cricket there, and how, instead, the fringes of full-bodied lakes were ideal not only for services but also even to take a nap thereafter. Lakes, like trees, did not come with a price tag and made human contact with laundrymen who came to wash or locals who undertook minor fishing. For the rest of the day, after the laundrymen and fisherfolk left, lakes were open and inviting for sex work.

Male sex workers, though, mostly preferred the comforts of public toilets. These spaces were for male workers what lodges were to female workers: the first choice and home ground. Public toilets could be spotted everywhere in the city, at all major transport terminals, at older shopping complexes, marketplaces, close to public parks and markets and in nearly all major neighbourhoods. They were simple in structure – usually, a single building partitioned into two with one doorway each for male and female entry and manned by a male staff who collected the nominal amount depending on what you would like to do. Public toilets around transport terminals also had bathing facilities. It is mainly these, more well equipped, toilets that male workers preferred to locate around. After the overtures between the worker and the customer, they would move straight into the toilet, where services were offered. Earlier models of public toilets for men, even until the late 1990s, had a basic channel in the form of a trough running at ground level so men could stand in a row and urinate into, plus one or two squat commodes for defecating. Models built later had bidets installed on walls with thin partitions between them and commodes with cracks snaking all over the ceramic. Both models were equally preferred by workers, as they individually offered benefits of either space (in the former trench model) or privacy (in the latter partitioned model). Unlike female workers in lodges, male workers in toilets could not spend lengthy extents of time or rest, but this was not necessary for male workers since, as we discussed in the earlier chapters, there are no social restrictions on two men spending extended lengths of time in open public space for conversation or rest.

> … [giggling] why do you think they are called 'comfort stations'? It is because the whole city knows where they can get some comfort and joy. They are our lifeline. Since everyone else just does their business and goes, no one cares what we are doing there. In fact, no one even notices why *two* men need to go together into one

commode cabin. When no one was around, during public holidays on bus strike days in the past, we had the whole place to ourselves.

Our narrators spoke at length about the toilets around the city: in the Upparpet area, near Ulsoor Lake, attached to the Indira Gandhi Exhibition Ground, near the Ayurveda Hospital, at Ananda Rao Circle, and so on. Some of the workers mentioned how they left their real and code names on the walls of the toilets to allow a potential customer to survey, like a Yellow Pages directory – the customer would finger through them and quietly ask around those men loitering around the toilet if they were the 'commando' or 'chocolate' scribbled across the wall.

> Sometimes, I just wait outside, and even from his expression, I could make out that he has read my name and wants to see me. But sometimes, if he was not good looking or seemed threatening, and if he asked me whether I was 'dada', I pretended ignorance ... though that was my name for twenty years.

> I have written my name in every toilet around the city. I am eternal!

Cleanliness and hygiene of the toilet were secondary, as livelihoods were paramount for our workers. They spoke about how they were genuinely concerned about contracting infections or walking around smelling of a public toilet, having inhabited one for hours each day, but that income reigned supreme.

> At the end of the day, when I take a bus home, I sometimes smell of urine, and some of the stuff is actually on my trousers. Bus conductors sometimes ask me what the hell this is, and I tell him I am a toilet cleaner, but when things become really bad, I take a quick bath in the same toilet, and then it is safe to go home.

Public toilet cleaners, manual scavengers and male sex workers regularly crossed paths in these spaces. This was a meeting emblematic of the desperation of advanced marginalisation and pseudo-invisibility, with all parties engaging in their respective occupations – one fulfilling core human desires and the other fulfilling their responsibility in a divinely ordained social order or as a 'spiritual experience'.[3] The only difference is that urban gentrification requires the services of some and hence maintains the presence of their occupations, while it seeks to exterminate the presence of the other occupation altogether.

Another haunt that male sex workers frequent have been public parks, both in an era when these spaces were truly open to all as well as in the contemporary era where parks are gated, secured, sometimes ticketed and off-limits to the immoral and disfigured. Again, because no one would suspect two men – especially if dressed and groomed just about decently enough – to indulge in such nauseating activities when entering a park. These Gardens of Eden provided

---

[3] As put forward by Prime Minister Narendra Modi in 2007.

enough nooks and crannies to offer services, benches and tree shades to welcome long conversations and to just walk around when desired. Open parks – without security guards and their batons, without green and yellow barricades and gates with locks dangling on them, without boards proclaiming time limits and park etiquette, without manicured lanes and exercise equipment – offer free entry to all and do not have any time limit. They can be frequented day and night, by families, the elderly, the athletic and the transgender. Almost all our narrators who were transgender workers mentioned open parks as desirable workspaces; not those in affluent neighbourhoods or close to schools, but those in more working-class localities and those with sparser foliage in grounds where boys play in the daytime.

Transgender workers felt safer and more secure in such parks than anywhere else. They narrated how in these spaces were they far less prone to violence and glares from people, and how they could even sleep and rest. In fact, a couple of our own conversations with transgender workers were in the relaxed confines of parks around the peripheries of the city. They appeared visibly at ease in these spaces than anywhere else to have conversations at length and seemed to care little about people walking by. Interestingly, though, one park that was reported as the 'best' for sex work among transgender workers was the sprawling Cubbon Park, which at first seemed a bit contradictory since it was teeming with people who would naturally intimidate and hound out transgender individuals. Our narrators told us how this was 'paradise' since the place was so huge that it contained everything.

> Everything comes in one package in Cubbon Park. That's why we loved it. You want a lake? There it is. Want a grove? You even have a choice of bamboo or other types of groves. Want to rest under the big rocks? Plenty of them. And trees and trees everywhere.

> Cubbon Park was all mine. I knew every single vendor there, every single constable and could even recognise some regular families. Of course, I knew to keep away from them, but eye contact was always there, with mutual recognition. They didn't want me and I didn't want them either, but we had to share the park, so we did! This was my ground, and all other community members [transgender sex workers] had to get my permission to get in and operate. Of course, I offered it to them, provided they came to me. No, not to pay me ... I had enough money during my days, but to come for my *blessing*. You could not do your business there without me during those days. I lived up to my name. When I was born, my grandmother exclaimed how I was neither boy nor girl, so she named me after the great goddess on the hill. I lived up to Her name!

Spacious arenas such as Cubbon Park have for long witnessed a decorum in apportioning time between male, female and transgender workers.

Transgender workers narrated how they did have skirmishes occasionally with female workers, especially during evening hours, but that a mutually agreeable time division was followed for the most part. While female workers would operate in the daytime in the park, transgender workers would operate after dusk and until sunrise and male workers would operate throughout the day but restrict themselves to designated spots in the park. There were also areas chalked out for sex work, which workers would abide by and restrict themselves within to gain their own privacy as well as to keep away from walkers and others strolling through the Park. These mostly included secluded corners with thicker groves and bushes or large boulders and behind benches near these areas; workers rarely came out of these areas, especially in the daytime, but narrated to us how they rarely felt 'restricted' since there were innumerable such areas around Cubbon Park, which gave ample space to stretch out.

> The TGs [transgender indivduals] have a problem about this, since they can't really be seen too frequently around Cubbon Park – the park will end up losing walkers, and they will end up losing customers too. Also, they knew that if they are seen too easily, security would be beefed up in the park, affecting everyone in one go. So they operate in their restricted areas, and in those areas, I know they do very good business. But we women have little issue about this, since after servicing our client, we can still go around the park as though we are anyone else, or meet our friends.

Large spaces, such as parks, not only allowed for services but also served as venues for solidarity and sharing, especially among male and female workers. Whereas a single woman sitting on a bench for too long would be frowned upon by the crowds that frequented the park, groups of two or three women sitting on the vast lawns and talking to one another would not attract the slightest glance or raise eyebrows. They were able to rest, relax, eat, work and socialise in boundless spaces like Cubbon Park and ease their minds too.

Anonymity was achieved relatively easily not only in parks, but also in large bus stands such as at Majestic or KR Market. These were areas that the workers narrated as ideal places where they would simply blend into the swarms and where the sight of transgender individuals would be tolerated by the floating crowds. The KR Market area was far more liberal towards the presence of transgender individuals, visible even today, compared to the Majestic area, and certainly far more inclusive of them compared to the MG Road area where they would be violently hounded away by police and other 'concerned' groups of Citizens. Bus stands supplied a torrent of customers from within the city and outside, and provided an ocean of hordes to disappear and meld into when required to vanish. Bus stands furnished workers with benches to relax on, spaces on platforms to take a nap, water to drink and wash hands and faces, vendors to buy snacks from and, most of all, vast stretches to just *be* in. The last luxury, what ecological spaces also facilitate, is what allows street-based sex workers to gain a sense of legitimacy in the human landscape of the city and what admits them for a short while into the Populations. The opportunity to just *be* there is an integral part of claiming one's right to the city, to add to the colourful cacophony of the swelling throngs of people, to earn one's labour and enjoy its fruit and to feel at one with the metropolis.

Workers narrated how they enjoyed the breezy freedom of just *being* there in these bus stands, but not without a sturdy demarcation of territory among themselves and with intricately calculated long-term investments in building rapport with the wide variety of actors in the area to allow for their presence and their livelihood.

> This platform is mine. It has always been my area, and I share it with other male workers when I am away for any other work. I have a nice relationship with TGs and female workers who sit on other platforms, and chat with them when services are few, but otherwise, this is literally my second home. I can be here all day, and no one will question me. After all, we men need not worry much about questions.

> Sometimes, I get a few looks when absent-mindedly I put on too much lipstick one morning, or if I wear a sari that unnecessarily attracts attention. What type of woman would sit in a bus stand dressed so well, with no company – obviously not the one going to some wedding all by herself. But those people quickly forget about it when their bus arrives, and then they have disappeared from sight. I know a small tap in the corner where I can wash my hands before eating and bathrooms that I can easily use.

> There used to be this middle-aged woman who used to glare at me every morning when she came to take a bus to work. I think she knew what I did. But so what? She's waiting to go to her work, and my work is right here. So we are equals. She can't possibly come and ask me whether I am a prostitute, because she doesn't have the guts, but sometimes [sniggering] I wish she did – I was ready to shout out 'Yes, I am one!' to embarrass her. That opportunity, unfortunately, never came. But bus stands are like that. People's stares and memories are only temporary. We, however, are permanently there.

Bus depots, which are designated areas to park buses, were another such avenue that provided not spaces to 'be' but sites to actually offer services in. The Karnataka State Road Transport Corporation (KSRTC) bus stand has not only running buses but also those parked for long hours. Almost all our narrators who operated here mentioned how the insides of buses were convenient locations for quick services to be offered. Male, female and transgender workers narrated how they would wind their way around parked buses, find one that was sufficiently secluded and offer services there. However, stationary buses were similar to lodge rooms in terms of the creative possibilities of crime.

We TGs have to get used to being targeted at every moment. Each morning is a sign that we survived the previous day. I made friends with one client, way back in 1999, and he too enjoyed coming with me into buses. No one to disturb and lots of space. He always had this habit of smoking immediately after my services ... he sometimes offered me a cigarette too ... they didn't taste as nice as *beedi*s [a thin, inexpensive and popular Indian cigarette]. But he might have hatched this during one of his smoking sessions. Once, he casually paid me in advance, like I always demand, and we walked mechanically to our usual bus. But, like in the movies, suddenly, some guy emerged from behind the bus, another one leapt out of the driver's seat and one was already sitting on one of the seats. He had planned this. They didn't rape me but took away every bit of money I had, and to humiliate me, they left me stark naked to lie on the corrugated floor of the bus. I then waited for a short while, heard another parked bus being boarded, realised it was my friend who was also serving a client and quickly shouted out to him for help – he was an angel, asked his customer to wait and immediately ran and got me a new sari he bought off the street in front of Sangam theatre.

Not just parked buses but even moving buses with passengers have been used as venues for sex work. This was an interesting narration by three female workers we conversed with. They described how it used to be a difficult negotiation, but successful at the end, to convince the drivers and conductors of overnight buses to allow them to provide sex work in the very last seats of the bus, especially on routes where the bus was sparsely occupied. Overnight buses with shorter routes were the most preferred as they offered the possibility to offer services on the night route with one or more customers who accompanied them (paying for the workers' tickets too), reach the destination in the middle of the night and take the same bus back to Bangalore to reach by early morning. This required very strategic bargaining with not only the conductor and driver for the overnight route but also with those who staffed the bus while returning, to avoid any suspicion. Bengaluru Metropolitan Transport Corporation (BMTC) buses, that is, those that operated within the city, were impermissible for this arrangement, as the workers could run into trouble very easily. KSRTC buses, on the other hand, were more accommodative towards these arrangements.

Long before the Volvos conquered the highways and the interstate roads became crowded, these buses were ideal to conduct business. Ninety-nine per cent of the buses were off-limits for such things, but some conductors and drivers were nice. They didn't mind. And what did we do with the other travellers? Well, they were either sleeping or pretended not to realise what had happened. In one case, both my customer and I noticed a young fellow with his big-eyed looks who probably wanted to give us a moral lecture – we both winked at him, and he immediately went back to his pretended sleep! Some conductors demanded free services too, to allow for this, which I once said okay, but after that offered him a discount on my bus rate. My bus rate is usually higher than my lodge rate.

The KR Market area for long hosted bus operators who ran privately owned and managed intercity and interstate buses, before they were gradually shifted out to other locations in the city to overcome the sheer space constraint in this area. Kalasipalayam, to the immediate south of the KR Market square, was synonymous with private-bus operators. Our narrators reported that though this area was the most accommodating towards them, it was impossible to try out the same bus arrangement with private-bus operators.

> Hmph! Their morals are much higher. They think they are some purists. I even offered them more money, but they looked down upon me and told me that their buses were not brothels. What utter nonsense! Of course, they are! If I were some flashy madam who is a high-class escort, they would allow me with open arms. You know those buses where you have beds to sleep in? What do you think happens there? Some take a trip to their real destination, but some take a trip to another dreamland, with these escorts.

Women and transgender workers also benefit from trucks that are parked in wholesale vegetable and fruit markets. Besides KR Market, another such area is Yeshwantpur, which today is a bustling centre that has been overrun by flyovers, malls, upscale apartments and the metro, but it was for long an area synonymous with its RMC[4] Yard frequented entirely by traders engaged in wholesale agricultural produce, loading and offloading workers, truck drivers, individuals in the vegetable and fruit business, transgender individuals and female sex workers. Our narrators explained how the site – a regulated agricultural marketing yard serving as a crucial nodal point to trade produce that has been brought from rural areas all around – was a hotspot for female and transgender workers who operated throughout the night, when the trucks were brought in and after they offloaded the agricultural produce. Their other purpose, as confidently narrated to us, was to serve as spaces for sex services by these workers who would utilise either the bed of the truck after it was emptied of its cargo or under the truck between the rear wheels. They narrated how more upscale trucks, which had container facilities that could be shut and locked, were not offered to the workers for this and would not be preferred by workers in any case out of safety concerns. Open trucks and trucks parked for lengthy hours were preferred for sex work, as they had no issues of permission from the truck drivers (often customers themselves) or occasionally had to pay only a negligible price to rent them for a short while. Transgender workers narrated how they were able to operate freely and in full swing after offloading hours that were usually after 2 a.m. to 3 a.m., and that these areas were convenient to them since they were close to their *hamams* too.

---

[4] RMC stands for Regulated Market Committee.

Yeshwantpur railway station was nothing like what it is today. You never saw a single fancy luggage trolley in that station. They were mostly working-class people from Peenya going back to their towns in rural Karnataka or Andhra, or to some village around Bangalore. Sometimes, they too stopped by for our services after dark, but our customers were mostly those in the RMC Yard. There were thousands of rats and lots of dogs running around, but there was a flourishing business for us too. Loading workers were drunk and collapsing, but they knew exactly which empty truck to take us to. The traders also had their convenient spots near the giant sacks and crates. At the end of it, we smelled like cabbages and cauliflowers. Truck drivers particularly preferred us, and [grinning] one even said that we here in Bangalore were better than any other *hijra*s they met on the way!

The areas around Yeshwantpur, such as the Peenya industrial area, Jalahalli and Vidyaranyapura, formed a belt of thriving sex work that stretched right up to Yelahanka. These areas, quite unlike the centre of the city, were not filled with lodges, parks and shopping arcades. These were areas, before their transformation, that were arid, with acres of eucalyptus groves, dry bushes and long stretches of wasteland bordered by behemoth factories and the expansive air force station that kept to itself. It was here that some workers, as we saw in the last chapter, brought their customers when they could not afford lodge rooms or wanted to operate away from the city. Though sex work in these areas was neither insignificant nor sporadic, it operated at a density far lower than the Majestic or the MG Road or the KR Market areas. The density of work in the Kalasipalayam wholesale vegetable market, south of the main KR Market building and east of the private-bus operator areas, was particularly high and burgeoning, as this area attracted a swarm of people apart from those in the agricultural trade. Occasionally, in this area, even pushcarts and *tonga*s provided spaces for sex work throughout the night. There was no dearth of these spaces in KR Market and Kalasipalayam, narrated the workers, and customers were in endless supply, creeping out of the niches in the maze of gunny bags and mountains of produce, crawling their way to the countless bars in the area and then seeking out sex workers. It was, and for the most part remains, a macabre olfactory harmony of the redolence of vegetables, liquor, sweat, rags, jute, spittle, metal and grease.

Shady travel agencies also joined in the tapestry of spaces, and cruising spots for sex workers of all hues and offered the full range of services to all kinds of customers. KR Market was particularly interesting for the range of unconventional areas that it offered. One narrator described them quite colourfully:

Oh, so many spots! It was a heaven. If you didn't get any other space, there were the tarpaulin sheets of vendors you could hide behind and do your business. There was the bamboo bazaar, which offers a speciality – it blocked out the noise from the street and blocked out the noises that our customers make, so no one else could hear them on the street. The bullock cart stands were also another favourite.

And if you were lucky, sometimes the PWD [public works department] abandoned huge cement pipes that we could easily crawl into to offer services. These were really nice, but they were often taken up by beggars and old people who used them to sleep for the night.

A male worker also revealed a very interesting site that appeared to be an exotic genre of public toilets:

> Not many people know this, but KR Market and Chickpete areas used to have a couple of bathing *hamam*s. These were not public toilets and were privately owned and operated. Basically, men could have a bath there. It was used by truck drivers and loaders who came from outside the city. The disadvantage was that we were not allowed inside, of course ... we had to wait outside and give the necessary signals to men coming out. The advantage was that the customers were cleaner since they had just bathed [laughing]. Today, I think there are just one or two of these remaining in the area.

Male workers in the area have retained another haunt, besides public toilets, which include the open grounds attached to SLN College in Kalasipalayam, as well as those alongside the Vanivilas College in the same area. These are open for services even during the daytime, as workers narrated to us, and are ideal spots for a quick service. This has also been the case with large pile-ups of abandoned tyres that skirt the area around the old Mariswamy Matth area, which offered small crevices to provide services, entirely unsuspected.

Bathing *hamam*s, bamboo curtains, tyre pile-ups, tarpaulin sheets, cement sewage pipes, *tonga*s and jute sacks – all notable features in the KR Market tapestry – are a wide world apart from the spaces that make up the MG Road tapestry. Here, our narrators explained, there has always been far less tolerance towards open street-based sex work compared to the Majestic and the KR Market areas, but also that this area was dominated mostly by 'high-class' sex workers who were more sophisticated in not just appearance but also in their language and articulation, their familiarity with the artefacts owned and operated by their more upscale customers (such as cars, more sophisticated mobile phones or hotel ambiences) and, of course, their caste and economic class.

> Those women are not like us here. They are fairer, wear better clothes, know how to properly get in and out of cars, sit on a bike and not look awkward behind the rider. Those escorts look just like the [dominant caste] lady who employs me to clean her house in the morning. You can't just lie around near a tree or stand in front of a shop.

> [another narrator, interrupting the above narration] Does this mean that it's possible for a high-class sex worker to employ a street sex worker as her domestic help? God, what an interesting world!

Working on the MG Road area brings along with it a different vocabulary and familiarity around artefacts and spaces. As revealed in narrations such as the one earlier, it is impossible to stand around public spaces in that area in the same manner that workers do in the other areas narrated here. It would attract unnecessary attention with passers-by and would certainly be noticed in full view if one openly solicited with the overtures employed in the Majestic area or tried out offering services even in crevices and pigeonholes. Moreover, there were no lodges one could disappear into and no religious sites for solicitation or rest. There were also no stationary buses or trucks and certainly no wholesale vegetable markets or agricultural yards. Here, workspaces for several decades included the long walkers' stretch that lined the northern border of MG Road until the metro and its architectural cargo arrived, along with the public toilets around Trinity Circle and Ulsoor Lake at the eastern end of MG Road, the toilet near St Patrick's Church on the southern part of Brigade Road and the spattering of parks within the very elite neighbourhoods in the area that were once un-gated and unsupervised after dark. Workers narrated how, in daylight, they were suspiciously looked at if they frequented the long northern-border stretch of MG Road that was elevated above the road, which had foliage extending from the Mahatma Gandhi statue until the Brigade road signal.

> Men and women who walked that long stretch were so well dressed with their white shoes and colourful shorts. But they always gave us a dirty look. I don't think they realised we were sex workers, but they glowered at us since women like us weren't really supposed to be there. We looked strange there but got enough business after dark when the walkers stopped coming, and our customers began arriving ... they didn't have shorts or shoes. They didn't have to dress for us.

> It's a bit stiff on MG Road, but you learn. Our older sisters who retired from sex work told us, don't do this, don't do that, don't touch this, don't go there. We have to learn that the benches there are for *those* kinds of people to sit and not for *us* to lie on. In Majestic, I could sit on any pavement for long, but that wasn't possible on MG Road. We can't just sit in front of a watch shop or a bookshop. It's not just that we will be shooed away immediately ... we simply won't get customers!

The dominant spaces around this area for sex work were usually leafy green areas, which were once commons for everyone before they became club goods for the few. Residents of the area, who belonged to a very high economic strata and usually held or retired from senior positions in government or business, or perhaps were old Bangaloreans domiciled there by virtue of inheriting homes and apartments, would frequent these parks with pet animals or with children all throughout the day, and disappear into their warm yellow glowing homes after dusk. It is at this time that workers would trickle in and begin spreading themselves out towards their territories and positions. Transgender workers, like everywhere else, found solace in these parks to find and solicit clients, but they were unable to rest, eat or spend too long hours.

There's an uncle who used to walk at a strange time of around 7:30 p.m., when many of us slowly came to the area. This was in about 2001. He wouldn't look at me, maybe because I was a man and I looked like any of the cleaners or drivers in this area. But I once saw him shouting at a poor TG worker in the area. I eventually realised he wasn't actually shouting, but trying to get the point across in a booming voice that no one was going to ask for blessings or give money in this area, so it was better to get out. He was probably too naive to understand what we were all doing here, or maybe he knew things but was too embarrassed to explain in his roaring voice that these services were not welcome here.

One common issue among all workers in that area was that though spaces for solicitation and meeting points for customers were aplenty, services had to be offered mostly indoors, in houses that clients led them to. Workers narrated that the customers here were relatively safer, compared to the chilling gang-rape experiences in lodges or buses, but there was always a light cold fear even with the most 'decent-looking' clients.

Customers in Majestic are brute goons, but in this area, they are cultured goons. If you get in trouble in KR Market, there are always other drunkards who will come to your rescue with expectations of free sex after saving you from some rowdy. But here, if the customer pointed a live cigarette on your breasts and wanted to torture you for some thrill, there was *no one* who could help you, and screaming would get *you* arrested, not them.

Parks had to be shared with drug traders and other criminal elements who met throughout the night, which was also potentially risky in these areas, especially for transgender workers. More wary customers, too, preferred not to avail of services in the park out of fear of such individuals, which is why they routinely moved to rooms in acquaintances' apartments or other spaces such as cars within which they had familiarity and control. This is why it was important for workers to become familiar with operating inside cars, entering apartments without being too conspicuous, speaking minimally so as not to give away their coarse and uncouth tongues and to understand English, including reading and writing some morsels. Though there was a disadvantage in the cultural unfamiliarity with some artefacts in the area, there were some interesting advantages too.

My friend who works as a cook in one of these rich apartments said that people don't really know each other the same way that we all know, even those who died or got married in our neighbours' extended families. She told me that they wouldn't know even if the neighbour was dead. Though that's really strange, it's also really great for us. They just sit inside their apartments after they come back from work and don't even *look* outside. Even if there's a bomb explosion, those people will probably realise it only after they see it in the newspaper the next day. The streets and parks there were completely deserted after dark and we could easily operate. So even though they stared angrily at us during the daytime, their area became ours at night.

Sometimes I see some escorts going around in their own cars in the area. But they are in their world, and we in ours. No client-sharing, no fights, no territory battles. But then when the police come, they come only for us, not for them. I've heard that senior police officers have their own women and don't want their juniors to arrest their own escorts! So, quite easily, they arrest us instead.

You know which park was the safest? [long silence allowing the other narrators and us in the room the chance to guess] Forget it, you'll never guess – it was that small patch right in front of Mayo Hall where that statue [of the celebrated Indologist Reverend Ferdinand Kittel] is. And you know why? Because it was bang on the main MG Road, and long before the metro arrived, no one ever thought it should be patrolled!

Another space that the workers narrated that was ideal for cruising was around the many old educational institutions in the area. A long tract from Richmond Circle all the way to Brigade Road is endowed with schools and colleges with their venerable-looking establishments, endless boundary walls and pavements all along their margin that spill over with school students during the daytime but are virtually deserted at night. These have been standing firm, with their chrome-yellowing stone edifices, airy arched windows, flanked by green canopies and settled with calm assuredness on their copious grounds for a century and more, all huddled together within dozens of acres. The distinguished administrators of these hallowed institutions, who have produced illustrious Citizens and have educated and provided livelihoods for generations of Populations, might not have had even an inkling that right outside their estates of learning and empowering were acts of immorality and desperation, or perhaps they were in convenient denial of these livelihoods. Entering the school premises at night was virtually impossible for street-based sex workers in this area, but soliciting clients in front of their stone walls and gates were, for many years, effortless. Workers told us of how they had negotiated a 'don't ask don't tell' agreement with the night watchmen of these academies, which in the days of yore were relatively easier negotiations to maintain. Gate watchmen in institutions such as these were usually semi-permanent workers who were easily recognisable in their khaki outfits and who swore deep-hearted allegiance to the school or college administration to maintain discipline in the thoroughfare, whether it was towards students, parents or sex workers.

I stayed in the same slum as the main-gate night watchman of that old school. He knew me and knew exactly what I did here. We took the same bus together here from Ejipura and got off at St Patrick's. We walked the same paths to work every day and took the bus back the next morning. We never made eye contact. Or maybe *he* didn't make eye contact. Didn't matter, as long as he guarded his gate and I got my usual customers.

Students, parents and sex workers also trudged common paths in yet another space in this area – neighbourhood shopping complexes. Though there were not many complexes like in the Majestic area, these were not very well guarded during their tenure. Shopping complexes sat in the prime centres of practically every middle- to upper-middle-class neighbourhood in Bangalore, swarming with shoppers during the daytime and, after 9 p.m., hosted street-based sex workers who circumnavigated their mouldy stuccoed ochre walls and grey cement floors. On MG Road, the now locked and ready-to-be-demolished Shrungar Shopping Complex was a dense cruising point for women and male workers, as was Spencer's supermarket and the areas around the Public Utility Building and the Mayo Hall court complex. Not a single one of these buildings could be entered into by the workers, but orifices always existed.

It was *I* who found the way to enter the underground parking lot of the Utility Building. I was the very first. I found the perfect way to squeeze through and take my customers there. But then the problem began with my friends who were working around the Victoria Hotel.[5] In an inebriated state, I once bragged about this achievement of mine, and the next day, those scoundrels beat me there! What a betrayal! Could I say anything? I trusted them so much, but they brought their men there one by one after that.

The best of the spaces called the shopping complex was exploited in Majestic, a land we now return to, where, as enlightened to us by workers stationed there, the 'air was freer than on MG Road' and 'there were better customers than in KR Market' and hence enjoyed the best of both worlds. Three important shopping complexes in the Majestic area, besides a few others, were for several years congregating points for especially female workers – Alankar Plaza, National Market and Janata Bazar. The first plaza is frequented by crowds of shoppers who grazed the area for inexpensive and lurid clothes, tawdry accessories, legal and illegal DVDs and small items useful around the house. The second market has also been synonymous with inexpensive items, especially electronics, and in its heyday was the staple watering hole for those who wished to pick up kitschy electronics and illegally produced DVDs ranging from Kannada flicks and

---

[5] An old restaurant where Winston Churchill was said to regularly read his morning newspaper, and where Central Mall now stands.

compilations of old Hindi films to even Milos Forman's *Amadeus*, which were clumped haphazardly and strung up like seafood in a South East Asian market. The third bazaar, however, was a more staid complex built in 1935 as the Asiatic Company and converted in 1966 to a dusty but well-stocked government-run supermarket, a number of nodal offices and a few other shops. These three complexes had passages and areas for carefree movement, rest and solicitation. There were watchmen posted there during night time, who could be negotiated with, but in general, were laid-back about surveillance. For the longest time, there was no surveillance or restrictions on the kind of people who could roam the area. It was common to see people of all hues and economic strata criss-crossing paths in these complexes, with something for everyone – the anxious middle-class job applicant, the weary transgender individual taking a bit of rest, the wide-eyed working-class shopper, the sleepy inebriated homeless man taking his regular nap on the steps or the sex worker awaiting the glance from a customer that served as the harbinger of one's negotiation skills.

> Janata Bazar was my heaven. The boundary walls were low enough to jump across with your customer at night after everything had died down. I used to always take my men to the top of the portico behind those lion statues, where you can even lie down and offer any services you want to, as long as it was not raining. The iron spiral staircases were really comfortable to lean against and sit under … and speaking of stairs, sometimes, the hatchet door to the terrace was left open by mistake, and all I had to do was take that iron ladder up to that opening from where the entire terrace was open and all for me!

Workers narrated how it was possible to use the area during the daytime to stroll around and perhaps even buy something once they had enough money, besides soliciting customers and meeting other street-based sex workers to chat and gossip. After dark, they narrated, the action gained momentum, and they positioned themselves in their respective spots around and within these shopping complexes, taking their customers either to their little caves in the complex building, to a lodge or to a parked bus, entirely depending on the service required or the privacy they could command or simply how much customers could afford.

> If the customer wanted just oral sex, I could offer it right in the complex itself, maybe in front of a shop shutter-door if it was dark enough. If he wanted to just touch me, there was even lesser privacy required, and even behind some pillar or cargo carton would be more than enough. Maybe even that area near the transformer room was good enough, if it was open. However, when the demands went up, it meant walking all the way to your regular lodge or some other space where more time could be spent.

> I found out how to switch off the tube light on one corridor of Alankar Plaza. This was long before they put more serious-looking security guards there and when

TGs and us could easily roam the place at night. Because of some electrical issue in one corridor, they connected a tube light with a stupid flimsy wire that they hung across a shop name-board and put a switch there. I tried to switch it off once, it worked, and then so many possibilities started jumping around inside my head. I negotiated with my customers in front of Janata [Bazar], crossed the road, took them inside to that very corridor in Alankar and simply switched off the light. One fellow got scared and began shouting at me, threatening what he would do to me if I robbed him, but I then calmed him down, saying that this was my spot and I didn't have any intention of mugging him by shutting off the light. After that, I realised that it was sheer luck that *I* didn't get robbed sometimes.

National Market was my spot for years, before they threw me out along with the illegal CDs [laughing]. So many, so many spots, even right in front of the shutters, which I could easily slip into. In fact, even when the police conducted combing operations once a year back in the 1990s, I used to run and hide in there. And by the way, there was this really nice old Muslim uncle who ran a shop selling fake watches. He used to allow me to use it for rest during the afternoons, after closing down his shutter with a small gap below. No customers, we agreed, but I was welcome to rest. No one is like that these days, not even his useless nephew who took over his shop. [Facing her palm towards us] You don't need to agree with our work, but at least, like this uncle, you can allow us to just be there; what's wrong with that?

A couple of parking lots in the Majestic area also provided the hunting grounds for workers to cruise, rest and meet. These were very unlike the giant pay-and-park lots that are present in the area today that protect hundreds of vehicles; these were simply muddy vacant grounds pockmarked with bushes in the lanes between the main streets in the area, the entrance of which had a long horizontal steel rod that acted like a boom barrier with a few bricks dangling on one end, manned by a person during the daytime and tied down permanently at night. Though the barrier obstructed vehicles from coming in, humans, decent or immoral, could easily pass through from underneath.

I would stand near the Jamia Masjid just around Triveni theatre after 9 p.m., long after all the prayers were over. Stray dogs took over the area at the time. Once I got a customer, it was a long walk to the parking lot, but worthwhile, as long as it was not raining or as long as packs of dogs didn't fight in that patch of land – those were my only two challenges. Long before mobile phones came, I had to wait in one place and then take my customers to the parking lot; by the time mobile phones came, the place was gone. Once, about twenty years ago, a huge car, which I had never seen before, came up to the parking lot at about 11 p.m., right in the middle of my offering services to a customer. I thought I was in deep trouble, since my customer could just run, but I would be stuck. Turns out, there was an escort inside the car – I knew her since she started her business on the street and then got her 'promotions' – and she and her customer who was driving needed a place to quietly park. Another way to 'pay and park' [sniggering], you see? I operated the whole night for so many years in that parking lot, until one sound acted as my stop signal: the *suprabhatam* at 6 a.m.

The popular battering hymn played at sunrise for twenty long minutes across South India served both to awaken a principal Hindu deity from slumber and also to signal sex workers to cease their services in this locality. It turned out that the hymn was blared out every morning out of a small tinny tape-recorder placed at a tea stall around Alankar Plaza. In the group discussion among female workers who operated around the Majestic area for decades, when we veered around discussing shopping complexes, one participant, who was in her fifties and had ceased sex work a few years ago, intervened:

> Many of you don't know that this tea fellow was there long before Alankar became a plaza. I don't like this plaza at all since what was at that spot before it was my place, and I lost it. Yes, I'm very happy for you, and you need to earn too, but don't go on and on about the plaza in front of me. My theatre was right there, and I saw the place being brought down and it felt like my own house being demolished.

Alankar Plaza was itself a replacement for a cinema theatre of the same name that stood at that location for years, like more than twenty cinema theatres that were bestrewn all over the area. All one had to do was take one trip by bus to arrive at this land of jollity to shoppers, cinema lovers, tourists, families, everyone. As we know, the locality gained the moniker 'Majestic' from a theatre by that name which prominently stood in the area and became the namesake for the very centre of Bangalore city. But Majestic was neither the first nor the most important theatre in the area, either for cinema or for sex work. All theatres had the footprints of sex workers, particularly female, imprinted all over their walls and aisles for decades, and sex work, according to our narrators, was as freely and habitually served in cinema theatres as much as in lodges, trucks or parks. Cinema theatres during the late hours, and especially when screening low-budget soft erotica, became the natural choice to seek and offer sex work. As we saw in the previous chapter, like all other places, cinema theatres too necessitated careful negotiation with their staff and required meticulous planning and zoning, not only with other sex workers operating in the same theatre at the same time but with other members of the audience, who, like in intercity buses, probably knew what was going on but turned a blind eye towards the last rows. It required multiple visits to the theatre (which was not inexpensive), reading the area attentively for various particulars, building rapport with the ushers and ticketing staff, and, as one narrator related, perhaps even carrying out some marginal vandalism.

I carefully broke the backrest of two seats in the last row corner. In any case, no one sat there since it was full of mosquitoes hovering around and there was red spittle on the wall corners. For months on end, no one even cared to repair it. Those were how things were: the theatres were pretty bad but the movies were pretty good – now, it's just the opposite. My customer and I climbed in, unless he was too fat, and I provided the service with no one looking. It was especially easy during the scenes when there was a lot of fighting or during songs. And most movies had only those two things, one after another.

Most sex work was conducted in cinema theatres during the late shows, which were usually screened after 8 p.m. or in some cases after 9:30 p.m., but it was not unusual to offer services during the morning shows that commenced at 10 a.m., when the halls were empty, there were no crowds to dampen the sound and the songs and battle scenes rang out in high decibel volume for at least two hours. These sound curtains and the general darkness assisted sex work to flourish in cinema theatres in this part of Bangalore. Some narrators gallantly described how they were almost exclusively 'theatre workers' and how this was the safest place to offer services. Many of these narrators were retired workers who were, at the time of our conversations, well over the age of sixty. In one of our group conversations, workers narrated, one after another:

> I didn't need to bother about rain or sun and didn't need to worry about police raids in lodges or elsewhere. I didn't have to care about drunkards since the theatres didn't allow them in if they were rolling drunk. There was little fear of knives and glass pieces to threaten you. The theatre was the best. My regular halls were Kailash and Kapali, but I would sometimes venture into Prabhat or Movieland if my regular ushers in those two theatres were away for a few days. Anyway, my place was the theatre, and I don't remember how many times I ever offered services anywhere else….

> … but unlike you [referring to the earlier narrator], I didn't restrict myself to two or three theatres – they were *all* mine. You tell me a theatre, I have serviced there. Sagar, Kalpana, Bhumika, Himalaya, Geeta, Alankar, Menaka, Tribhuvan, Santosh, Sapna, Sangam – *each and every one*. I knew every ticket staff, every usher, every watchman. I serviced in theatres for more than fifteen years, but I don't remember watching even one movie for those fifteen years. When I see these malls there, Alankar or Pothys or Coupon Mall, I can only see my comrades the theatres, not those unfriendly malls….

> … true. The theatres were much more peaceful. Pradeep theatre in Kalasipalayam was for us men. There were some female workers there also, but it was mostly for men. And like in toilets or parks, there was no limitation for morning or night shows. We had theatres like Rajeshwari[6] where we dominated, but we had full

---

[6] Located in Marathahalli, at a considerable distance from the Majestic area.

liberty to operate throughout the day. Maybe by some stroke of bad luck, if a family with kids suddenly landed in the seats in front of you, you had to restrict to the basics like touching or using your hands on the client, but otherwise, we could lie down on the row below the seats and do whatever we pleased....

... yes, yes, but theatres were good mostly for all of you. For us TG workers, theatres welcomed us *only* for the late show, and never the good theatres like Sangam. We could go only where B-Grade movies were shown, and we had to go in groups of three or four and then fan ourselves out. Like all other things, it's easier for you than for us. But yes, in theatres, nobody else realised our presence simply because they could not see us in the darkness....

[a much younger female worker interrupts this conversation with an assertive tone] ... but those were *your* days. You know how things are now? Every day is madness because we have to scramble like squirrels jumping from one place to another to find a place to do our work. Getting customers is not so hard, but getting a place is impossible. Do you know where we have to squeeze now? You never had it that way. Yes, we have many *sangha*s [associations] now, but where do you offer sex service in the first place?

[another younger female worker continues] ... she's right. It's nothing like how these *akka*s [older sisters] have described it. Yes, some of the things are still there, but it's just not possible, even if there's no police. In fact, it's not just the police, because people like that lodge manager who you were talking about earlier ... oh now ... he has now become [in a sarcastic tone] pure and pious and tells me, 'People like you are a problem here' ... it's the same case with the hardware fellow ... they just can't be negotiated with. And ever since that flyover was built up in KR Market, and the metro station just around it....

The conversation moved in a direction that we did not predict. For the younger workers who participated in the various group conversations that we hosted, there was barely a mention of a theatre, little amusement at the thought of a salubrious green park, almost no account of trees or buses, no utterances about lakes and fewer stories about toilets. These younger workers, who claimed that they constituted the bulk of the street-based workforce today, spoke about negotiating the city that brought to mind not open urban spaces and convivial places but rather a trapeze act where one had to leap and swing from one disappearing patch to the other. The revelation of sites where sex work is offered on the streets in present-day Bangalore appeared to be more of a list of useful hide-and-seek spots than venues for offering quality street-based sex work. Workers spoke of some elbow-room behind giant sugarcane stacks, under mobile phone towers at night, garbage pile-ups eclipsing a small tract where they could service, space under the inclined shelves where shoes are stacked and sold on the streets, the dried-up pool under the bust of Rajkumar at Upparpet (and how one could 'easily' jump the gap from the foot overbridge above the thespian's bust to the parapet of the Central Bank building) and the dark green metal cobbler kiosks that lie scattered all over the city offered by them to sex workers after cobbling hours.

What does street-based sex workers' Bangalore look like? What did *these* people feel about the elephant? What is critical for us is to understand that the parts of the elephant that these people felt were not invisible to the rest; rather, the other people discerning the elephant did not realise that there were more than just seven people. There are an innumerable number of cohorts of people who are aware of the other parts of the elephant that they have not touched; the problem here is not exactly what the fable had described. Everyone stroking their part of the elephant – be it the Information Technology Enabled Services (ITES) workers or the privileged nostalgia brewers – know very well that other parts of the elephant exist. They are hence not really blind. What the Citizens and some of the Populations do not know is that their parts of the elephant are not *their* parts alone, and that these parts are being handled and claimed by other pseudo-invisible people as well. The parable of the seven blind men and the elephant has to be slightly altered here. In the revised parable, scores of people touch various parts of the elephant, are not in denial of the parts they have not touched, but are blind about the fact that there are others, too, who are touching their sharp tusk or swinging tail. We are all well aware that Bangalore is not just a trunk or a tail or an ear; we are not blind in that respect, like in the original fable. But we are indeed *homo myopis* claiming that the part that *we* touch is only *ours*, while actually it is as much someone else's part too. We find it hard or disagreeable to believe that the right to the elephant – whole or in part – is everyone's.

The threads of the spatial tapestry of urban space are shared by many and, in some cases (such as bus stands), by an enormous proportion of the population. However, even if the warps and wefts are shared, the tapestries that are woven out of these appear different for different people. The problem begins when parochial and privileged minds wish to claim that the elements and motifs that make up their urban tapestry are exclusively *theirs*, with an intermittent welcome, a quick entry and exit, only to those who are socially and morally legitimate. Devotees at temples, or those meandering around parks, shoppers at plazas, complexes and parking lots, families at the cinema, users of public toilets, tree enthusiasts, tourists at lodges and in buses and the thronging millions who use bus terminuses – do most of these realise that the residuum of this city also uses the same threads to build *their* city too? Do they realise that the city's outcasts even have a city of *their* own? How far would these freer participants in the urban humanscape agree and coexist with the rejects of society for whom all these spaces and places are pivotal to their life and livelihood? Continuing with the revised fable, when we wish to assert a new and more jet-set gentrified imaginary of our part of the elephant, or even its whole, we suddenly realise that there are more people around us who we think should not be there. An entire machinery is deployed to ensure that the elephant will hereinafter belong to just these seven blind men, and not too many more. That entire apparatus, loaded with the ammunition of economic privilege, political clout and moral aura, is set about in full fury against street-based sex workers with a raucous battle cry to ensure that they are cleared away from the elephant.

Violence against street-based sex workers by law enforcement agents to 'clear them out' is a global phenomenon and has been routinely and rampantly inflicted on these pseudo-invisibles, even during the 'golden era' of sex work in Bangalore that promised to last an eternity but began corroding from the early 2000s onwards. The despising of this occupation has been dutifully practised in nearly all spheres of human civilisation – the literary, the religious, the administrative, the artistic – for millennia. 'Prostitute' has never lost its reliability in being a choice expletive to insult women who break glass ceilings above and glass walls around. Utter the term 'immorality' and the image of the (usually female) sex worker conjures up in the eye of the mind as the paragon of that vice. In Bangalore city, the fire of abhorrence against these pseudo-invisibles was lit at first with a measured pace and then inflamed further with sudden heavy jolts of gentrification and revanchism in recent decades. Urban transition was not just the fuel for this fire, but the very kiln within which street-based sex work began to be extirpated from the streets and spaces, an upheaval in these workers' lives that was stoked by the very same ancillaries (who we met in the previous chapter) who transmuted into adversaries. The galaxy of people and tapestry of places would slowly crumble over a long twenty-year period in the process of creating a Bangalore that was supported in substructure by the many, built for the few and imagined by the fewer. An entire ecology around street-based sex work in these areas in Bangalore unhurriedly but aggressively (often violently) disintegrated, pushing many workers to either further invisibility than ever before or towards digital platforms, leading to a gradual melting away of their grasp on their city.

The city has *always* changed. We used to talk about it even as teenagers in the eighties. We've heard enough and more about it from the older generation. We welcome harmonious change as it has genuinely brought good to us in the past in some instances. But this sort of disharmonious change is poison to us, sapping away our life bit by bit, and wounding us badly. Still, the most hurtful trend is how people, our accomplices, are forsaking us as part of this change that is happening in Bangalore. Their enmity towards us is based on morality and decency that they have recently acquired from god-knows-where. I can't separate the change in the city and change in attitude, with our old friends withdrawing. For us sex workers, this is our *kali yuga* [age of upheaval].

5

Upheaval

Bangalore city has been continuously and repeatedly reimagined for centuries, but the pace of wholesale reconfiguration over the last two decades, of what and who Bangalore is, has been matchless. Janaki Nair has shown how even social movements in Bangalore have been mostly gentrified, which she has interpreted articulately as an 'ideology of beauty', which we encapsulate here. Crusades against the prevention of the 'misuse' of 'public' spaces by 'anti-social elements' have enjoyed the full support of the middle- and upper-middle classes, and have been backed by the corporate sector, who wish to 'rehabilitate' the city's image as peaceful, air-conditioned and content, with their own upmarket concerns around image, aesthetics, planning, administration and environment. On aesthetic and environmental grounds, even bottom-up political rallies and strikes, struggles for civil or worker rights and protests by distressed economic groups were, over time, diverted from strategically effective locations, such as in front of the state legislature and in public parks, to designated plots some distance away so they could be hidden from view. Indubitably, this has been a textbook example of revanchism. These 'concerned' citizens and their protests put a spotlight on the core spaces in the city, spaces that were actually an axis for informal livelihoods which were seen as inconveniences or as anti-social (except if they catered to the recreational requirements of the comfortable and the affluent). There was little appreciation among these upmarket protestors that Bangalore's green spaces were not only Cubbon Park or Lalbagh, but in homes across every class and character in the city – be it expansive gardens within colonial bungalows in Langford Town or simply rows of potted plants in front of workers' quarters and shanties around the old mills and markets of Bangalore, or in scores of lakes and tanks, wide trees on the streets or religious groves (all these described extensively in Harini Nagendra's aptly titled *Nature in the City*), which is what made Bangalore a garden city in a genuine sense. In fact, as Janaki Nair[1] revealed in a telling anecdote, campaigners for aesthetics suggested at one point, in a spirit of high revanchism, that the 'heterogeneous crowds' who thronged the high court complex for their businesses should be forbidden to enter Cubbon Park that lies right beside it, lest they ruined its 'elegance and beauty'.

[1] Nair (2005: 226).

But more than even the Populations, it is the pseudo-invisibles, such as street-based sex workers, who routinely constitute these 'heterogenous crowds', posing as aesthetic, moral and political threats to both the past and the future of this beautiful city. New spaces, new artefacts and new actors broke into their world, suddenly and gradually, and transformed the spatial and behavioural dynamic of street-based sex work – an occupation that is integral to the compass of informal labour in the city. In their individual lives, these transitions have had jarring implications on their bodies and spirits, on their families and livelihoods and on their very existence. And, on an aggregate, the sexscape of Bangalore has experienced tumultuous transformation under the crushing weight of the neoliberal gentrified transition that rumbled above it. In this chapter, we wade through Bangalore's transition experience, with them as the nucleus.

To trace this experience and bring out its full fury, we realised that it would be most effective to compound their oral narratives (which we have used to flesh out Bangalore's sexscape over the last two chapters) with archival material sourced from popular print media such as newspapers and magazines and documentation housed by the organisations that support them. As we had explained in greater detail in Chapter 2, to richly texture the urban transition experience, we combed through newspaper reports and media narratives from 1998 to 2018 to complement the spoken narratives from the sex workers we conversed with. The outlook towards these workers by the print media, details on police atrocities and justifications for these abuses and the general popular discourse around these workers are only evident in the journalistic material. In this manner, the narrative and archival sources build the diegesis of Bangalore's urban transition among these workers. In this chapter, we lay this saga out in two parts, the first of which are accounts of betrayal by their former ancillaries and the trauma of losing their core workspaces, and the second is their experiences with their arch antagonists, the police. Finally, in order to fully fathom the intensity of the upheaval of urban transition, we develop in this chapter a series of maps that we curated based on their oral narratives, and how their spaces have been acutely corroded, how *their* Bangalore has shrivelled and dissolved, leaving them stranded. We begin with the stories of how their city melted away.

Et Tu, Brute?

The pavement was no more a comfortable place, and the public toilets and their staff began behaving strangely. The trees, groves and lakes slowly disappeared, as did the open parthenium-infested tracts. Theatres and complexes began disintegrating. Street vendors and small shops began giving cold shoulders. Autorickshaw drivers and bus staff appeared to not know of them, and sleepy watchmen turned into hostile security guards. Parks began growing gates and barricades overnight, and lodges cloaked themselves with a veneer of rectitude through the years. Shiny new buildings came up, shopping centres became plazas, bare grounds became metro stations and bus stands could now only be used for boarding buses. Sleek eyes with a blinking red dot began to be installed on pillars that still had their bases reddened by callous spitting, and groups of hunters with large cameras and microphones suddenly decided to unearth their nefarious activities to reveal to the shocked Citizenry what their city had become. The Populations pulled the plank on them, standing quietly and nodding silently when they were violently attacked and driven out of their workspaces; they behaved more genteelly than the gentrifiers in the policy boardrooms. Only their customers and the city's flora retained their conviviality towards them. The city morphed, sometimes at a glacial pace and sometimes with intermittent jarring shards of change, from a place where they could freely roam and work (with the occasional police escapade) to a patchwork of forbidden tracts and valleys where the police were only the most violent among other foes.

> Yes, the police are the most dangerous, but now they're not the only problem we have. Everyone and everywhere is the problem these days.

Lodges became deluxe lodges within a span of a few weeks, with a new coat of a lighter coloured beige or moody-grey paint that gave them fresh relief from older greens and browns and made them look airier and more open. A few decided to stick a prefix 'New' to their existing names while many others renamed themselves with anglicised names such as 'Elegance Lodge' that radiated a sophistication that cannot be captured by 'Bhuvaneshwari Tourist Home'. Corridors began to be lit up with sharp-bright socket lights instead of yellowing forty-watt bulbs or tube lights blackened at their edges. Rooms began to be tiled with vitrified tiles and installed with air conditioners, a far cry from rooms whose windows had wooden or aluminium shutters and which had mosaic floors that retained stains beautifully.

> Lodge managers began snubbing my requests. Not just the younger new fellows, but even the usual older fellows who practically ran brothels in their lodges in the eighties. I even heard that customers who asked about the availability of 'services' were given dirty looks and were told that 'this wasn't that kind of a place', as though he was running some *ashram* [eyes rolling].

> I didn't like public toilets from the beginning since my clients were more sophisticated men, who couldn't afford the costlier gays on Church Street but wanted sexual services in a less smelly place. So, I used to take them to lodge rooms myself, like how the women sex workers usually did. But from the last five or six years, they allow only either families or two men who are dressed better. So I had to buy a clean white shirt to look like some banker, and I kept wearing the same

shirt when I went from lodge to lodge with my customers who looked anyway like bankers. We looked like two colleagues on a work trip.

Some of the lodges still allow us … there are so few welcoming lodges now. But even in them, I thought at least the bell boys and cleaners would still allow us to do our job in the rooms. But they too look at us as so badly when we come out of the rooms with our customers. All because they now think they're very high up morally.

And this is also the case with eateries. The managers don't chat with us the way they used to, and waiters constantly tell us 'finish quickly' to make us leave soon, especially when there's a crowd of families or working men. Once, signalled by the cashier, the waiter came and told me quietly 'switch your phone off'. When I asked him why, he told me in a hushed tone, 'We don't want you booking your customers in our hotel – we don't want our other customers to see prostitutes here'. Oh, for so many years, we would get looks from others sitting around us, but they used to just get back to eating. Now, can I say anything when he talks like this?

A very interesting revelation that came up was in not just visual gentrification, but even aural.

That hotel near Balaji Paradise lodge, which used to serve great *bonda*s [a deep-fried potato snack, popular as street food in India] and tea, it has suddenly turned very holy. [The hotel's manager] used to play only Kannada film songs and sometimes racy Bollywood songs back in the 1990s. You know what he plays now? Some Sai Baba stuff! I can't believe it. I asked him jokingly why he changed his music, and he told me with a smile that he wanted to create an image that he was a clean fellow. His customers, he said, might not get attracted to the Sai Baba *bhajan*s [devotional songs, usually Hindu], but they would surely go away if he played some loud film songs. And he quietly added that he didn't like Kannada songs anymore. If he were not Kannadiga, I would've told him a thing or two.

You're right! I didn't realise it till you said it. They play more decent music these days in those eateries. Surely to look better. Even their chairs and tables are now better looking, and I look strange sitting on them. And the music is much more polished, sometimes only instrumental. I don't know why they can't play those beautiful old Rajkumar songs – maybe Kannada songs are not fashionable enough, and they don't want to come across as too local.

But if the sprucing up of many lodges and eateries was antagonistic to street-based sex work, the ultimate death knell was the closure of many more lodges, especially in the KR Market area. There is little data to show how many actually disappeared (mainly because many were operating off the record), but a walk down memory lane with a few of our narrators revealed to us, as they pointed one building after another, how many had disappeared. In their place were glittering shops, or at least those with names on sleek flex boards, selling mobile phones, paint, floor tiles, clothing, and so on.

> From 2005 to 2015, I can't tell you how many disappeared. I'm not joking – on so many mornings, I woke up and took my usual walk down from Upparpet to KR Market, and suddenly this one's permanently locked up, that one's been scaffolded for demolition, another one has just been reduced to rubble within a week! God knows where all those staff went … why did they just pull them down? I've really lost count of how many have gone; they had such nice names too. For so long, Majestic meant 'lodge' more than theatre. There were more lodges than anything else, and all were always full.

> [a more articulate narrator joins in] But do you know why so many are gone? See, it's not that they have just gone, but that so many new hotels have come up too, pushing them out of business. The problem was that, first, business was getting really bad for most of them. People don't want to stay in those untidy places and instead prefer the newer hotels, which are cheap if you book early enough. Another problem was that most businesses and trades have moved out of Majestic and Market to many other places, so who wants to stay here? The existing trades are already facing serious competition from online sales, so few people come here and do business with them. But there's an even more important fact. They want Majestic and Market to *look* better. That's why the new hotels instead of lodges, where we are forbidden to even stand in front of, let alone get a room. Majestic meant lodges and lodges meant us. Lodges became so full of us that this became another reason they wanted a cleanup – *us*.

For transgender workers, who could not access lodges even in their heyday, streets and open spaces were their sites for solicitation and work. Their spots were pavements, behind large trees and boulders, empty plots and beside lakes. Each of these has experienced gentrified transition over the last twenty years, documented well by academic and popular literature. Wooded groves (known as *gunda thopes*, or just *thopes*) that had multiple uses for ecological as well as socio-cultural and economic benefit have gradually eroded over time, with sweeping tracts of groves disappearing in and around the city. Bamboo groves and other wild copses were aplenty in the city and around it, and were hotspots for sex work among transgender workers, besides male and female workers too. A drive around the periphery of the city would reveal the abundance of eucalyptus groves as well, which also served as ideal spaces for bringing your client from either within the city or sourcing them from the outskirts. Groves[2] had social regulatory systems around them and were crucial for poorer migrant communities, in especially the peri-urban areas, for food, firewood and fodder. They have been gobbled by the recklessly expansive urbanisation of the city

---

[2] See Mundoli, Manjunatha and Nagendra (2017).

(or reused in some cases as garbage dumps), and only a few remnants still remain around the ring roads that encircle the outskirts where transgender workers can freely enter. These disappearing commons – erased as a result of infrastructure construction or residential development, and in many cases, within the city as a result of manicuring into gated parks – have also erased sites for sex work. Where boulders and parthenium bushes once stood, those spaces have now been converted into sites that are 'better looking', if not into commercial complexes and other public infrastructure. Thickets around lakes, too, housed sex work by transgender workers, to the extent that Rohan D'Souza and Harini Nagendra, in their research,[3] listed sex work as one of three main categories of livelihood around the lakes they studied, such as Agara Lake. Their work has shown how surveillance and security of lakes such as this have recast these livelihoods as 'illegal' which must be prevented in order to 'save the lake' for more recreational (or religious or artistic) purposes among the more affluent, in a classic revanchist move. The case of Agara, according to their study, has been fortunate for these workers as litigation complications have allowed a nexus between the police, security guards and workers, a situation that has not been the case with most lakes around Bangalore that have been manicured and trimmed to suit a certain brand of aesthetics. The need for idyll has overruled the need for livelihood around lakes. Also, these livelihoods have been accused of befouling lakes more than the effluent from apartment complexes or industries that surround these lakes. All this, of course, when the lakes have survived in the first place.

This congested metropolis was decimated of its lakes and tanks, from nearly 400 in the late 1800s to just under eighty in the present day. But for most of this history of lake extermination, the structures and neighbourhoods that came up on lake beds were not antagonistic to sex work, with the exception of buildings such as the Vidhana Soudha. This does not condone the deliberate extermination of lakes, but it provides at least a second-best option to continue sex work, even without the lake. Our narrators recounted many lakes from their childhood, but appeared to not be too concerned about their disappearance, except in the case of transgender workers who were the most affected by the loss of lakes and groves. On the other hand, it was interesting to hear from them about how refurbishments around existing revived lakes were more inimical to sex work than the outright vanishing of the lakes themselves. For street-based sex workers, this is a double loss. First, it is a loss of the commons where solicitation, service and recreation were possible. Second, it becomes a loss when the infrastructure that replaces it forbids sex workers to cruise around. But this need not always be the case. While urban transition and the resultant loss of ecological sites such as lakes and groves is a crucial issue, in many cases, what replaced it was at least welcome to sex work. A transgender worker narrated:

---

[3] D'Souza and Nagendra (2011).

When the lake was dying and full of algae, no one came near it, and at least we could operate there. Even if it was really dirty, our customers didn't seem to mind. I mean, where else do we go now that the city has become less friendly to us? But they closed down my lake for about six months and revived it. After that, they put up a footpath around it, put gates and a security guard and neatly kept me out. The lake was saved; my livelihood had gone. Just like parks.

Transgender workers narrated to us how their conditions have, expectedly, been the most compromised, as they have had to battle not only the alleged immorality of their occupation but also their very presence around these remodelled and barricaded commons. The popular, academic, journalistic and literary or artistic literature on the condition of economically poor urban transgender individuals is copious with accounts and analyses of threats by the state and society towards their existence and legitimacy as citizens, and we will not attempt to cover these deep complexities in their entirety. However, as we will be able to see across this book and especially in this chapter, the corroding away of open and shared urban spaces due to neoliberal urban transition has affected them the most, compared to male and female workers, because it is transgender workers who are dependent on urban ecological commons and open shared spaces for sex work. They are disallowed into other enclosed areas and are unable to secure residence in most neighbourhoods, making their livelihoods also insecure. Open urban spaces and ecological commons such as lakes and parks often remain their refuge, which have been encroached and gentrified recurrently.

Parks have had a turbulent history in this garden city. Scholars such as Janaki Nair and Harini Nagendra have documented the politics of parks in Bangalore, and several civil society organisations have taken up the environmental and livelihood concerns around parks for decades. Our narrators were also full to bursting about parks.

I used to frequent the small parks around Gandhinagar [around Majestic bus stand]. Slowly, park by park, they began putting up nice green and yellow fences, and then, one fine day, they put up a gate too. What's worse, they locked those gates after people had come and gone. I didn't realise it until the day they locked it. I used to get my customers and jump over the fences, or squeeze through the half-open gates, but one evening, I brought my customer all the way here, and then saw it locked. He just walked away muttering something, making me look like a fool.

[another narrator continuing the conversation] But *akka*, even the locks are okay. We can probably get our customers during afternoons or late mornings after the walkers have gone. But the problem is the security guard. If someone told me ten years ago that there would be a security guard for a park, I would have laughed, wondering who would want to steal bushes. Now he stands there not allowing me in at all. So what if I am a TG? I, too, can get into a park at least to sleep!

They won't allow me to sleep at a bus stop anyway, and I only had parks left. Now those are gone too.

[a third, female narrator joins in] Also, I hate it when they allow these young couples to get into parks but not us. As it is, Sundays are completely off for us since the parks are filled with families and children the whole day. But on weekdays, or when we really need some cash, these students come and take up the place. Is that not indecent according to the guards? We are doing this for our daily bread while those couples are wasting their time in there. What else … their love is more decent than our work.

[a fourth, female narrator continues] Correct! Correct! No one asks them anything. In the old days, the constable used to shoo couples away or threaten to tell their parents, and instead, we could pay him 25 rupees to do our job for one full day. Now it's the reverse. These rich lazy kids can pay the 10 rupees to enter the park and spend the whole there just staring into their phones and giggling, while if I go in there, they complain to the guard that there is something immoral going on.

[a fifth, male narrator joins in] That Journalist's Colony Garden near Kalasipalayam – have you seen it? They almost put makeup on it, and it looks superb! But no use to me, since the regulars there know me and my job by now, and there's no entry for me.

Besides securing parks with barricades, gates, locks and guards, another strategy that has been regularly employed to keep certain kinds of people out has been to ticket them. While the idea of ticketing a public space may seem audacious at first, those who endorse the gentrification of a park would only wholeheartedly uphold monetising its entry not to earn revenue but to maintain a certain image of the park and keep it away from the homeless, transgender individuals, and other immoral activities such as sex work. While a sum of 5 rupees or 10 rupees may be laughed at as a minuscule amount, this may not be as affordable for sex workers.

Look at it this way. A person who wants to use the park for jogging or having a picnic on Sunday can afford 10 rupees, because it is for a one-time entry, possibly once a week. Even to pay it once a day is very affordable for them. But we have to enter and leave the park several times a day. We get a customer from outside, pay the entry fee, sometimes even for the customer, and leave the park after the service is done. We then have to get another customer from elsewhere and enter the park once again. Another payment. And then again, and again. When they began ticketing my usual park, I first thought how a small 10 rupees entry fee would affect me. In a single day, I realised what a huge burden it was because I ended up paying 40 rupees to 80 rupees if I had four customers! And it's a good part of what I earn per day, even on a good day. Repeatedly exiting and entering the park costs a fortune for us. It isn't fair.

[another worker joining in] That's right. It's also not fair that sometimes we have to prove our purpose there even if we want to rest or sleep. The poor TGs are forbidden even if they can pay, but in our case, even if we pay and enter, after sitting there for ten minutes, the guard comes up and asks what we're doing there. In some instances, I have even had regular walkers passing comments to me asking 'whether I have started yet', which is very humiliating. Yes, I am a sex worker, but I am not some loose woman.

[a transgender worker adds in] And we are not devils. Do you know how many times, when I sit on a bench just eating peanuts, I have seen families keep their children some twenty feet away from me? So many have pulled their children away from the area where I am sitting, and I have even heard them discipline their kids by warning them that I will kidnap them. Sometimes, the security guards tell us to sit in a particular place in a park far away from children's play areas. After repeatedly experiencing this, I decided to stay away from parks altogether.

[another transgender worker continues] What you are all saying is the same case with lakes nowadays. Gates, fences, railings, pavements, jogging and children. There's some board there that says all kinds of things, but I can't read. Neither can my other friends. I was told by a security guard it was about what was allowed and what was prohibited. For me, the message on the board was simple, even if I couldn't read it: *this park is for them, not for you.*

Parks, open spaces, lakes and small green patches have been routinely fenced and blocked away to achieve multiple simultaneous solutions – beautify it, get it back from the indecent anti-social elements, restrict entry by ticketing and keeping opening hours, guard it and, at the very maximum, allow food vendors to operate there. A mind-boggling 1,000 parks have been 'developed' all over the city, including in its peripheral areas, and of these, nearly 750 have been assigned a security guard. Compared to a summary list of parks in the city, which numbers to nearly 1,300, the proportion of 'developed' and 'guarded' parks is very sizeable, leaving only a few hundred parks 'undeveloped'. In fact, the Bruhat Bengaluru Mahangara Palike (BBMP), the municipal corporation of Bangalore city, also displays 'saved' parks, which informs us that practically every single park in the city has been 'saved'.[4]

Guards, too, have multiplied and morphed. The omnipresence of security guards in a city as a labour force has had a strong association with neoliberal urbanisation, with the sprawling of private property over former agricultural or scrub land in the city's outskirts, and with the replacement or modification of

---

[4] This data in this paragraph has been sourced from the BBMP's 'Developed Parks List', 'Parks with Security Staff' and 'No. of Parks Saved'. The data was obtained from OpenCity. in for 2015, which is an urban open-data platform for public data, gathered from authentic sources such as the BBMP.

publicly owned buildings or open spaces inside the city by transferring them to private hands and management. Importantly, they have also emerged as convenient instruments to protect the interests of capital and upkeep image. Their economic and cultural proximity to those they are trained to restrict and discipline assists in this convenience, simplifying the efforts that Citizens and the state have to undertake to encounter deviant individual figures at the ground level. Security guards have become a standard fixture in the metropolitan urban humanscape, their appearance ubiquitous and almost synonymous with city life and in urban space. During decades prior, the groggy scruffy khaki-clad 'watchman' in sandals, slouching on a wooden stool or chair with a baton in hand, sitting in front of government buildings, educational institutions, factories, theatres and residences of the wealthy, was an occasional sight. In the neoliberal city, the 'security guard', affiliated to a firm, no more the khaki-clad elderly watchman but the young first-generation immigrant to the city in a much more impressive-looking bluish or greyish uniform with multiple stars on shoulder straps and uncomfortable shoes, slouching over a mobile phone, has become a permanent fixture. They are scooped up by the thousands from the pool of millions of cheap immigrant workers in the city, and are appointed as foot soldiers of gentrification and protectors of privatised or ongoing-privatising urban space and structure, themselves usually the victims of dispossession and economic distress back in their native lands. They are welcomed as necessary immigrant labour and slotted into the Populations but rarely provided quality employment and living. They fit beautifully into the imagined city, to further its cause.

So many security guards think they are mini police. I first thought they were in a good job, but my friends later told me that they are actually not much better than us. They don't offer sex for income, that's all. The rest is the same. But their attitude is really bad. Yes, I have been beaten by a security guard even when I began sex work in the 1990s, but that's because I tried to enter a cinema theatre even after it was closed. These days, every corner of the street and every building has security guards, and they have a special eye for us.

[a transgender worker continues] Then think of us! They can't stand the sight of us and are kept there to ensure we are nowhere in sight. Forget sex work, one of them even told me that we are not supposed to even be *seen* near the Pothys mall. I asked him what if I wanted to buy some clothes from inside, to which he pointed towards a series of vendors with cheap *saris* selling on the street. And in parks, these people are the very worst. They enjoy seeing couples kissing but hate us lying on the grass.

[another transgender worker adds in] Back in 1999, I fell out of favour with my guru, and it took two months before I entered my next *hamam*. In the meantime, I slept in construction sites and in front of shops. There were no guards at the time. I can't think of such a situation now, with a security guard manning every construction site. I'm only there to sleep, and sex work is not going to bring that building down or curse it. After all the tarpaulin sheets are taken off, once it is almost complete, I will leave the building. But who listens? The guard doesn't want to hear even if I'm very sick and need a shelter to sleep in for even one day.

[a female worker continues] Yes, yes, migrant security guards don't know our culture here. It's only after *they* came that all these restrictions began.

[another female worker continues] You can't really say such things. By the way [giggling], you are also a migrant from Shimoga. They know this culture very well. I'm sure their own sisters are sex workers wherever these migrant guards come from. But they act so 'shocked' at our job, calling us all kinds of names. Who are *they* to call *us* names? We are the locals here, and they are the migrants, but when there's any trouble, people and police will treat *them* as locals and *us* as outsiders.

[a male worker interrupts] I also agree. That's wrong. Completely wrong. Do you think only the migrant security guards are the problem? I can't go to my public toilet now. The fellow there is a hardcore Kannadiga, with those yellow and red stripes across his wrist throughout November. But now toilets are off-limits for us.

The fortressing of formerly unmanned (or laxly manned) buildings and complexes has been a serious obstacle to street-based sex work, for which security guards have served as the ideal troopers. Merely putting up gates and locks are insufficient, as the staff of these buildings told us. A shop manager at Alankar Plaza and his staff narrated:

I have been here for more than twenty years. Long ago, I used to notice that there was some movement in the basement and around the corridors at night, since you could see footprints in the dust in the morning and some cigarette butts lying here and there. No locks and chains are enough. Those people know how to get in. So, we have had to put a man there in front. He does nothing all night, but at least now they are a little afraid to walk around. [wiping his forehead] All this doesn't look good anyway.

That's true, sir. Unlike in the old days, the shops are now open until late, maybe even 10 p.m. We can't have these people loitering around here. Can you imagine if potential customers eyeballing and window-shopping our wares noticed these elements around? They might think I am involved in that dirty stuff too. We can't allow business to suffer. That's why we put that guard there and asked him to be extra vigilant about these types. And also, they should be taken somewhere else anyway, since we don't need them here. What are they contributing? I feel embarrassed walking through them as a decent woman while getting out of the shop every evening. What purpose do they serve?

As a male worker narrated to us, the change in the guarding of public toilets is an accompaniment to the transition in public toilets in Bangalore as well.

During our conversations with narrators, we also attempted to enquire from the city corporation and the state public health departments about public toilets with regard to their number, locations and change in design, but we failed to receive any proper information from them and were pushed back and forth between these two institutions citing that the other had the information. We were fortunate to obtain a list of public toilets as of 2016.[5] The list ran up to nearly 500 toilets (including information on facilities, year of construction and rough location) which seemed like an impressive number at first glance, but upon speaking about this to male workers, we were informed that this was a low estimate.[6] The workers compared this number to the area and population of Bangalore and said that not only was this insufficient but actually an inaccurate figure. To follow up on this topic, we arranged a conversation with a few male workers only about public toilets in Bangalore, and the issue that turned up in their narrations, more than manning or facilities (which we have seen in earlier chapters), was their disappearance.

Public toilets were said to have disappeared by the dozen, with no warning, practically overnight. Narrators recounted how there were so many more toilets in the KR Market given the immense floating population in the area, even as late as just prior to 2010, but, especially during this decade, they were simply pulled down to either keep the place clear or to make way for another construction. We were enlightened by our narrators that public toilets were first, genuinely, very unhygienic in appearance, smell, sanitation and flimsy in construction with tiles dropping off and the sanitary-ware ceramic cracking routinely, but after the late 1990s, the Infosys Foundation had funded the construction of dozens of public toilets that were of far better quality and appearance. However, while this was a boon for the appearance and incentive for the usage of public toilets, it also meant stricter manning in the new toilets and overhasty demolition of older ones. There has been, in general, a demand from civil society organisations for a significant increase in the installation of public toilets in the city as part of strengthening public health infrastructure, but for male sex workers, the pulling down of toilets by the dozen is a livelihood concern.

> I don't know why they razed so many of them down – they were necessary to urinate, and for income too. Now, both activities are being done dangerously. People are urinating in the open, and we are facing difficulties in offering sex too.

---

[5] Again, sourced from OpenCity.in.

[6] A report in *The Hindu*, dated 1 July 2021, also affirmed that the number of public and community toilets in Bangalore city was significantly low, when compared to the same for Chennai, Hyderabad and Ahmedabad. These three cities have a community and public toilet ration per 1,000 inhabitants, per square kilometre, per ward and per 100 kilometres road length (while Chennai and Ahmedabad have twenty-five and fifteen toilets per 100 kilometres road length, Bangalore has only five). The article also evidenced the need for the city corporation to update its data.

I'm sure this had to do with driving us out as much as it was about cleaning up the place. You may think I'm unnecessarily imagining things, but you know, even if we can afford to get into the new toilets paying the entry fee each time, they don't want us in there. The new toilets are manned only to do toilet activities, and the old ones have disappeared. I know so many of them that have been replaced with some shop or have just been left as open areas to make the place look pretty.

Toilets can now only be used for urination and defecation, like bus stands can now be used only to alight buses or wait for them. There are only singular uses for these areas.

A female worker, who had planted herself at the Majestic bus stand until 2005 and then shifted to KR Market after a brawl with other workers in Majestic, narrated:

Do you know they now ask you if you have condoms inside your handbag? It's so humiliating. Well, actually, I do have condoms. The social workers come and give you a stash of condoms for your safety; the bus stand staff see this and then come and ask what we were doing there since this was a bus stand for buses only. I can see a drunkard lying there the whole day and young college-going students doing nothing there, with buses coming and going. But we can't be here. When I asked a bus conductor once what crime I committed, he simply said, 'Oh, *you're* here, that's the problem', as though I was some cockroach spreading some disease.

[a male worker continued] True. Like toilets, these were our areas. Platform 12 was all mine, but now the vendors inside Majestic terminus and the bus staff have a problem. If not one, the other. The shop owners have known us for a while but have suddenly turned ways in order not to get into trouble. The bus staff know we are not here to take buses and shout out that we are inconveniences to genuine passengers who are finding it hard jostling for space. I went to school with that rascal, that conductor, but now he thinks he's the transport minister and I'm some stray dog spreading AIDS around.

[another male worker joins in] I tell you, this is all part of creating a more fashionable Majestic. Things were much simpler in the old days, with fewer instruction boards about 'public nuisances', no CCTV cameras and many more toilets. Everyone could be as clean or dirty as they wanted to. But now we all want to look more modern and glamorous. I can see it everywhere. They want their Majestic to look different. One or two policemen have even told me that on my face, glaring at me like I was some rat.

The BMTC staff are now, allegedly, serving even as informants in a casual capacity to the police of the presence of sex work in bus stands and around parked buses. It was natural that given these emerging attitudes, sex work within moving buses would also be prohibited.

Why moving buses? Even in standstill buses, we are thrown out now. While no one really cared about it in the old days, and we had to bother only about dangerous customers, the dozens of buses parked in the depots are off-limits to us. Over the last couple of years, I've had bus staff telling me to my face, 'What do you think the bus is, a brothel?' I never had anything like this told to me from the time I began work in parked buses in 1995 to about 2010 or 2011. They think buses now have some kind of purity. And it's far worse for TGs. Despite a little more recognition by society, most bus stands and buses are forbidden to them.

On speaking to a few bus conductors and junior staff of Majestic bus stand and KR Market bus stand, they explained:

Sorry, sir, our bus service is meant to go to work or college or school or home, or for any other proper purpose. Not for prostitutes. We have been able to clean the buses and bus stations of beggars, drug addicts, drunkards and those eunuchs who are here to create trouble. They are otherwise okay in buses, but the moment we see them haggling our passengers, they are out.

Upon relating this to a transgender worker, the response we received was:

Yes, yes, that's true. But you know what? The worst place is still not the bus stand. You can do *something* there. The very worst are the metro and all those flyovers that came up around them. They took away a lot of land for that, which we could use, and now you can't do anything else there except take a metro. Remember the MG Road area?

With respect to transport, the element that came up most often in our conversations was the metro, as the supreme hallmark of the futuristic city and consequent dispossession for sex workers. Most conversations on transport and public spaces veered towards the metro, despite the fact that the metro is not the largest carrier of commuters in the city and is a pale comparison to metro services in megacities such as New York. The construction of the metro in Bangalore, as in Delhi, was celebrated with great pomp and splendour, more for its role in providing the ultimate modern facelift to the city than for its actual service as a seamless public transport. Scores of street vendors and small traders, hundreds of families in their shanties and thousands of people who took shelter on the street and public spaces lost their tracts.[7] For sex workers, though, it brought with it an incomparable loss of operating space. Even the very first operational metro line, from MG Road to Baiyappanahalli, dispossessed them of their principal cruising areas on MG Road, Trinity Circle, near the Ulsoor police station and all the way

---

[7] See a 2007 report by CASSUM (Collaborative for the Advancement of the Study of Urbanism through Mixed Media) for more on this.

up to Baiyappanahalli, where transgender workers conducted thriving sex work around the groves that filled the area. Most cruising spots were located around where the metro stations stand now, around which a great many businesses and eateries have sprung up, unwelcoming to street-based sex work.

Metro! *That's* the one which has made our lives the worst. Do you know how many of us had to move away to unknown areas thanks to those stations? I'm not saying that we should not have a metro. But the first thing they did was move the TGs out, and naturally, we too had to move. The construction took so many years, and we were unable to go there since the sites were totally cordoned off by security guards, unlike how construction sites used to be in the old days. I have seen Shivajinagar bus stand being constructed, but the site was not as guarded and we could go there after dark. The metro construction at Majestic and elsewhere was totally guarded. And finally, when they opened it, it gave us the message that we were not allowed here. Many of us tried and got shooed away. The rest of us didn't even attempt to go there.

Well, a few of us still operate around there, those of us who know where to stand, but providing services is completely out of the picture. When MG Road station came up, the big problem was not really the station but what was built around it. Do you remember that long pathway from the Gandhi statue to Brigade Road? That's now completely built up, and you can't even sleep there. Yes, a drunk man can sleep there, and all those people in fancy shorts and shoes can sit around. But not us. And *definitely* not TGs. Every now and then, they put up some public function there, and we just can't fit in, we can't stand around, and if the new guards knew us, it would be the end for us.

The metro at Majestic came up on that land just behind the intercity bus terminus, a land that was open and free for us. While returning from my job and just before changing buses at Majestic, I used to spend about half an hour there with friends and regular clients. It was so nice for us male workers. Free and airy. In fact, there used to be a lake there even before that, which was paradise. In the evenings, just before dark, we could offer our services on the banks of the lake. The lake went, but the land there was also conducive to sex work. Maybe even for just some cigarettes and conversation. Then the metro came, and I didn't know where to go.

That's the same case with the Baiyappanahalli station and at the other end near Natraj theatre where the metro dives into the ground. I can't recall a lake there, but it was just scrub and open space. That was more than enough for us. Solicit customers there during the daytime and service more customers after dark.

Wait, wait, the best story is the KR Market metro station. It's so stylish that I didn't find the words to describe it to my wife and children when I first saw it. When you go down the escalator, it feels like it's immersing in some holy river and becoming pure [laughing]. It completely masks the wild forest of people and activities above.

Like some five star hotel. Of course, to my family, I made it look so nice and then took all of them for a ride on it. Only I knew that I couldn't meet my customers here anymore. All the old places have gone, and the new ones don't welcome our work.

When I was really small, I saw Majestic bus stand come up. Of course, at that time, I didn't do sex work since I was six years old, but after I began many years later in the 1980s, I heard from older women workers at the time that the lake has gone, which is a loss, but the bus stand was okay for sex work. So, you see, if we lost something important, the next thing that came up in its place was open to us. So it wasn't so bad. Not like it is now.

That's correct, do you know what I was talking about Alankar Plaza? At least that was for a long time open for us. But these new places are impossible to get in. There's an Aishwarya Mall now coming up, and even though it is not finished yet, I can already see that it won't be friendly to us. And even if it isn't malls, we can't stand anywhere near the renovated shopping complexes whose only purpose is to make the place look good.

Do you know Shrungar on MG Road is going? Even until five years ago, that was the only place left on MG Road for us. They beat us very badly if they find us near the metro station or the shining glass shops. And the rest of the people just look on, since the police tell them we are anti-social elements doing prostitution and trafficking and gain their silent support.

Oh wow! Shrungar is going? I haven't been to MG Road since they kicked me and two friends out of there for being dirty men. But you know, the gays on Church Street are still there. Maybe if I knew English, I could still operate on Church Street.

[the previous narrator responds] Church Street is worse than MG Road. I can still at least try to hang around near Barton after eight at night, but Church Street is completely off for us, after that pavement beautification which served only the shorts-shoes people. Not for us pant-shirts.

The loss of pavements is as much regretted by street-based sex workers as ecological sites, lodges, shopping complexes and bus stands. These spaces, which were open to even service provision back in the 1980s, slowly forbade service but tolerated solicitation, and then began barring even solicitation. While street-based sex work is still solicited on some pavements of Majestic and KR Market, what remains today is a feeble remnant of the spectacular theatre of the sex work industry that the pavement used to be. Some pavements are impermissible altogether, such as the ones that have been remodelled by the project TenderSURE (Specifications for Urban Road Execution), to which lengthy stretches of roads and footpaths have been given (for a stunning bill that runs into the hundreds of crores of rupees) since 2012 to create lovely pedestrian-friendly footpaths, bicycle lanes, bus bays and wide luxurious walkways all over the city without the usual obstacle-course experience that most pavements are. The website of the project proudly announces that the core idea is to 'transform the public realm', the city corporation's document on it includes 'proper landscaping to increase the aesthetics of the roads and city' as one of its salient features, while the central government's Ministry of Urban Affairs website on urban transformation states that this project is about 'getting the urban road right'. This project is, even visibly, the *pièce de résistance* of urban gentrification of Bangalore and one of the most long-term threats to street-based sex work in the city. While only a portion of the targeted roads in the city has been provided with this facelift as yet, the earlier narrator's experience will assuredly be the general case among street-based sex workers when the project spreads through the 100 kilometres of targeted roads in the main parts of the city. Ecological losses and manicured minimalist replacements of existing street greenery have been well documented,[8] as have been compromises on livelihoods that depend on informal systems in the urban public space.[9] It took a decade after their official recognition for street vendors to gain licences, whereas the TenderSURE project was given immediate priority as it catered to 'world-class aspirations'. This ended up being more of an imposition of an idealised-West visual imaginary of the sidewalk as a material space than an informed and inclusive collective aspiration to improve and empower the everyday lives of people.[10]

The steady loss of pavement space for street-based sex workers is a direct deprivation and impoverishment of the site that gives them their very name 'street-based'. On second thought, it might be more appropriate to name this category 'pavement-based' sex worker, as solicitation usually occurs not strictly on the street but on its pavements, and a gentrified assault on pavements that are recrafted to suit mainly the genteel Citizen pedestrian and few others is an invasion on the sanctum-sanctorum of solicitation in street-based sex work. They are fabricated for Citizens, served by the permitted Populations and verboten for the pseudo-invisibles.

The slow decay and eventual renovation of shopping complexes in Bangalore, whether constructed by the city corporation in each neighbourhood or privately set up, has also been a serious loss for these workers. Complexes such as the Jayanagar Shopping Complex built in the 1970s, which was a commercial focal point of Asia's largest suburb, have been on the drawing boards of the Bangalore Development Authority (BDA) and the BBMP for nearly a decade. This has worried shop owners and street vendors circumambulating the complex,

---

[8] For example, by Nagendra and Gopal (2010).
[9] For example, by Keswani (2019).
[10] Sanath (2018).

many of whom have operated here since its inception. Not only in Jayanagar, concrete-facade shopping complexes, which have housed hundreds of tiny shops and swarms of vendors for decades, have been due for either complete demolition and replacement with a mall or gentrified renovation to accommodate more upmarket sellers. Even as these Populations struggle for survival with the phantom of gentrification clouding their present and future, pseudo-invisibles have practically nowhere to go, as they are simply invisibilised during official deliberations and in popular conversations around these trends.

As we have seen thus far, the pseudo-invisibles of this study have been forsaken not only by planners and Citizens, but by these Populations as well, over the last decade. As much as they have been victims of gentrification and have had an abrasive experience with neoliberal urban transition, they have equally been advocates of these processes against those beneath them in the urban social and labour hierarchy. Desires for gentrification and revanchism have been employed regularly as battle cries against sex workers by the working class, in the very areas where they were ancillaries for a long time. Those individuals around street-based sex workers who were associates have morphed into adversaries and eschewed their tolerance.

We can't even just sit on the footpath anymore. [looking at the other narrator] In Church Street, you say the footpath is not meant for us. It's the same on that street along Gubbi theatre in Majestic – it's *so* clean that we can't go there anymore. But, you know, in Majestic and KR Market, not just the footpaths, even the shopkeepers and vendors have turned their backs against us. I am struggling not just with *where* to go to, but also with *whom* to go to if I need something.

For so long, they were our friends and they helped us so much, and we, in turn, used to negotiate with the goons in the area to help them. It was really like a strong bond of friendship, but now that's not the case. Those selling vegetables on the street are worse than those selling shirts and pants. They shoo us away, calling us names and shouting that our presence will ruin their business. But I know it's not just about business. They don't want people like us there, even if we help them in their business. The shopkeepers in Kalasipalayam are slightly better. Some of them still just look the other way, which is okay for us, but many have now suddenly become priests and monks who think too pure of themselves and their surroundings. They're not even Brahmins but worse than Brahmins.

I used to thank god I'm not in some brothel in Bombay or Calcutta. I've been there once and seen them in cages. But I slowly realised over the last few years that we are in the biggest open cage where we can't go anywhere, work anywhere and hide anywhere. Shopkeepers used to give us water and would allow us to sleep near their shop. Now, only that coffee seller near the Rajkumar statue tolerates me. No one else. Not even the beggars, and not even the groundnut sellers. I was once called 'prostitute' and thrown out of the shop. They are all above us now. Or we are below them, whichever.

[a transgender worker continues] So how do you think it is for *us* then? They say we are not allowed on this footpath and near that shop. A jeweller openly told me that it didn't look good if I were seen around. Look good to whom? I had blessed his brother's son twenty years ago, and now that brat is just going around with his father's and uncle's money. Doesn't that 'not look good?' Everyone's a hypocrite. It just doesn't seem like my city anymore. I've been here for thirty years, now there's no place, and everyone's my enemy.

A few small shopkeepers and street vendors, from the other side of the battle, related:

I don't know why those women have to stand around here. I can't recognise the men who do this dirty stuff, but the women I can make out in one instance. It's really bad for business. Many families who come here, and even good women who come to buy a bulb for the house or to ask about a pressure cooker part, how can they stand here comfortably? Am I in the middle of a brothel, or is this a street?

As much as pavements, a monumental loss for many female workers has been the steady decimation of single-screen cinema theatres in the Majestic area, among other areas, and their replacement with either malls with multi-screen cinema theatres or shimmering shopping complexes. From the 1940s until the 1960s, a string of theatres were opened in the Majestic area around KG Road – Prabhat, States, Sagar, Kempegowda, Himalaya, Geeta, Nartaki, Majestic, Alankar, Kalpana, Menaka, Abhinay, Kapali and Tribhuvan. There were cinema theatres everywhere else in the city too (totalling more than 100 by the year 2000), but nothing that could match the concentration in this area or the dedication to Kannada cinema during its golden era. Lakshmi Srinivas's work,[11] from which we borrow here, carefully documented how the urban informal street economy immediately around these theatres was woven intricately with the running of the theatre and, therefore, indirectly with the film industry as such. She documented how street vendors sold a full range of products, from those that added to the movie-going experience to those that had little to do with watching a film, such as luggage, wallets, caps and handbags, which were emblazoned with pictures, names and poses of film stars. Her ethnographic studies also reveal a crucial part of the social experience of cinema watching in the yesteryears, which is that women from the middle classes would never watch a film in a theatre alone; it was always a family experience and to dress appropriately for, and that women who went alone to these halls were committing an unnatural act.[12] This was despite

---

[11] L. Srinivas (2002, 2005, 2010a, 2010b).

[12] However, there appears to be no mention about sex work going on in Bangalore's theatres in any of her works, which we find surprising. It may be partly due to the fact that her respondents may have either deliberately not mentioned their presence, or that they may not have been aware of sex work in theatres altogether.

the allocation of 'ladies seats' many decades ago or 'ladies ticket queues' until the mid-2000s. This is an especially important revelation for this study because it revisits the notion of the decent public woman (which we saw in Chapter 1), and that sex workers were hence the few categories of women who would openly go to a cinema theatre by themselves, for a show that was usually late or very early, and sit in areas of the lower and upper classes in the hall that no other women would usually sit in. Cinema theatres were, as we have seen in the earlier chapters, a sought-after cruising and servicing area, especially for female sex workers, who enjoyed a freedom that was unavailable in lodges, buses, parks or elsewhere. Our own observations on cinema theatres were striking. Upon referring to older maps of Bangalore and locating the same sites on an observation walk around the area, we could see that out of around twenty theatres in the Majestic and KR Market area, half of them had disappeared, and of the other half, nearly all had been subjected to bold facelifts either indoors or on their outer facades. Those that had disappeared had either completely turned into shopping malls (not always with multi-screen theatres attached) or shopping complexes. Upon asking our narrators, a whole train of names were brought forth, many with smiles and twinkling eyes:

Sagar, Kalpana, Kailash, Kempegowda, Himalaya....

Geeta, Majestic, Alankar, Kapali, Tribhuvan....

Prabhat, Sangam ... and by the way, I've heard that Nartaki and Santosh are going to go in the coming years.

The existing ones are also becoming expensive, and customers generally these days are either not interested in theatre sex work, or most of them expect us to pick up the ticket cost. We can't break even given the rising ticket costs these days.

The pattern rhymed like poetry – Alankar and Prabhat became shopping complexes (much more concrete in appearance and less sophisticated compared to the glass and air-conditioned malls) with their names retained. Kailash, Himalaya and Tribhuvan, on the other hand, also became shopping complexes but with new names: Sagar became Pothys Mall; Kempegowda became Coupon Mall; Kalpana became Kalpana Mall; Sangam, Geeta and Kapali remain rubble at the time of writing this and await a new showy building, while Majestic remains an open ground. Bhumika, Menaka, Abhinaya and Nartaki have been zealously renovated, while only Movieland, Santosh, Sapna and Triveni remain at least in external appearance. Even in the more cosmopolitan areas, Galaxy, Plaza, Bluemoon, Bludiamond and Liberty disappeared, making way for lustrous and vivid structures that housed metro stations, malls and office spaces. The old hunting grounds moved on, giving way to a more shining Majestic and an assuredly dignified and upright movie experience, at any time of the day and for anyone – as long as you were a member of the Citizens or, in this case, even the Populations.

Anyone wishing to experience a typical family recreational Sunday evening with shopping, eating and movie-going would travel all the way to Majestic from anywhere in the city, because nowhere else, apart from, say, MG Road, would you get as wholesome an experience. Autorickshaw drivers, who in Bangalore have an old notoriety for refusing to travel where you want, would not bat an eyelid if you wanted to go to Majestic or KR Market. We attempted to ask a few autorickshaw drivers about sex workers, and responses ranged from complete silence to a shrug, to even a denial that they exist here. One of them decided that the best way to deal with these nosy researchers was to suggest:

Shall I take you to Pothys Mall?

Late in the evening, and as we have seen in earlier chapters, autorickshaw drivers would even know, if you were a single male traveller, where to get 'services' and would gladly take you to a lodge, cinema theatre or bus stand where street-based sex work was available.

Ha! Not any more. Now, they smile and say they don't know what you're talking about when a customer asks them where women are available. The same fellows who used to allow us to sleep in their autorickshaws and with whom we would chat.

That's true. Even those we knew in person now turn the other way, as though now they are too high for us and don't want us to pollute their 'clean' autos with our presence in it. For us TGs, it's one less place.

He doesn't bring customers anymore, and runs the other way when he sees me from afar. This is not the first fellow to do this. I've had this experience with a few other drivers too. But this was a guy I was quite close to. No free sex, but lots of friendship and long talks about things. When especially *he* went, I just stood there and thought, 'Oh, you too?'

Street-based sex workers sighed how Brutus, after Brutus plunged a dagger into them, turned their back on them, abandoned them, pulled the plank, and how they were pushed away place after place, from a city that was theirs to roam and work freely. While until the early 2000s they had very serious issues only with the emissaries of law and order, their losses of space and social capital have been far more extraordinary than for many others among the marginalised – though even among them, the impoverishment of city space has been ascending in severity from male to female to transgender worker. Our narrators stated that only health workers, social workers, a few lawyers, journalists and researchers (whom they refer to as 'college teachers') were supportive towards them. There were new enemies among old ancillaries, new threats within old places and new fears.

I once took an auto from my home to Majestic to stand in my usual place at 7 p.m. after my other day job was done. I knew his face, and he knew mine, but we didn't know each other personally. Instead of taking me to that place, he suddenly sped ahead and landed me up in front of Upparpet police station, handing me straight over to the police as a public nuisance. I felt like a helpless chicken being taken straight to the butcher.

No one liked us anyway, even twenty or thirty years ago. It was rough and involved a lot of careful relationships. But all these people around us were far more collegial....

[another narrator completes her sentence] .... yes, of course, *akka*, except the police.

Primum Hostium

The police have always been the first among adversaries, the *primum hostium*, of street-based sex workers all over the world. In Bangalore city, too, verbal and physical abuse against street-based sex workers have been inherently high in their traditional operating areas across public spaces. But when these public spaces have been subject to large-scale transformations, when they shrink or even disappear altogether – as we have seen throughout this chapter – violence against street-based sex workers skyrockets. For over two decades, this has been the standard story of the worker–police relationship. The use of strategies by the police ranges from aggression on the streets or in police stations to public humiliation and raids in private or public spaces or to even bare display of individuals by television media (a theme we shall take up in the next chapter).[13] Upon asking any police officer or constable in the area, the answers are the same: 'clean up the city' or 'restore its decency at any cost'. The police are the mercenaries of everyday revanchism in the city, and their tentacles penetrate nearly all living and working spaces of street-based sex workers. With full support from either bluntly antagonistic actors who pose as the city's conscience or from former ancillaries of sex workers who are part of the city's Populations, spatial and social marginalisation are deployed in full force by the police.[14] There has been ample

---

[13] *The Hindu,* 5 June 2007; PUCL Press Release, 30 March 2014.

[14] Detailed information on the police atrocity against sex workers in Bangalore can be seen in two major reports, submitted by two Bangalore-based organisations – the Alternative Law Forum and Sadhana Mahila Sangha. Most of the material in this section has been broadly based on ALF (2014) and SMS (2013), besides our conversations with the workers and newspaper reports.

evidence of this globally, and a rich treatment of this theme by the academic literature, which interprets these activities as territorial control, flexibilisation of control and for the production of space.[15] Mira Fey[16] has spelt out how the role of the police has sometimes been crafted as that of the 'protector' of women in prostitution (opposing the abolitionist position on sex work but at the same time posing as male rescuers of weaker females from male threats). She draws her arguments from Michael Lipsky's[17] conceptualisation of police officers as street-level bureaucrats and Wendy Brown's[18] interpretation of the police as an expression of the masculinist state's bureaucratic and prerogative powers, in the understanding of the shortcomings of putting the law into practice in the sphere of protection. As practitioners of the law, the police have had a sturdy track record in aggressively enforcing rules about a range of things such as dressing, waiting on the streets, sexual identity and what a 'worker' ought to look like – all these with the intention of restricting sex workers from public spaces, and to displace them away from city centres because they are 'inappropriate' or 'illegitimate' users of these spaces and hence might be even criminal or anti-social.[19]

When we spoke to our narrators in Bangalore about police atrocity in public spaces, they began by first talking about police atrocities in their homes. This was seconded by the documented evidence too. Let us begin by looking at the police's reach in their private spaces.

It has been common for law-enforcement agencies to conduct what are reported as 'raids' or 'drives' on hotel or lodge rooms that are treated as 'brothels'. Police routinely raid lodges where sex workers regularly operate. But a trend that has surfaced over the last decade and more has been raids even in private homes where immoral activity is suspected and routinely lumped with human trafficking. Workers who live with families – children and the aged – rarely conduct their occupation at home in order to escape stigma and to avoid children being exposed, but the raids ensure public disgrace and exposure of children.[20] Sex workers end up attacked and exposed even in their domestic spaces in the name of raids and rescue missions, with even their adult children criminalised in this process.[21] Instances were related to us where neighbours with whom they have discord (over unrelated matters such as water supply or garbage) settle scores by approaching the police with false information, with the police promptly following up, arriving in plainclothes and arresting or exposing them. Two workers narrated:

[15] Herbert (1996); Pitman (2002); Kerkin (2003); Hubbard (2004a, 2004b); Kunkel (2016).
[16] Fey (2017).
[17] Lipsky (1969).
[18] Brown (1992).
[19] McDowell (1995); Duncan (1996); Mitchell (2003); Nayar (2015).
[20] *The Hindu*, 6 August 2013.
[21] *The Hindu*, 8 February 2014.

I would obviously undertake this job far away from home, in the main city, away from my ailing parents and, more importantly, away from my kids. When they came home and started shouting at me, accusing me of running a brothel, naturally my kids too were exposed to the attention of our neighbours and local community.... How can I possibly run a brothel in the same house as my parents? I have nowhere else to shift house. How do I show my face around my locality now? What do I tell my kids? Won't they be ridiculed by the other children around?

They just barged into my house wearing regular clothes, announcing they were police. Bad enough, they kept asking me embarrassing questions. They even gave a suspicious look at my daughter, and asked me whether I have 'plans for her too' in the future. I was speechless....

This is routine in houses of individuals belonging to sexual minorities, too, ordering them to vacate the place by publicly humiliating them.[22] A male worker among our narrators, who was 'discovered' to be homosexual by a few locals, stated:

You don't need the police to create trouble. My neighbours threatened to have me evicted from my own home, stating that this was a 'decent neighbourhood'. Funnily, I've lived here in this locality all my life, and it has now suddenly become a 'decent' place that wants me out!

I work as so many other things – sometimes as a cook in a street-food cart, sometimes as a delivery person, sometimes helping out in shops. My neighbours know all this, but for them, I'm only a sex worker and nothing else. Do you know how difficult it is to get work once you're exposed as a sex worker? Especially a male worker? They think you're the very worst because they can imagine a woman sex worker, but a man doing it must be very, very perverted.

Whether sexual minorities or not, the final outcome is that workers are often thrown out of their neighbourhoods and made to constantly move around. This has been the case, especially in the last decade, as many workers narrated. For especially those belonging to this economic strata, building and depending on social capital is a complex, time-consuming and indispensable process, given their economic vulnerability and constant need for other kinds of employment throughout the year. Moving from place to place interrupts this process of investment in social capital, and sex workers have to begin from scratch or fend for themselves over and over again. This results in serious long-term debilitating effects on maintaining financial and health security within the family, setting up a stable home, eking out a future and maintaining a sustainable livelihood.

Often, they are pushed out finally to the city's peripheries into other working-class neighbourhoods. In these new places, they end up in hostile

---

[22] *Times of India,* 9 June 2000; *Deccan Herald,* 5 August 2001.

and abrasive encounters either with the incumbent sex workers there or with intimidating elements such as local goons. Clashes spawn with incumbent workers in the new areas as the operational dynamics and relational equations in these outskirts have been already set and cannot suddenly accommodate new sex workers migrating from within the city. Finding new accommodation and ensuring security and education for their children in these new areas are also huge challenges.

> Oh, the sex workers in the outskirts? We knew they wouldn't exactly welcome us, but they will never accommodate us since their routines and processes are already set, and they won't compromise on them.

> Thugs within the city where we used to operate for years and years – we negotiated with them over those many years. Can we now suddenly negotiate with thugs in the new areas we are pushed out to? These are so complicated interactions.

> Our families are within the city – how can we now possibly travel so far away from home for this work? It's so impractical.

Pushing sex workers into the peripheries keeps them disconnected from community and outreach workers as well, who supply them with free condoms and assist them in gaining access to routine medical checkups. An outreach worker who was a key informant during fieldwork, who operated around the area of KR Market, lamented:

> It was much easier to find them and get them together, even until recently. I could just go up to a crowd of them and distribute free condoms and other medical precautions. I could easily convince or compel them to follow me to Victoria Hospital for a regular check-up. However, after they have scattered in recent years, I have no idea where everyone is. I would have to walk kilometres around to get all of them together for these purposes.

She continued to describe to us that similar experiences were shared even among other organisations, especially those working on health issues among sex workers and those that are cash strapped. While some organisations such as the Sadhana Mahila Sangha (SMS) still benefit from being able to get together workers who are dispersed, this is not the case everywhere.

Atrocities targeting them in private habitations and pushing them out to peripheries bring their own variety of humiliation, but attacks in urban public spaces take more extreme forms. In 2014, Bangalore recorded 144 cases[23] under the Immoral Traffic (Prevention) Act (ITPA), 1956, as part of the police's drive

---

[23] *The Hindu*, 12 September 2014.

to clear the city's public spaces of street-based sex workers. The police claim triumphantly that, subsequently, the number of sex workers had declined in places such as Majestic bus station, city railway station and pedestrian subways. However, the Karnataka Sex Workers Union (KSWU) alleges[24] that the numbers indicate an 'abuse' of the ITPA, as this Act is used to criminalise sex work de facto within 200 meters of any public space. They pointed out that practically every space on the street in a city like Bangalore is a public space within that definition. The ITPA does not criminalise sex work per se, but, as the Lawyers' Collective that works for sex workers' rights points out, it results in de facto criminalisation through the prohibition of soliciting, brothel and street work, and this has effectively undermined sex workers' ability to claim legal protection in public city spaces. The law is defended as being necessary to prevent trafficking and child prostitution. The law first prohibits brothels or deems premises shared by sex workers as illegal, including their residences. The law also punishes adults who live off the earnings of sex workers. However, as sex workers are beaten down most by Section 8 of the ITPA, the Lawyers' Collective explains that the criminalisation of soliciting is one of the most obvious legal problems for sex workers, as they are arrested even when they're not soliciting; most plead guilty finding themselves in a vicious cycle of criminalisation. This, of course, is only part of a larger battle towards basic rights of citizenship and as workers.[25] Over the years, the police have used a range of strategies, apart from the ITPA, to arrest and detain sex workers.[26] The police frequently refer to the Karnataka Police Act, filing cases of nuisance and obstruction of duty against sex workers.

Participants at a public meeting on 'Sex Workers Rights Activism in India: Achievements and Challenges' in 2009 in Bangalore agreed that the major challenge faced by sex workers and sexual minorities was stigmatisation and violence perpetrated by the State through the police.[27] Workers' narratives on police atrocities revealed public identification, verbal abuse, beatings, being chased around with batons, and so on. Attempts to complain against routine detention or extortion were met with further violence. Police officers would often publicly abuse in obscene language or even call out their names over loudspeakers.

---

[24] *The Hindu*, 12 September 2014.

[25] *The Hindu*, 8 February 2014.

[26] *Police Violence against Sex Workers in Bangalore: An Interim Report* (cited here as ALF 2014), was submitted to the Panel on Sex Workers constituted by the Supreme Court of India in the case of *Buddhadev Karmaskar v. Union of India (2014)*. This report has been prepared by members of support organisations in Bangalore working with the SMS and other sex workers' organisations, include ALF, PUCL (Karnataka), Janasahyog (Bangalore) and Vimochana.

[27] *The Hindu*, 10 December 2009.

You know that area around the Trinity metro station? Starting from there, right up to the MG Road metro station, we used to see policemen in their white jeeps zipping across the street announcing over a loudspeaker that there were anti-social elements and prostitutes in this area. It turned out that they were announcing messages in social interest for those who were in the area after 8 p.m. Are we some worms to trample upon or poisonous snakes to be scared of?

Many workers are accosted on their way home or when merely running errands. Police routinely confiscate mobile phones (a trend we take up in greater detail in the next chapter), which are then convenient tools of misuse and to blackmail family and acquaintances. As we have seen in earlier sections in this chapter, even regular bystanders on the street, shopkeepers, hoteliers, clients and others have been prone in recent years to become antagonistic to sex work around them, and may even conspire with the police to physically attack sex workers in open public spaces whenever disgruntled.[28]

I sometimes keep rolled-gold in my handbag. Sometimes I keep two metres of cloth tightly folded in my bag. I keep these things because over the last few years, there has been the risk of random people on the street complaining to police constables about prostitution and racketeering. When the police come to me, I can easily say I'm selling the rolled-gold or supplying blouse pieces to some tailor. These are the things we have to do these days.

When sex workers approach the police if they are beaten or abused by local goons or even their customers, their right to remedies is routinely denied by the police (including women constables), who at times refuse to lodge First Information Reports (FIRs) or investigate or produce them in a court,[29] by mocking about how a sex worker could possibly be 'sexually threatened', since the provision of sexual services was their job in the first place![30]

In 2003, there was a case of a sex worker even ending her life after she was beaten viciously in public and left in pain, unable to bear further agony and harassment.[31] In the same year, another sex worker was arrested, and a co-worker was summoned to the station by the police to prepare a concoction of chillies. The concoction was then inserted by the police into the arrested worker's genitalia. This incident caused a huge uproar, and it was picked up by the Karnataka High Court. The High Court eventually passed a direction that any officers engaged in such violence would be suspended, and severe action ought to be taken against them. Very recently, too, in 2017, around two dozen sex workers were beaten and abused in public and then detained in the police station under

---

[28] Also reported in *The Hindu*, 10 December 2009.
[29] *New Indian Express*, 3 March 2002.
[30] *The Hindu*, 6 August 2013.
[31] ALF (2014).

the command of the deputy commissioner of police of the region. The women were reportedly detained from 11 p.m. to 3 a.m., subsequently sermoned about how 'we' wanted a 'clean Majestic'.[32] It is evident that physical violence against these workers is often undergirded with the motive of 'cleaning up' the city even at the cost of human rights and due procedures of law and order. They are required to inhabit the city either as 'decent individuals' or leave the 'decent city' altogether.

In a detailed conversation we had with Prof. Rajendra, a senior member of the People's Union for Civil Liberties (PUCL), it was explained to us that gentrification was only one of the grounds that the police use to further violence on street-based sex workers. Though entirely outside of the legal ambit, the notion of the 'moral upkeep' of the city and society was the premise upon which verbal abuse and physical brutality were brought into action by the police. There were no legal grounds for this, but there was enormous popular and political sanction. The latter provided the fuel for violence and mistreatment in public spaces and private spaces, and in the most extreme forms while in the police station. Only in the case of barbarities such as the usage of the chilli concoction in the 2003 incident does the public, media and judiciary proactively gather in support of the human rights of sex workers, but there is very little outrage in the everyday micro-brutalities that these workers face at the hands of the police. Prof. Rajendra continued to explain how these grounds of morality are a convenient premise on which even female police staff routinely harass sex workers, particularly female and transgender workers; female police staff face far less censure for abuse towards women on the street and, in fact, might even be viewed heroically as holding up female morality in public space. All over the world, too, the police (of course, with the cooperation of local agents such as merchants and other actors on the street, as Svati Shah has also shown) advocate harsh treatment mainly on the basis of morality. It appears, therefore, that gentrification and morality take turns in serving as facades to one another.

If the police were not bad enough, neighbourhood watch groups mirror the attitude of law enforcement authorities by perceiving sex workers as outside of the ambit of the 'public' and hence having lesser rights to public spaces. Terming their presence as 'eyesores' that aggravate 'hooliganism', 'nefarious activity', 'unseemly public displays' or 'full-fledged prostitution racketeering', some neighbourhood groups have even accused the city corporation of doing little against these 'encroachments' that keep residents away from public spaces.[33] During our initial conversations with workers, too, there was visible discomfort on the part of our narrators to hold even casual conversations in the vicinity of a police station or in a public park. On one occasion, at a discussion we had with two former workers

---

[32] *New Indian Express*, 23 March 2018.
[33] *The Hindu*, 5 August 2005 and 21 April 2007; *Asian Age*, 7 May 2000.

near Cubbon Park (when we were just beginning fieldwork and did not realise the intensity of the problem), one worker suddenly interrupted our already shaky conversation:

> Could we please go somewhere else? The police here don't know me at all, but whenever I see them, I feel very scared.... [after we begin walking to a better location] ... I'm sorry I asked us to leave that place, but about twenty years ago, I wouldn't have had to request this.

This was a far cry from the transgender worker we spoke to (quoted in earlier chapters) who claimed Cubbon Park to be 'entirely hers' back in the day. Shakti, as we shall call her here, is revered across the transgender community in Bangalore as one of the oldest surviving individuals in their cohort, and possibly the most dominant transgender figure on the streets and spaces of Bangalore in the 1980s and 1990s. Her blessings were said to be sought even by individuals from other *hamams* and by other gurus across the city, attaining a kind of padrino (or actually madrina) status, and she ensured, in her own words, that 'peace was maintained with the police and within the community'. Currently residing about 80 kilometres from the city and living in retirement with her fair share of medical ailments and coterie of disciples attending to her and ensuring restricted access, we too decided to make an appointment well in advance, gain sanction from other senior individuals in the community and visit her. We paid obeisance to her as one of the richest sources of information on transition in the street-level micro-politics of sex work in Bangalore up until 2010, from which a great many narrations and experiences emerged, which we have presented all over the chapters of this book. Shakti spoke volumes on how the police were indeed always the biggest threat, but that there were also times when they realised that the transgender community (and, for that matter, the street-based sex worker community) were actually valuable leads and informants for other more dangerous forms of crime. Since they were well versed with the street and its menagerie of actors such as vendors, beggars, goons, the homeless and others, they had accurate knowledge on the exact whereabouts of traffickers and kidnappers. There were instances, Shakti related, where the police actually collaborated with her to trace and pin down terrifying criminals who were genuine threats to order and morality in society.

> I have faced the police baton on my back and thighs countless times. But as my hold on the area grew, inspector after inspector became friends with me after they realised who I was and what valuable use I could come to. I received so many pats on my back, and I was allowed to roam free. Remember I said Cubbon Park was mine? I maintained complete order and discipline there in the community. Nobody needed to fear when I was around. Neither the TGs nor other people.

I can't name people here because they may still be at large and perhaps after my neck, but I have traced and spotted many criminals around the Cubbon Park, Corporation Circle and Majestic areas. I reported their movements to the police on a daily basis. All before the mobile phone came in.

This, however, was not long-lived. As the city became cleaner, glamorous and righteous, the tables turned on them, and whatever few specks of amicability that were shared by the transgender community and the police were extinguished to nought. Shakti concluded, wiping her forehead:

> We TGs helped the police trace goons and criminals because only *we* knew where they were. Even traffickers and kidnappers. Now, we are the traffickers, kidnappers and criminals.

Transgender individuals have often complained (as we have seen in so many instances by now) that they are at the very bottom of a hierarchy in sex work, where those who are called 'escorts' who service elite clients are right at the top, as are those who can speak fluent English, dress well and frequent pubs and restaurants late at night. Transgender individuals are typecast as criminals by default, even by senior police staff.[34] When extortion from the police is resisted, transgender individuals are swiftly booked for robbery and theft.[35] Bangalore-based transgender activist Akkai Padmashali has said:

> Booking us under false cases is not new. When I used to stand on roads in the year 2000, I ended up paying 30 rupees to them [the police] regularly. Whenever we failed to pay, they so easily booked us under robbery, extortion and theft cases.[36]

Sexual minorities, in general, have had to face flak for simply 'being present' in public spaces or appearing as potential troublemakers to visitors. Some 'concerned' people have even written to newspapers calling for the removal of posters of models who are known to be homosexual or about gay individuals being permitted into public spaces such as parks, or have even commented that the city has unfortunately transformed from a pensioners' paradise to a 'home for homosexuals'.[37] Police harassment against male homosexual couples casually sitting around or even detaining gay or transexual individuals and extorting money is not uncommon.[38] It has also been unexceptional that individuals from sexual minorities who are booked for a variety of crimes are reported for their

---

[34] *Asian Age*, August 2005.
[35] *Bangalore Mirror*, 18 June 2018.
[36] Ibid.
[37] *New Indian Express*, 18 October 2002.
[38] *Times of India*, 9 June 2009; *Asian Age*, 7 June 2000.

crime with a sexual-orientation prefix (for example, 'Murder of Pharmacist: Four Homosexuals Arrested'[39]) in a manner as to suggest that their crime and sexual orientation were associated, or even for purely the sensational value of the orientation. In one instance, the police had arrested a man for petty robbery, and on discovering his homosexuality, pushed him around the city to identify other homosexuals.[40]

In response to increased police atrocity, a coalition of sexual minorities was formed in April 2000, who held a discussion with the then assistant commissioner of police. However, his response at the time was that homosexuality was an offence under Section 377 of the Indian Penal Code (IPC), that prevention of crime was their job and that these were not human rights violations because such groups were not legally recognised. He also added, interestingly, that the 'public' were, in recent years, exerting tremendous pressure about homosexual men present in parks and other recreation areas.[41] It is quite sure that these attitudes remain, despite the de-criminalisation of consensual homosexuality in India in September 2018.

On speaking to police offers in the Majestic area, we gathered that their attitudes to sex workers are not only based on the grounds of social morality and crime, but that of *image*, easily ascertained by statements we received from one police officer after another:

> They don't look like workers, they are not here for proper work. That's why they are nuisances to our city.

> Sir, don't talk to them [sex workers] for too long, they are all criminals, here to destroy decency.

> Sir, why are you talking to this criminal woman? You don't know her activities, sir. Madam, please stay away from these women. Or are you here to help them get a job? Then that's good. Let them do something else.

> They were always a problem. I don't know why they can't operate wherever they live instead of coming here to these central areas and creating a headache for us. If we decide to let them be because we are tired of always chasing them, the public will keep pestering us.

> Our job is to keep the streets peaceful. And the various shopkeepers and others are here to help with that. They let us know anytime there's some racket going on.

---

[39] *Deccan Herald*, 5 August 2001.

[40] *New Indian Express*, 3 October 2002.

[41] www.bangaloremag.com (accessed on 25 June 2018).

I always receive phone calls from shopkeepers around the area to come and get rid of these kinds of people. What do these people [sex workers] have against everyone? Why do they want to do this and operate *here*, of all the places?

My superior is proud of me. Do you know how many of these prostitutes I have cleared out of the Mysore Bank Circle and near Alankar? Tell me, madam, will you ever go shopping to Alankar or Coupon or Pothys, with your husband and children, if these people are standing around?

We got rid of most *hijra*s from around Majestic. But this prostitute problem still remains. What sort of women are these? They are an insult to all women. Our culture pays great respect to women, but these are not proper women.

Suppose some tourists come to Bangalore and get off at the railway station. Imagine if they see these *hijra*s standing here and there! What will they think of our city? They will laugh at us, especially the police, since we are just standing around doing nothing about this nuisance on the roads.

They are a bad example to the youth. The boys look at them and think all this 'goes on' in the city. The college girls may even think this is a good way to earn quick money. What will their families think? What will our society and city become? Is this modern? All these prostitution activities going around right in the middle of everything? We are here to make sure that they are not bad examples. Let the young boys and girls look at the software people and learn how to have a good job.

These standpoints stem not simply out of a traditional prejudice against sexual minorities or sex workers, but with the powerful backdrop of gentrification trends in the city, with emissaries of the state ensuring the operationalisation of revanchism through brute means.

However, rough force is only one strategy. An ingenious initiative from the police force established in 2017 and 2018 in Karnataka state is the 'Obbava Squad' (named after a valiant woman Onake Obbava who single-handedly fought Hyder Ali's soldiers with a pestle), which operates in other towns beyond Bangalore as well. This is a small but potent all-women constable force, trained rigorously in self-defence and the law and wearing special uniforms, deployed to patrol across public spaces in the city to ensure the safety of women and children (besides also working with schools and social workers on self-defence). The idea was to excise unwanted elements, such as pickpockets, louts and alcoholics, from especially bus stations. Journalistic reports even stated that this was the 'answer to daytime soliciting at Majestic',[42] and that 'the foot over-bridge, populated by sex workers is now free of them, allowing other women to walk on the bridge without being solicited'.[43] According to these reports, sex workers were supposedly occupying

---

[42] *Deccan Chronicle*, 28 August 2018.
[43] *Better India*, 28 July 2018.

the foot overbridge and causing an embarrassment to other women who were mistaken for these workers, but now, with the squad, sex workers were 'feeling the heat'.[44] Reports have even been brought up in newspapers about how squad members take workers to the nearest police station and fine them, all in the name of cleaning the city and 'helping women'.[45]

> There were these young women in army clothes. I first thought they were just going somewhere by train, but then they came straight to me. I was late in realising what this was, but my friends told me later that this female squad is going around rounding us up to clean up the place. This is so cheap! First, the male police harass us, and now women themselves. I tried telling them that I meant no harm, but they said that my presence there and my activities were harmful enough.

One of the motivations of the regular police force is the paternalistic but unsound belief from the part of the state and popular culture, which we have discussed in detail in Chapter 1, that all sex workers are trafficked individuals, and not workers with a sense of agency, who must be viewed keeping aside the lens of social morality. Sex workers are regularly labelled helpless victims and administered various training programmes and rehabilitation drives to those who are 'willing to reform'. But the process of 'rescue' of these sex workers often involved beating, dragging by the hair, abuse and looting by law enforcement personnel.[46] Consequently, the arrested workers are placed for indefinite periods in state-managed detention homes to be 'reformed', with no access to legal representation, and their dignity seriously compromised. Another similar strategy was to file cases against sex workers under the provisions of the Karnataka Prohibition of Beggary Act, 1975, which defines a beggar as any person other than a child, who, 'having no visible means of subsistence, wanders about or remains in any public place in such condition or manner as makes it likely that he/she exists by soliciting or receiving alms'. The result is, again, transportation to state homes or beggar homes. State home shelters in Bangalore often accommodate these workers with women who are homeless, who have faced domestic violence, who are abandoned, unwed and pregnant, who are mentally unsound with no guardians and who are other victims of the ITPA, who altogether find each other's company extremely challenging. Workers are subjected to constant harassment in the form of perverted invitations and lewd risqué comments from the staff, which was extremely traumatising for them. Shelters have also been criticised for being extremely unhygienic with poor sanitation when it comes to lavatories, bathing rooms and waste management. Rehabilitation measures do not acknowledge the fact that many sex workers also engage in other economic activities such as

---

[44] *Bangalore Mirror*, 28 July 2018.
[45] *The Hindu*, 5 March 2019.
[46] SMS (2013).

domestic work, a fact well known to most worker associations and civil society organisations who are never consulted by law enforcement when 'rehabilitating' workers. Naturally, when rescued and forcefully placed into shelters or prodded into precarious occupations, the economic situation of these women worsen. They lose their other jobs and their financial and social resources, are not able to pay their utilities or rent and lose whatever self-established stability they have. Shelter homes also cut off support systems of sex workers, be it family, CBOs (community-based organisations) or friends, which further isolates them.[47] KSWU members added:

> In many cases, their families may not even know that they are in the shelter home and they have to continue there for twenty days or more, until some NGOs came to their rescue.

> We are not beggars. We are not allowed to get out of there until and unless someone from our family or guardian comes to take us from there. And the place is so far away, how does anyone even know we are imprisoned here?

The regressive perspective of state and law enforcement was epitomised in the recent move by the Government of Karnataka to label sex workers as *damanitra mahila* ('oppressed women' in Kannada), which emerged as the result of a report in 2018 titled *Status Report of Women Who Have Encountered Sexual Violence* and produced by the committee headed by the Minister of State for Women and Child Development, in the process of studying the situation of sex workers in the state. In the twenty-two-member committee, only three members were sex workers. They conducted a 169-question survey among 17,000 workers in Karnataka with promises of free housing and loans to the workers, but respondents' right to privacy was routinely violated during the survey through perverted questions such as the nature of their clientele, HIV status and their fraternity. The members of the KSWU questioned the survey.

> Why does the department want to know the nature of my clientele? Whether they are college students or not? How many clients I entertain in a day and how much I earn? How are these questions in our interest? Whether we introduced others to sex work? No questions assessed our access to safe drinking water, food, housing, land, sanitation, electricity, health, child care and education.[48]

Such typecasting of sex workers either as trafficked or oppressed is a symptom of the larger agenda to reinforce control over their bodies and physical spaces, allocating locations for them against their will (such as state homes or labour

---

47 SMS (2013).
48 Karnataka Sex Workers Union, press release 18 March 2017, Bangalore.

rehabilitation training centres) and engineering a marginalised position for them in the city landscape. This emerges as a convenient manner in which sex workers, among other undesirables, can be forcibly migrated away from the visible public spaces in the city and kept at a safe distance away from the respectable and stylish city.

The Unkindest Cut

Towards the end of countless hours of conversations with the workers, they began speaking among themselves about how the problem was not 'change' since that has been continually happening practically every day since the city was born. We learnt that it was also not about the pace and recklessness of change, a much talked about topic in most informal conversation around Bangalore, but about how the transition over the last twenty years, which, since about 2005, has been particularly pernicious to street-based sex work in the city. When we spoke about spaces, it inevitably drifted to people (of course, since space is socially constructed); when we spoke about people, it meandered towards spaces (of course, since the existence of people is defined by the spaces they have constructed). Morphing actors, remoulded or disappearing places and transformed attitudes gushed out in their narrations, dripping from which were new fears, new threats and new deprivations. In the old days, the police were brutal in their interactions with street-based sex workers, showing no mercy or humanity whatsoever. This, the workers related, was mostly on the grounds of social morality and the easily misemployable ITPA. But the nature of change in the city over the last two decades have plugged holes in their ship and planted landmines throughout their terrain, on the grounds of creating a spectacular metropolis that is home to fine people and for big (local and international) capital to invest in and apportion.

Most workers were familiar with the ambitions of converting their city into Singapore or Silicon Valley, but they explained how they assumed that these would restrict only to the more gilded areas and not to the entire city. Even in their wildest dreams, they narrated, they did not realise that their old compatriots, the local vendors, the autorickshaw drivers, eateries, bus staff and even lodge boys, would abandon them and quietly watch them descend into utter misery. This, they repeatedly said, was the unkindest cut, as this desertion demonically pranced around urban transition and the loss of workspaces. They could not believe that their grounds would be taken away one by one, and that the assemblage of structures and spaces would be eaten away in front of their very eyes. The maze of streets and spaces that tightly tethered their workplaces into a tapestry where street-based sex work thrived is now a labyrinth that stonewalls them at every corner, threatening them not to trespass or plunging them into point-blank range of their old nemesis, the police. We see, through the maps we have constructed here (Maps 5.1–5.6), based entirely on their narratives, what their city was and what it looks like now, what a city meant to them and what is left of their city now – a stark contrast that displays not just city change in the sense of heartfelt regret or nostalgia but the loss of a sexscape.

A layer of informal labour and livelihood is being scratched out through a variety of strategies, a long-standing character in the dramatis personae of the public space is being expunged, all in the name of the fabrication of a vista named Bangalore.

Maps

The purpose of these maps is to demonstrate the stark losses in street-based sex workers' accessibility to their traditional sites of solicitation, service and recreation, in the three focus areas of Bangalore city – MG Road, Majestic and KR Market areas. In these six maps, while the streets are completely accurate, the buildings and structures (with the exception of noted heritage structures and other landmarks) are caricatured.

Maps 5.1, 5.3 and 5.5 show what their city was once to them – a chaotic, jagged, but freer jumble of sites. But, as seen in Maps 5.2, 5.4 and 5.6 in complete contrast, large black shaded swathes present the losses of spaces and structures to the sex work industry.

The important point to bear in mind is that the disappeared spaces in Maps 5.2, 5.4 and 5.6 have been shaded entirely based on the narratives of the street-based sex workers and members of civil society organisations we spoke to. These are streets that have become off-limits, or, if the streets are still open, buildings such as lodges and older complexes that have become non-tolerance zones for sex work or have been replaced altogether, or gated and monitored parks, or disappear/ed grounds. The structures and spaces that are not shaded in Maps 5.2, 5.4 and 5.6 are those that were in any case not part of the sex work landscape of the respective areas. The rest of the areas shaded black are now closed off in terms of any association with street-based sex work.

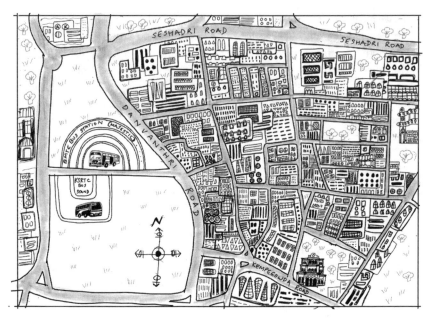

Map 5.1 Majestic area

Source: Artwork by the authors.

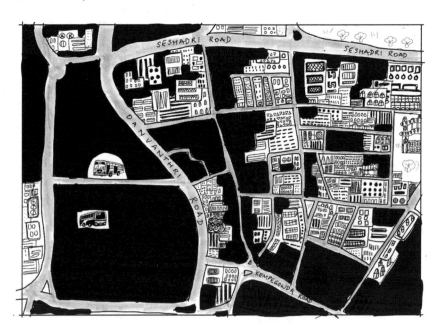

Map 5.2 Disappeared spaces of Majestic area

Source: Artwork by the authors.

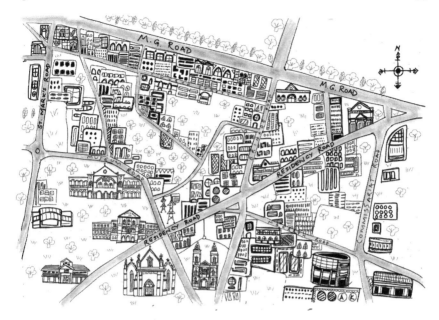

Map 5.3 MG Road area

Source: Artwork by the authors.

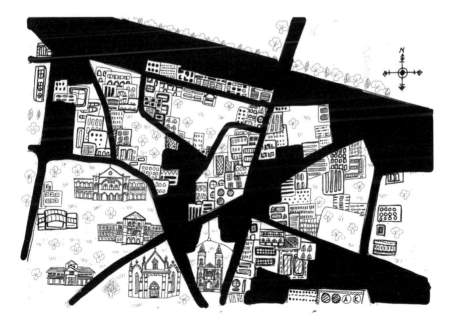

Map 5.4 Disappeared spaces of MG Road area

Source: Artwork by the authors.

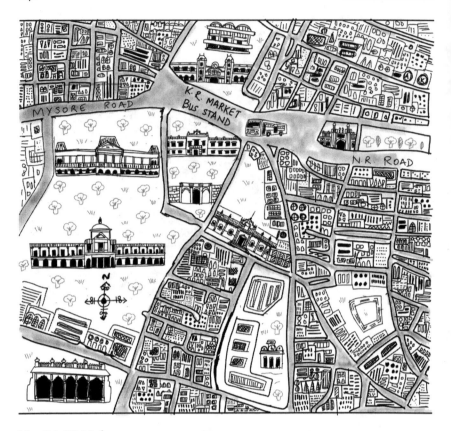

Map 5.5 KR Market

Source: Artwork by the authors.

Map 5.6 Disappeared spaces of KR Market

Source: Artwork by the authors.

6

Technology

'When did you use your first mobile phone for your work?'
'Much before any of you did for *your* work.'

This, with its gentle sarcasm, was the manner in which we began conversations with our narrators on the use of the mobile phone in their trade. With a two-decade-long overhaul of the city to befit Citizens and (legitimate) Populations, street-based sex workers, among other pseudo-invisibles, have coped with this divestment of urban workspace and consequent everyday oppression by migrating to digital platforms. Unlike sex workers of higher-economic strata who operate via the internet for motivations that have little to do with disappearing urban spaces and ground-level aggression, our narrators have needed to resort to using the mobile phone and, subsequently, mobile-phone-based internet, to sustain their occupation and their very existence. The pervasive use of mobile phones in sex work or the internet is neither new nor unique to Bangalore. Global trends in sex work have increasingly seen the adoption of mobile phone technologies for operations, support and collectivisation in this sector – that is, a wholesale movement to a digital platform – but what is interesting in our case here is that while the employment of mobile phones was an early development in the sector, dating back to about 2001–2002 (according to our narrators), it became a device for sheer survival only eventually because their traditional worksites had begun to disappear, or gradually became forbidding. In other words, what makes this a novel development in sex work in this particular case is that the technological experience has been intensified as a response to neoliberal urban transition, as much as it has purely for improving efficiency in business.

Naturally, experiences with moving operations to mobile phone platforms have been mixed for these workers. But we must bear in mind that their engagement with mobile phones is not the only exclusive technological experience among street-based sex workers. Our conversations on the phone regularly veered to other technological devices that have graced this city over the last decade, and new actors that have adopted cutting-edge technologies, who have been on the prowl in recent years. While technological artefacts such as mobile phones may be individually owned (hence the associated experiences with these technologies arising on account of their individual ownership of the artefact), other technological devices that street-based sex workers are engaged with are externally enforced. In other words, the technological experience of street-based sex workers in Bangalore is not restricted to mobile phones (individually owned artefacts) alone – it includes other (externally enforced) devices such as closed-circuit television (CCTV) cameras and native-language television media. CCTV cameras as a new feature of the modern 'safe' city dovetail elegantly with the concept of subjecting city spaces to intense surveillance to keep watch on urban undesirables that include not only criminals and deviants but also sex workers. These have formed a new source of hazard for workers over the last decade or so. Yet another externally enforced source of hazard, a force to be reckoned with, is native-language television news media, which is not a benign, unbiased or neutral reporter of happenings but actually a *techno-cultural predator* that routinely conducts self-assigned gentrification operations, covertly or overtly discovering and publicly disseminating instances of immorality and delinquency in mainstream society in the city. This faction of television media zealously assists in the reproduction of sociocultural institutions and practices using the aid of advanced technologies to not only report but also broadcast and diffuse information.

All three technological experiences – migration to mobile phones, CCTV surveillance in city spaces and media-led gentrification operations – understandably have had very complicated fallouts for street-based sex workers in Bangalore, and not simply for their everyday experience in terms of intimidation and surveillance. These experiences have an additional intensity: that the politics of these technologies (that are at the foundations of the experiences of these pseudo-invisibles) are intersected by yet another sphere that sex workers have known first hand – body politics.

As we shall see in this chapter, the body politics that these workers have traditionally encountered, embraced and battled, and the politics of technology that these devices and mediums are infused with, do not just 'incidentally affect' one another but actually *mirror* one another within this sphere of work and, in addition, are set within the neoliberal urban transition experiences of Bangalore's street-based sex workers. The politics of technology that this workforce comes up against is complex, significantly because it intersects with body politics in this line of work. This is because both (the politics of technology and body politics) share strikingly similar concerns in the territories of self, community, support, resistance, negotiation, commerce and power among these workers. Let us unravel this marriage between the two by first listening to the voices of these workers in their technological experiences.

Hands, Ears and Voices

It is easy to assume that within the human landscape of the city, it is the Citizens who would be at the forefront of technological adoption, especially of innovations that are relatively expensive. Populations would follow next, while pseudo-invisibles would be late adopters, if they adopted the technologies at all. This standard format is to some extent commonsensical, given especially the affordability of these new technologies. However, the trajectories of technological adoption may be even completely in the reverse direction, as mentioned previously, which appears to have been the case as far as street-based sex workers and mobile phones go.

> Probably, you didn't think about us owning phones during that era [2001 or 2002], because of the nature of our work. For long, we couldn't flaunt these phones everywhere, starting from home and to the streets.

By virtue of the clandestine nature of their occupation, they claim to be actually one of the initial adopters of this technology. Even if they were not actually the first set of adopters (on par with very wealthy businessmen, politicians, celebrities, and so on), it is for sure that they were certainly not laggards in adopting this technology, as one might assume subaltern groups to generally be. So much so that we can suppose that long before several other activities in the mainstream economy moved to digital platforms for business, the sex work sector was already familiar with the medium. The fact has been that their marginalised status in the economy and society hid from view the rampant diffusion of mobile telephony among them even as far back as in 2001–2002, when this artefact was yet to graduate from a luxury toy among the affluent to a useful commodity for the upper-middle classes, not yet a prosthetic to everyone's hands, and before the overwhelming force of urban transition began clearing away indecent operations in decent spaces.

> I remember, really, really long ago, when a social worker who was helping me get regular check-ups needed to urgently call his mother, and I gave him my phone to use. Oh, at that time, it was two rupees for a call, when you could buy a cup of good coffee with that amount. Though he thanked me profusely for my help, I don't think he realised, at least at that time, how important this would be for his work. No one really had a cellphone those days.

> Things are different today. Like everything else. Only the really old women, say, over fifty years old, don't have a phone in their hands and still get customers purely by standing around Majestic or KR Market. No one will shoo them away because they are too old to look indecent, but they are really poor to afford or maintain a phone. I gifted one to an older worker, but soon, she just kept it at home because the packages were too expensive for her to maintain it. In fact, these days, only if you're really poor or destitute will you not have a phone.

It was informed to us by transgender workers that the penetration of phones as a routine platform to solicit customers was the lowest in their community, as compared to male and female workers, simply because of unaffordability. Like very poor and old women workers, these workers also mostly use traditional and behavioural cues to solicit customers on the streets, sans a phone.

> They come to *hamam*s with just their clothes and an empty stomach. When do you think they can earn enough to buy a phone, and then, to use that to get customers? Probably we may be mugged for the phone, apart from the usual violence we face.

We gathered that more than women workers, it is the male sex worker community that overwhelmingly moved to soliciting through the mobile phone. The reasons were endless – the explosion of clientele, the scope of a long-term customer relationship, vaster geographical access, secrecy, and so on, which they have been able to gain through platforms such as Grindr or Planet Romeo. Indeed, the homeless male sex worker who operates exclusively in the last few crumbs of ecological commons or public toilets that remain in Bangalore cannot be compared to the more well-dressed and sophisticatedly articulate young male worker who stands on Church Street. But in the final observation, both live and work through their phones.

> It's just superb. Now, the younger, newer workers don't fancy standing in front of a stinking toilet, if a toilet is there at all. It's all Grindr. After all, if two men meet at a location on the street as directed by the app and then walk away somewhere else, who is ever going to ask questions?

It appeared very clearly that the days of writing across toilet walls, gesturing with tongues and eyes and making subtle facial expressions while standing around public toilets, were all disappearing. Again, we were informed that there is a clear, and obvious, economic-class element in ownership, access and operation of mobile phones among male workers, but the reality is that the contemporary sex work era is overwhelmingly inclined towards the digital sphere even among economically lower-middle-class and working-class male (or female) workers who own and operate devices for sex work commensurate to their affordability. These range from simpler GSM phones, which have no touchscreen and no internet access, to the middle-range smartphones that are affordable with savings from a few months' earnings, to the high-priced phones that are operated by younger workers and those with greater monetary clout. Naturally, a gender digital divide exists between male and female workers in terms of not only ownership of the device but especially its sophistication. While, as we know from earlier, that there are still women workers who do not own or operate a device, among the male worker cohort (according to our narrators), there is probably not a single worker without a device (even though everyone might not use internet-based apps). This, they said, was because male workers were usually employed in more remunerative jobs outside of sex work and could afford devices and internet access more easily than women. As two women workers put it:

> See, we women are usually employed as domestic help or something like that, apart from sex work. Where do we earn enough for these phones and for internet? Men, on the other hand, do sex work but also autorickshaw driving, masonry, hotel waiting ... so many other jobs are open to them so they can afford it.

> [another woman worker, following the conversation] That's true, but there's yet another important thing. When we women work, we have to support our families. So all the money goes there, not for a fancy phone. But for men, not only do they earn well from other jobs, but many of them don't give a rupee to their families. Goes straight to alcohol, or phones or whatever else they wish to spend on.

There was another interesting issue that was related to us by women workers, which was, for a long time, a source of annoyance, sometimes serious trouble, and was resolved only recently. This was the issue of a mobile phone constantly ringing at home from customers or other workers, which frequently raised eyebrows and antennae among those who coinhabited with them (particularly husbands, parents, in-laws or older children). However, with the advent of devices that could harbour multiple SIM cards, they could activate or deactivate the connection and phone number that was dedicated to home or sex work depending on where they were, in order to maintain strict silos between home and (usually concealed) sex work. Also, they stated, it was very common for people these days to spend hours on the phone speaking and texting friends and relatives, and hence there is relatively lesser suspicion unless there was some explicit talk of price or a suitable place for services. Some women workers narrated how those clients with whom they develop more intimate relationships recharge their phones regularly (with more expensive internet packages that allow for video streaming and photograph sharing) or sometimes even buy newer and better phones which deepen the intimacy and length of the relationship. In this manner, phones allowed them the secrecy of solicitation operations in sex work that was traditionally bodily impossible to conceal when standing in public spaces.

All workers narrated to us, enthusiastically, how the phone was truly a boon for solicitation. They expressed vividly how it was a fantastic platform to put forward expectations, declare limitations, advertise a variety of services one offered, share photographs to one another (that is, between customer and worker), write messages to the customer (or to the worker) to improve quality of services or for monetary negotiation, attract one another's attention to agree to services (sometimes almost as if the customer were wooing the worker), maintain contact well after services and keep a repository of customers' and workers' numbers. They expressed how it was now far safer to find customers and negotiate over the phone as compared to a pavement, bus station, marketplace, park, shopping complex or any other such open public space. One of the workers put it quite succinctly when she described how:

I am in the phone, which is much better than me being in the open areas.

This suggested a sort of vicarious presence of the sex worker's body in a virtual space. In the same conversation where the previous quotation was put forward to us, several other female workers opined in a similar vein how they felt that in many aspects, they were in some sort of 'safer world' in their phones than in the real world. That is, when their bodies manifested within that virtual space for solicitation, it was 'safer' than when their bodies inhabited the physical urban space. In other words, the phone allowed them to plant their bodies in a digital space for solicitation rather than planting their bodies on the streets.

Now I don't care about the sun or rain. I don't need to appease some street vendor or autorickshaw driver since my customers and I completely communicate through the phone. The need to maintain that difficult network with ground-level people, that's slowly going away. Maybe for better, maybe for worse. Well, maybe for better actually, since we can't really trust anyone these days. Not like the old days.

Workers who were more internet savvy were able to upload videos and photographs of themselves on social media such as Facebook or YouTube, subtly enough, to solicit potential customers for sex work. This fact was narrated to us in articulate detail by the same worker who stated the quote about being 'in the phone'. She revealed to us that there were dozens of sex worker groups in the application WhatsApp (of course, concealing the names of such groups) and how it was very difficult to gain entry into these groups. Entry, she described, required consent from many workers incumbent in the group who may have known the woman (or man, in the case of male worker groups) applying for entry and who they knew was not a police informer, a trafficker or abuser. The purpose of these groups was not only to share information about availability on a certain day or time but also to share pictures and videos of solicitation and for solidarity. One worker described how if a customer contacted her and she was not available or willing to offer services to him, she would forward his text message onto the WhatsApp group so that someone available and willing would respond to the customer. This sort of advertising and matching was easily possible on digital platforms, providing them with a world where they could insert an incarnation of themselves without being bodily hurt, which was rampant when soliciting in open spaces.

Often, female workers received phone calls or text messages from anonymous men who sought their services. These new customers had obviously received her contact details from other past customers. When this was narrated to us, another worker chimed in:

I feel like I'm being passed around.

Of course, while that statement was conveyed to us with a smile and with a tone of amusement, it strongly suggested that the phone facilitated the bodily commodification of especially female workers much more than they already were facing when viewed as 'prostitutes' in conventional parlance. In this manner, it appeared from the style of narration that passing phone numbers of women workers from customer to customer was perceived as almost passing the worker *herself* from one man to another, with its own deep psychological implications. Male workers who were in the room during this conversation seemed to be indifferent to this issue and even shrugged when prodded further about this interesting bodily experience in a digital space. The transgender workers we spoke with were completely blank when asked about this feeling.

However, this was not the only issue. More accounts on detrimental experiences began pouring in from our narrators and filling our conversations. In a group discussion, one of the workers stated quite articulately that though the phone allowed a wide scope for operational freedom within individual-to-individual transactions around sex work, it was also a tool for creative forms of oppression and exploitation against workers, particularly female and transgender workers, and they hence had little strategic freedom in terms of control over their engagement with the phone. In other words, while they could be dextrous with the phone as a prosthetic to their hands and bodies, they had little control over things when other external agents such as the police or goons gained a grasp on it. Many workers related how there was an interesting trend in police atrocity against female sex workers that has been established as a de facto modus operandi when arresting or detaining a worker – take her phone away and begin threatening her using this device. Workers narrated that while in the good old days it was usually a baton lashing or a standard overnight detention at the police station with rampant sexual abuse, the first move by the police now was to confiscate their phone, browse through their contact list for other workers (never male customers or social workers), threaten to call families and even publicise the worker. One worker poignantly said:

It has happened so many times, I sometimes think the police know more about my own phone than I do. They take my phone, almost automatically each time, and hold it in their hands and wave it throughout their questions to me. Sometimes they scratch their unshaven cheeks with its edge too. But when they clutch it throughout the detention and interrogation, it really feels like I am *handcuffed*. Like they have tied up some part of my hand and are holding it till they release me.

Though an interesting metaphor, one cannot really accuse this of being an exaggeration if understood that clutching the phone was, metaphorically, an act of restraining their hands. Another worker, following this 'handcuffing' statement, added how the police now actually do not need to restrain them up or keep them in custody for twenty-four hours, and related her personal experience:

> I too used to be questioned with my phone kept on their table or in their hands. But over some time, I think they too got tired of keeping me there, to avoid any publicity, and then they began to just confiscate my phone, telling me to 'go home'. Now you tell me, will I move from the station? Will I budge until I get my phone back? They're really cheeky. They know how to keep me standing outside the station, maybe for hours, without having to force a finger on me.

In effect, they had restrained her entire body at the station, without touching her or directing her movements, by simply restraining the phone. It felt almost that she could not leave the station with a part of her body behind. Another worker said, similarly:

> They don't need to clutch my hand anymore … they now only need my phone. It's as good as tying me up.

A disturbing trend revealed to us by workers was how the police would, even on the open streets, just snatch the phone away from the hands of a worker, peruse through the contact list and begin announcing names out loud on the streets in full visibility in the hope of catching more women workers who may be around. One worker narrated:

> He just kept shouting out, 'Geetha, Aruna, Dhanalakshmi, Nagamma …' from my phone in his hand, right in front of Triveni theatre, a really crowded area where people were looking and wondering what was happening. In fact, Dhanalakshmi was standing right across the road and she froze stiff. She later wept seeing my condition that morning.

If the handover of the phone is not complied with, workers are easily threatened for bribes in cash or even with demands for unpaid sex. When asked what happens after such incidents, a few said that they had to change their phone numbers, which meant that they had to re-inform all their contacts about the new number, a laborious task if it had to be done every few weeks.

On the part of the police, the usage of phones to track down sex work is considered a ground-breaking move. We spoke to a few police staff in Majestic and KR Market, where confiscation of the phone was reported by workers to be rampant, and asked them about how important the mobile phone as a device was in their engagement with the sex work sector. With exuberant responses (and a chair kindly offered to us to sit so we could listen at length to their enterprising ventures), they said that this was the 'ultimate' device in combating the menace of sex work in our streets. They gushed about how it was a far cry now from the days of yore when their knights led the charge with long wooden batons in the crusade against immorality, and how now,

> … one click of my phone camera, and we have the prostitute red-handed causing a social nuisance. She can't say anything when we show her own picture to her. Sometimes, we needn't say a word – just click and then show it to them. No touching, beating, threatening, raising my voice, running after them, fighting, none of that. Let me assure you, we don't harass them. When we show the picture to them and they quietly move out of the area, the matter is over, and we delete the picture. After all, why should my phone be filled with these people's pictures? It's just to scare them – no physical abuse or harassment. Clean and neat.

A police inspector boasted to us about his ingenuity in establishing a routine among lodges and hotels in his precinct in central Bangalore to send a photograph of the guest register every day by WhatsApp to him so that the police are aware of movements within lodges.

> Just see this photo, from yesterday's WhatsApp message. The full register, with all details of who came and went. Of course, there will be movement that is not recorded here. We are not fools, right? We can easily find that out in a jiffy.

Yet another strategy by the police, according to our narrators, was to retain their contact lists and call other workers on that list posing as potential customers or old customers, lure them and trap them – again, with threats to confiscate their phones. However, the police were not the only culprits in using phones to trap workers. Customers with criminal intentions also lured female workers to desolate areas by directing them through the phone to 'preferred' locations for sexual services, and then robbing them, attacking them or even gang-raping them. The phone became the easiest medium to attract workers to such areas, which was hitherto a criminal strategy by customers to bring female workers to lodges and then subject them to gang-rape (as seen in the earlier chapters).

Not just physical assault, even monetary fraudulence was very common before digital payments became common. Fraudsters, posing as customers demanded photographs and videos on the pretext of solicitation and negotiation (that is, offering higher payment for services if pictures and videos are shared ex ante), did not show up for paid sexual services and instead shared the material from their part for a price or simply for thrill among their friends. To add, some of these individuals would even divulge to the worker how the material was now (or would be) everywhere and that she would have to pay him with either cash or unpaid sex to stop further circulation. One worker told us quite emotionally:

The pictures of my body are now everywhere, without me knowing!

When reflected upon, this becomes a case where the worker's body is practically held at virtual ransom for money or unpaid sex. Kidnapping women workers in the past was not easy, given the protection they had from sex worker unions, their own sororities of female street-based sex workers, from local musclemen on the streets, from male sex workers, from transgender workers and others. When kidnapping did materialise in the past, workers mostly submitted to unpaid sex because they could not afford to inform their families that they (as sex workers) were held for ransom – the families would abandon them immediately. Now, however, kidnapping the body *virtually* is all too familiar an issue with women workers. When we asked them how they got around with it, they said that they now offered photographs only with a digital payment that was a sizeable percentage of the actual fee for sexual services in person. This was not foolproof and opened up a whole new dimension of transaction and service, but did curtail incidents of illicit circulation and threat. The unkindest cut, however, was when women workers themselves shared (or sold) their colleagues' photographs and videos to customers as vengeance when there was some interpersonal rivalry or squabble between two or more workers. This was very rare, but not impossible, and is actually said to have happened on instances.

> Before the phone, with camera and internet and all that came, rival workers met at a desolate location somewhere in the outskirts to fight and settle scores or send some musclemen to harass a rival in public. Now, however, pictures, videos, contact numbers and other details, such as even personal stories and incidents among rivals, are available to harass and avenge. The person you are attacking may not even realise it for a long time until someone else tells her.

At the same time, the phone was now the voice, the ear and the forum for solidarity and outreach among workers and their supportive ancillaries such as health workers and social workers. Much more than it is used to settle interpersonal scores among workers, the phone, workers overwhelmingly related, was instrumental in even saving workers' lives in some instances.

> Do you know how many times I have received messages and calls that some other worker (usually a woman or TG) is in trouble? Maybe she needs some money, maybe some medicines for her parents or children, maybe she needs to hide from the police or some rowdies – reasons for trouble are countless in our lives. But with the phone, you can send out an emergency signal as soon as you want to. Not like in the old days when you bore it entirely yourself, or maybe shared the issue with your friends or intimate customers long after you needed urgent help. One message is enough, and we can do something even before the sun sets.

When a worker is accosted by the police or henchmen on the street, other workers have on many occasions signalled and alerted either their colleagues or even local goons they have befriended. Both male and female workers narrated to us how many friendships with other workers were entirely on the phone, often never having personally met these colleagues. In this manner, cliques of workers were formed on digital spaces, where one can inform their friends if they are in bodily danger, if they are being harassed by families, if they are on the verge of suicide or if they are in need of money (which can be transferred digitally too). Emotional and psychological support is hence both easier with immediate reach, on the one hand, but also equally hard, on the other. In case the worker loses or gets robbed of her phone during violent skirmishes, new problems arise. Text messages and videos or photos circulated on WhatsApp draw awareness towards visible atrocities among not only local informal sex worker communities on the phone, but have on occasions also reached sex worker unions and collectives operating at state and national levels, prompting public outrage and seeking of legal support.

> You know what we do these days? Just like those criminals can circulate our pictures, we can circulate theirs too. We can't physically trap them but we can trap them in the phone and share photographs, names, phone numbers and even secretly filmed videos of those customers who have either misbehaved or have not paid, as a warning to other workers to keep off these individuals. And if really, really necessary, we have WhatsApp contact with some good lawyers too, if we need to approach this legally.

Male workers and transgender workers in many cases have become much easier to contact now, which was not very easy prior to inexpensive mobile-phone internet. Some are known to even have open and visible communities on Facebook to display to citizens the opportunity to understand issues of atrocity, rights and livelihood concerns of sex workers, and where anyone is welcome to post instances of such transgressions against workers. Violence against workers can now be tracked online through such fora, prompting a huge number of male workers to emphatically tell us:

> We sometimes feel safer in that world than in the real world.

Transgender workers also echoed similar sentiments, though in a slightly different direction. Their concerns appeared to principally revolve around the immediate reach of their network and leadership.

> Maybe we don't do as much body show through the phone, even for good payment. But for us, it is important since now our guru is just one phone call away. Everyone's guru is the most important contact, since she has a direct link with local henchmen and sometimes even the police.

Not very long ago, a couple of times a year, we used to hear that someone didn't return to their *hamam*, and a body was found quite some distance away. Murdering TGs is not rare at all. They think we are rats or mosquitoes to just swat or finish off. But now, if you have a good phone and connection, you can immediately call someone for help when you know you're going to be attacked. Remember you heard from my friend that he got locked in the toilet by some mischief makers, completely naked? That will never happen now with a phone.

We don't have too many WhatsApp groups like women and especially men. But we'll get there soon.

Male workers are not as much on the receiving end of virtual assault, even by the police, and have immensely benefited with the migration of operations to mobile phones as compared to female and transgender workers. Most of the instances we discussed earlier appeared not to worry male workers, who were quietly listening throughout the conversations where our female narrators were spilling out story after story, anecdote after anecdote about their engagement with the phone over the last nearly two decades.

However, while technological experiences have been generally positive for male workers, experiences have been mixed for social workers and health workers. While, on the one hand, they are able to offer legal support by circulating contacts of legal and social services (or even human rights information, job offers, government schemes, and so on) on the phone to workers, on the other hand, it is also now harder to track those workers who have disappeared from the streets of the city and who have a negligible digital presence. Health workers have lamented for the most part that while identifying workers on site was much easier in the days when the streets were filled with them, migration to digital platforms have dispersed them and made it far harder to spot them. This was a particularly hard problem for health workers who had to already do an additional job of persuading them to come for medical check-ups and receive condoms. They were now perplexed as to how to pursue workers who were for the most part invisible in their phone networks. One staff member of a community organisation remarked:

They just conveniently disappear.

As exclaimed by this individual, street-based sex workers, while formerly unable to escape the helping hands of support workers, were now able to hide their bodies and selves behind a digital curtain. A senior staff member of an organisation working on HIV control, related to us:

Before they vanished off the streets and bus stands, all I needed to do was to step outside, and many of them were there for me to target for welfare. Now, they are so scattered, it's like finding a needle in a haystack. Virtually impossible. Some of them are scared, so they don't pick up when I call them. Others have disappeared without a trace.

Similar accounts were provided by the doctors we spoke to at Victoria Hospital:

> Earlier, with the help of social workers, welfare organisations and student volunteers, we could trace them and bring them here for check-ups. Now, since they're all working through the phone and only a few are on the streets, it becomes their responsibility to approach us. How many do you think will land up here on their own?

The staff at the Alternative Law Forum and Samara echoed:

> It's really helpful in a way if they are connected by phone, since we don't have to physically find them. But this is exactly the problem too – that we are unable to physically find those who are not on the phone.

> I manage a WhatsApp group with thousands of male workers in it. But the constant entry and exit of people from the group just can't be managed even if I appoint multiple admins to that group. Yet, I'll still say there's a lot of promise through this medium. So much support is still possible, even if there is chaos online.

Eyes and Memories

During our conversations with workers about shrinking open public spaces and ecological commons, an element that came up regularly was the installation of CCTV cameras practically everywhere in the city. In the years gone by, when sex workers roamed the free open spaces in the city, as we know, the supervision that they encountered was mostly from the part of the police, from acquainted individuals who knew their undercover occupation and from other groups concerned about public health or human trafficking. However, in the contemporary era, there are new concerns around surveillance due to the ubiquity of CCTVs in bus stations, railway stations, shopping complexes, parks, traffic signals (which are managed by the government and city corporation), and private buildings, shops and plazas (managed by private owners of these establishments). In our conversations, workers constantly referred to the threatening eyes that looked down upon them from every other pillar and wall surface:

> There are many more eyes now. The very fact that they look down upon you appears so scary.

> I can't go to that park anymore, since the cameras are all over. The young lovers seem to have little problem continuing their activities, but the bunch of [neighbourhood] association people who installed those cameras are on the prowl for people like us and, of course, TGs.

When we enquired with them about what they felt most intimated about, they narrated how, more than anything else, they constantly felt 'looked at'. As one worker put it:

> In the old days, at most, some young boys and unemployed men would stand around the streets of Majestic and KR Market and look at you all day. They couldn't afford our services, but wanted to just stare at us because they knew what job we were doing. After some time, they got bored of seeing us and went off for a smoke or to play cards or to sleep. Now, things are different. They quietly take pictures of us on their phones and circulate them. Those lecherous eyes have been replaced by these robot eyes. These new eyes look at us all day and all night, with no rest for us, or [gently laughs] for themselves.

The experience of being constantly looked at is for sex workers quite apart from, say, the experience of genuine criminals or for completely regular passers-by. While those with a purported criminal intent would feel intimidated (hence serving the purpose of CCTV surveillance), regular passers-by would probably not bother or might even feel safe with constant observation around them. Sex workers, again, particularly women, on the other hand, have a complicated experience. While, on the one hand, the feeling of being watched is a direct inheritance from the (non-technological) monitoring of sex work that societies and governments have undertaken from time immemorial, the intensity of being watched by CCTV surveillance is unmatched.

> Those boys that she was referring to who constantly looked at our bodies, now it feels like those cameras also have some vulgar intent. Yes, we know they are not living creatures, but there are people behind those cameras, right? Now aren't they taking turns to see our bodies? I can't throw stones at that camera and expect it will stop looking at me. They'll arrest me for a day and then simply replace the camera.

> Before CCTVs, we could easily shoo away men who used to just stare at us. But now, whoever is behind those cameras don't want our services and instead just want to watch us, and we can't even shout at them. I can't possibly shout at a camera or ask the person behind it whether he wants my services!

While sentiments about their bodies being watched with perverted intent might or might not be misplaced, what is certain is that the surveillance is certainly to maintain a sense of 'decency' in the observed space and to nab any sort of illegal solicitation of sex work in public or pimping. We spoke to many shopkeepers and security personnel of malls in the city where once theatres and complexes stood, swarming with sex workers around them in their heyday.

It's very important we install these cameras around our shops. Big malls, in any case, install them, maybe as a requirement, but we need to do this to ensure there is no robbery. I've been robbed too many times by these eunuchs who roam around here and extort money. I don't mind giving them alms, but there have been just too many robberies of my items. And, of course, those women standing around. You see, I don't want any suspicion that I'm helping them. Tomorrow, if a policeman comes here, I can easily show him who was standing here and at what time. He then trusts me and realises I'm a victim of these people standing here, not their accomplice.

I don't like the old Majestic, even though I have many nostalgic memories here and, within Bangalore, I consider this to be my native place. I would always accompany my late father when he came to his shop. But I want the new Majestic to be much safer and free of anti-social elements who dirty the place. Like you said, they don't commit murder or pickpocketing. But who wants to see these people loitering around? So I snap my fingers at some women or *hijras* sitting around, just point towards the CCTV, and they move out instantly. No noise, no fights.

How much can we, as security guards at this bus stand, keep looking out? Sometimes we have to look in multiple directions, sometimes we have to take rest. But everything is now recorded by these cameras. They're like my friend and partner in my job! Makes my job of clearing out unnecessary elements easier.

Now that this park is completely CCTV-ed, I can even take a nap on my chair without much risk, and it will do my work for me [smirking]. Don't tell anyone I told you this – we security guards are not supposed to sleep on the job in the daytime!

Our conversations with police personnel on CCTVs brought out how these constables and officers wish to create a 'safe' and 'clean' space for 'good, hardworking people' and 'families' (these terms reproduced here verbatim, implying that sex workers are neither 'good, hardworking' nor 'family people'). Further conversations with individuals in law enforcement revealed how there were ulterior unwritten intentions to remove elements such as transgender individuals, homeless individuals or beggars around city spaces. One police inspector put it very directly to us:

With this superb technology, we are now able to control all movements and all people in public. We are not doing anything secret, and everyone must know that they are protected. That's why they are there for everyone to see. And by the way, why should anyone be scared? If you're not doing anything wrong, there's nothing to be scared of. But if you're doing something wrong, we can see your every move. You decide which side you want to be on. Our job is to maintain law and order and make sure Bangalore doesn't become like some Bombay red-light area or some picnic area for the underworld. These CCTVs help a lot.

When we related this particular conversation to our narrators, though, they had a very different position on the matter. They quoted the oft-adopted bent of mind and strategy to 'rescue' and 'rehabilitate' women who are engaged in sex work, and how CCTV surveillance was sometimes used to target women workers more than even transgender workers and move them away from the public space to 'protect' them; or, to the contrary, how some police constables used to gesture to sex workers in an area that a CCTV is watching them (in the same manner that the shopkeeper earlier narrated). These workers related how the technology was meant to both supervise their presence and movements and to also abuse them – often simultaneously. One worker told us of the first time she realised what this technology was.

> A police constable and a shopkeeper, who were great friends, told me of these cameras. I never knew what they were for a full week after they were installed many years ago near that new mall. They mockingly told me that something else is watching my every move. Only then I realised that there's now something else that has got control of my body.

Quite strikingly put by this worker, other female workers also chimed in during this conversation and added:

> I really felt on many occasions that that camera was groping me. It didn't move but knew it had to look at me.

> I felt almost that something or someone was noticing and controlling every move of my body. That thing actually has an angry expression if you look closely, telling me in silence that it knows what I am doing here with my body.

When workers were adding to this conversation around heavy surveillance in the area, one of them said that the police even informed her that her movements were stored in the camera's memory 'forever', so she could not lie at a later stage when caught at a police station. At this point, during the group discussion, our respondents – male, female and transgender – froze. Many, mostly older workers, had genuinely not realised that this device was not just watching them but actually had the capacity to even remember their moves. We vividly recorded what our respondents had to say after this fact was put forth.

> You mean to say that thing has a brain to remember all this? I didn't know that. Now it has a memory for everything I did!

> So anyone in the police station can even conjure up what I was doing sometime last month? Even who I was with? My clients, my friends who are not sex workers, those who are sex workers – it can see all of them?

Oh God, save us all! I didn't realise until now that it can even do that. Now I am stuck inside its brain too.

The last utterance was particularly remarkable for us, in the manner with which it created a feeling in the workers' mind that her body was trapped in a device and its memory for all to see and recollect. Not only this statement but other narrations during the conversation about CCTVs and their omnipotence in facilitating the monitoring and controlling of bodies in open public space, seemed to impart the message that the bodies of these workers were supervised and observed by the minute, worsened only by the fact that their bodily movements were even stored in memory.

Often, new implants of neoliberal urban transition brought with them, like baggage, these new eyes. Just as it was related to us by individuals earlier in this chapter, malls, new multiplex theatres, bus stands, metro stations and other installations of urban modernity arrive by default with an army of sleek eyes that observe, capture and remember. This becomes a multi-layered problem for workers.

So I thought that the completion of the new flyover will end my problems, and I can stand there again to solicit. But then the flyover was by itself not a problem. There were two cameras installed on it even before the first car went over the flyover.

My old area is gone because of the metro station coming up there. But now, can I stand in the metro station? No one may stop me from entering, but there are so many of these CCTVs at every point in the station. Above the ground, Chickpet, Balepet, Mamulpet, Sultanpet, all of them are slowly changing. Below the ground, the place is infested with these CCTVs.

Shops at National Market and Alankar took some time to install cameras. Maybe they couldn't afford it initially. This was the case with small parks around Majestic too. But then, the cameras on the neighbouring buildings are enough to capture us. So we can't escape.

Now, when any new building comes up in Majestic, like that Aishwarya Mall now coming up, I know it will be off-limits for us. We can't stand anywhere around it because the cameras will come for sure. I know it too well.

And the new lodges or renovated old lodges have cameras right behind the bald scalp of the front desk manager. I feel that the manager and the camera are both seeing me at the same time. The fellow is seeing inside my mind, the camera is seeing my body.

CCTV cameras (as externally enforced technological artefacts) are by themselves silent observers, as probably also may be the humans in the state machinery or private establishments watching their content. The most fervid wielders of CCTV surveillance as a weapon are perhaps not those who own and operate these devices, but those on the ground who are antagonistic to pseudo-invisibles to hunt down undesirable bodies. But there exists yet another externally enforced technological medium, a far more dangerous predator that street-based sex workers now have to be very wary about.

Techno-Cultural Mobs

Native-language television news media has emerged as an aggressive techno-cultural agent, highly antagonistic to street-based sex work, and a self-appointed emissary of the forces of neoliberal gentrification of urban human composition. Using state-of-the-art technology to conceal audiovisual recording equipment, or often unabashedly openly recording and broadcasting the personal identities, families, solicitation operations and even fabricating conspiracies against the community, television media has emerged as a new demonic figure in the sphere of sex work. While the paramount motivation for creating and covering activities in the sex work sector is to boost television rating points (TRP),[1] what powers the motivation of television coverage of this sector is a newfound veneer of morality that coats the imagination of the 'desired' city. While neoliberal urban transition may, on first sight, appear to concern itself principally with state-endorsed corporate interest and an affluent urban imaginary driving the recasting of urbanity (as discussed across Chapter 1), the element of foraging and exposing human desirables within this imaginary is a task that is outsourced to actors far smaller than macro actors such as the state and law enforcement (which, also, we have seen in the earlier chapters). While the surveillance of individuals can, drawing from Foucauldian thought, be accomplished even at a micro level with individual, interpersonal surveillance of conformity to power, actors at a meso level, such as the media, adopt advanced technology to hunt and uncover individuals and groups, embellish their existence and livelihood with sleaze and convolution and broadcast this with blaring sensationalism.

This has been achieved in its most spectacular form with the pursuit of transgender individuals and allegations of sex-change operations forced upon unsuspecting 'normal' individuals by this criminal cohort. In an 'expose' by the Kannada television channel TV9 in 2016, a young transgender individual was accosted and accused by this channel, based on a mother's allegations, of

---

[1] TRP, a numerical indicator of the viewership of a television programme, has emerged as the motivational basis of conceptualising television programming content in contemporary India. While corporate interests may be justified in sourcing those news stories that attract larger audiences, these are often divorced from both news broadcasting standards as well as legal and common ethics.

forcefully castrating her young boy, with this transgender individual herself supposedly the victim of such a procedure. The ripple effects were felt by dozens of other transgender individuals who found the police and the media barging into their homes and invasively video-recording with no consent.[2] This incident was particularly traumatic for the young individual in question here, who was celebrated within the transgender community as well as by large sections of society for being one of the first transgender individuals to pursue higher education in a reputed college in Bangalore.

With street-based sex workers, however, the hounding of individuals – again, especially women – in public spaces has been rampant and habitual in Bangalore as well as other cities and smaller towns (such as Belagavi in northern Karnataka, for instance), with the express intent of unveiling the immoral and criminal horror that lurks in the streets of our upright and proper city. Almost all of our female narrators brought out story after story of how they have been spied upon by television cameras planted covertly on the terraces of buildings, or sometimes even had a camera and microphone thrust in front of their faces demanding to know what they were doing in front of the cinema theatre or plaza with little evident intention of watching a movie or shopping. In one instance, it was an entire crew.

> When one or two journalists came up to me while I was standing in front of a medical shop, I gave them the choicest of abuses, and they ran away. But one day, they came in a van that had all kinds of equipment in it and practically attacked us. No, not with sticks or batons, but with cameras and mics.

> Yes, I remember that day. I, too, was there. They rounded up many women, some of them beggars and homeless, and showered them with cameras. The man with the mic was not even asking us questions but rattling away with his own description of what was going on here. He even began by asking, 'What is going on in our city?' Later, when my friends told me they saw us on TV, I realised with great shock that they were covering us live.

> I've been doing sex work on the streets for thirty years. We never had this problem at the time, but that's because there were no such cameras, no WhatsApp, no online, and the only thing telecast live was a cricket match.

Workers also narrated their experiences on how, in a few instances, after the police picked them up from the streets and took them to the station, there was already a cameraman and reporter ready at the station to report this story.

---

[2] See 'Operation Anandi: A Sting Operation That's Filled with Bias and Lies' by *Ladies Finger*, published online 10 November 2016, https://www.newslaundry.com/2016/11/10/operation-anandi-a-sting-operation-thats-filled-with-bias-and-lies (accessed on 1 June 2020).

It's nothing new to be picked up by the police randomly. We've told you about this so much. So, that afternoon, I thought it was one of those routine police pickups that I have now gotten numb to. But to my utter horror, at the police station was a TV channel van, with two cameras and one reporter with the mic in his hand. He was ready there to cover the whole thing, and he didn't, obviously, ask *me* any questions; he spoke only to the police. Well, they let me go in an hour, but when I told my cousin who is a sex worker in Ballari [in northern Karnataka] about this, she said it was much worse there and that this police–media connection was regular.

While it was still not sure whether in all instances the police had requested the media to arrive, the police–media nexus in surveillance and control of street-based sex workers has solidified, as one worker told us:

> Not every time is there a media gathering outside the station when we are brought there. But it is quite common now for the police to threaten of 'media attention', that is, roping in the TV journalists and displaying us to the whole world.

And like how (as seen in the earlier chapter) the police invade neighbourhoods and private homes pre-emptively, this was conducted more hawkishly by television media.

> They hounded me even in my house, after once seeing me and asking me some small questions when I was waiting for customers at KR Market bus stand. I have no clue how they managed to find where my house is … maybe [mentioning a rival's name] informed them. But they barged in one fine Saturday morning, knowing I won't be there, and began asking my family all kinds of lewd questions. Cameras were switched on and recording. After I returned home that evening and heard about all this, I felt squeamish throughout that week.

> Like a sting operation on criminals, they came to my neighbourhood posing as something completely different, and spoke to my neighbours and the women at the public water tank about sex-work activities. All the while, their camera was hidden in their bag. My friends ended up being interviewed about sex work without their knowledge. The video didn't come on TV, but I received the whole thing as a WhatsApp message. All this is circulating!

> I saw that TV9 report on Anandi on YouTube. And many other videos like that by other channels about our TG community are also put up on YouTube. We have done no wrong to anyone. But you should see the comments below the video! They are more hostile towards us than even the police. But getting those comments is the whole point. I don't know – do these channels get money when people watch it on YouTube? They can't do this for any other purpose than money, right?

Do you think they'll ever do this to the high-class sex workers? The ones hired by the politicians and higher influential people? Do you think they will ever record them, openly or in hiding, and bring them out? This is to hunt only us poorer workers.

It was not the aggressive reporting on the ground but also the final televised or uploaded product of the investigation that was sensationalist. Programmes on this theme display fancy graphics and thumping background music with menacing harmonies that create an ambience of sordidness and criminality, and a (male-voice) narration that swells and swoons with shock and exasperation on what has become of the city and how these women were destroying the sanctity of femininity. Naturally, it meant that the body and being of the immoral public woman was for all to see and critique, given the explicit (rarely blurred-out) faces of the workers telecast in full view, routinely with graphics and simulated visuals (such as circles and arrows) that highlighted their movements and activities in public and private. In their own words:

I'm sure audiences were looking at me with both shock and lust on that TV programme. I was showcased on TV for everyone to comment on my appearance and how I earned. For a few days after that, I felt nauseous just looking at a TV screen.

I'm doing nothing illegal. But I was on full view for all the world to see. My face and my body. The cameras scanned and broadcast every part of me. After all, that's what they were looking for, to show and earn their money. What is this? Some new form of mob justice against us?

There was no doubt that this techno-cultural lynching was possible with complete sanction from the viewers of these television programmes, who silently approved of this variety of techno-cultural surveillance by consuming these savoury snippets and anecdotes. The control of these bodies in public spaces (and in the process trespassing on their private spaces), especially among pseudo-invisible characters, is surely a collectively legitimised and valorised project, and not an undertaking that is singularly possible by the media alone.

Technological Experiences and Bodily Experiences

These narrations by workers may be stark and graphic, and valuable material in themselves. However, in order to understand the depth of the bodily experience of street-based sex workers when engaging with mobile-phone technologies, surveillance technologies and techno-cultural predators, it is important that we gain a conceptual grasp on the issue.

Assuredly, technological experiences are sociopolitical experiences as they are undergirded by sociological elements such as gender, class and agency. Sociopolitical circumstances set the context to study people's everyday interactions with technologies, due to which we cannot be blind to the gendering of these technologies, and therefore to the fact that their deployment and experience are the outcome of power structures, social constructs of gender and capacities for individual agency.[3] This can be observed in individuals' interactions with technological artefacts owned by them or enforced upon them. Individually owned technological artefacts (such as mobile phones) are often treated as extensions of one's body and self, as they assist in channelling expressions of selfhood or serve as platforms for livelihood creation or social collectivisation. Externally enforced technologies (such as CCTV surveillance) observe and control the presence and movement of the body in space and time, facilitating investigation and dissemination of information on these bodies. External techno-cultural platforms (such as television media) observe the presence, activity and agency of the body in both public and private spheres – within a context of social morality, public health and social order – and provoke the larger society to control and regulate these bodies. Whether these experiences are via individually owned or externally enforced technologies, understanding the digital embodiment of technology becomes crucial in helping contextualise technology-facilitated bodily experience.[4] The fluidity and co-evolution of the gender–technology relationship becomes further revealed, wherein different gender groups attach different and often diverging meanings to technology, and where gender identities (and power relations) are produced and negotiated simultaneously with technological development.[5] Undoubtedly, the technological experiences end up unanticipated, off-script, indeterminate, non-obvious and non-inevitable.[6] Drawing from feminist insights and adopting an intersectional approach by studying social location to comprehend the complex inequalities of these experiences among the economically and sexually marginalised, we see how all this, and, therefore, associated concerns of equity, justice and citizenship, are glaringly bypassed by policy.[7]

Surveillance technologies on movements in public space are structured through social categories; these technologies facilitate the formulation of new political relationships and reconstruction of social relationships.[8] Technologies of statecraft are immediately connected to technologies of surveillance, with

---

[3] Cockburn and Ormrod (1993).
[4] Powell and Henry (2017).
[5] Wajcman (2004, 2007).
[6] Akrich (1997); Monahan (2008).
[7] Eubanks (2007); Shade (2011).
[8] Nayar (2015); Lupton (2015).

the counting, monitoring and documenting of directed individuals and groups, who are discarded outside civil society, evinced as fundamental forms of state power. These practices have little to do with advances in digital technology and hark back to even colonial settings.[9] In more contemporary settings, new digital technologies have meshed with, extended and reinforced these age-old practices,[10] where individuals and groups who are monitored are often observed involuntarily and unawares. However, in most cases, the subject is made aware of and feels the potential of corporeal surveillance, and that political institutions legitimise the presence of this sort of wide-ranging surveillance and detailed monitoring of the body and groups in the public sphere as a prerequisite for 'security'.[11] In other words, this would be with the intention of discipline over individuals and groups, or for physical 'wellbeing'.[12]

Deborah Lupton even reveals the concept of 'ban-optic' surveillance, ever agile and fast-moving, which excludes certain threatening or contaminated individuals and groups from particular spaces through social sorting.[13] This social ordering strategy may be steered by locally powerful networks operating as an alliance of interests around spectacle, consumption and leisure, who construct negative images within public spaces on a discursive terrain by defining 'risk', 'insecurity', 'threat', 'pollution', 'vulnerability' and those who define what must appear as 'social and moral order', 'proper conduct' and 'natural and legitimate use of city space'.[14] These local-level interests could be even minor neighbourhood associations that absorb macro-neoliberal trends at their levels, defining and targeting 'prickly spaces' in locally monitorable areas that are out of bounds for 'inappropriate users' who loiter around and inhabit these spaces.[15] It is the wariness towards these 'inappropriate users' who threaten this order and proper conduct, and the urgent need to identify them and act on them, that demands increased policing and, in Henri Lefebvre's words, 'real spatial practices' such as surveillance.[16] One's citizenship (as well as the very sense of self) is therefore produced within a crucible of techno-cultural surveillance that is managed

---

[9] Cohn (1996); Lyon (2009).

[10] Crush (1992).

[11] Drawn from Svenonius (2018) and Lupton (2015), which, like other works in the huge body of studies on surveillance, draw from Foucauldian thought that in most cases the subject is made aware of and feels the potential of corporeal surveillance, and that political institutions legitimise the presence of this sort of wide-ranging surveillance and detailed monitoring of the body and groups in the public sphere as a prerequisite for 'security'. See also Norris (1997).

[12] Lupton (2015).

[13] Coleman and Sim (2000); Nayar (2015); Lupton (2015).

[14] Coleman and Sim (2000); Nayar (2015).

[15] Ranganathan (2011); Flusty (2004).

[16] Mitchell (2003); Nayar (2015).

by state, corporation and mainstream society, and which produces cultural images and practices. Therefore, rather than surveillance as just a technological extension that has social consequences, it is imperative to view surveillance as actually a sociopolitical process that has technological consequences; surveillance technologies are sociopolitical because they stem from social relations and political priorities, and these technologies are merely identification tools of social relations.[17] Hence, surveillance systems are not simply 'inevitable' developments that impinge individual privacy out of the necessity to provide security – they are social structures in their own right that actualise a micro-politics of social control, aggravating hyper-visibility for marginalised groups based on mistrust and risk, amplifying social inequalities and creating 'truth regimes' around guilt, trustworthiness, value and suspicion.[18]

The body is the final site of constructing and exercising such surveillance, whereby the transparency of bodies and blatant threats against selected individuals are only aggravated.[19] Individuals who are being monitored have even incorporated these technologies and melded them into their bodies with biographically specific meanings, mainly because they have little or no option to resist surveillance (as compared to privileged groups) and because their income and social capital depend on submitting to it.[20] More specifically, the surveillance of street-based sex workspaces serves not only a singular specific issue but overall to also improve the economic appeal of an entire city.[21] Their bodies are often under surveillance not only for their presence in public spaces but also as concerns for public health and social morality. However, not just aggressive or punitive surveillance, but also coloured by concerns of 'welfare' and 'rehabilitation', the sex worker's presence is monitored in a 'watch-care' system that normalises observation, paternalistic control and tutelage over them by the state and society.[22] A new form of voyeurism, harassment and involuntary circulation of bodily data emerges, which reproduces their deprived positions and throws out the idea and sanctity of privacy and anonymity.[23] In this manner, the sex worker is less a political subject aspiring for a body-positive, legitimate-worker, subject-citizen status, and more a delimited empirical subject around her bodily and socio-economic subaltern existence that is compromised of modernity in public space – thereby requiring greater targeted surveillance.[24] Here, not only

---

[17] Clavell (2011); Prasad-Aleyamma (2018).

[18] Monahan (2008).

[19] Svenonius (2018).

[20] Lupton (2015).

[21] Klauser (2007).

[22] Ghosh (2005).

[23] Kovacs (2020).

[24] Ibid.

the standard CCTV type of surveillance but also techno-cultural surveillance by the media controls the sex worker's bodily presence in space and time, with the anti-prostitution campaign having effectively used the power and reach of the mainstream media to represent the public woman in conjunction with local and state definitions.[25] The media in India, particularly the native-language news media, has completely changed the equation between television, social order and the marginalised, from a standpoint of wilful ignorance and fuelling inequality (as articulated eloquently by Jean Drèze and Amartya Sen)[26] to an actor behaving as a periscope, looking out for delinquency or detestability on the part of these distressed groups.

Historically (and, as also reported by our narrators here), the sex work sector has embraced technological change with negligible lag. From the automobile to the (wired) telephone, to the pager and finally to the mobile phone, the scope of solicitation, transaction, service, exploration, communication and risk management in this sector has kept abreast with technological developments in tandem with their progress in the market.[27] It was, anyway, one of the first markets to develop online, giving low-income female street-based sex workers (who encountered the police disproportionally) some of the advantages of high-income escorts, and possibly actually raising the supply of services by newer workers as well as new customers who may not have otherwise publicly transacted.[28] The proliferation and legitimacy of sex work have significantly progressed with the aid of mobile-phone and internet technologies – which allow the bypassing of traditional service providers, pimps and formal forms of surveillance – thereby simultaneously atomising and collectivising sex workers.[29]

Depending on local factors, nearly 80 per cent or more of sex workers in several locations have been observed to use mobile phone solicitation as a routine practice.[30] Visibility in open public spaces becomes less necessary with the phone, thereby escaping from the traditional adversaries of stigmatisation, the encounter with legal authorities or the general public, but, simultaneously, also creating difficulties for health and outreach workers to trace them, aggravating the likelihood of risky sexual behaviours and the inaudibility of indoor conflict and violence.[31] Sexual abuse and threats using non-consensual image exchange, disproportionately greater objectification of body parts (and the very personhood) of especially female sex workers, intimate image abuse, cyber-flashing, 'sextortion',

---

[25] Tani (2002).

[26] Drèze and Sen (2013).

[27] MacPhail, Scott and Minichiello (2015).

[28] Cunningham and Kendall (2011).

[29] Ibid.

[30] Shourie and Fernandes (2017).

[31] Lowthers (2015); Navani-Vazirani et al. (2015); Panchanadeswaran et al. (2019).

technology-facilitated sexual violence and digital rape by jilted customers or even other rival sex workers, have become rampant with increased use of smartphones, though it has also helped in counter-surveillance of problematic customers by workers themselves.[32] New fears of non-consensual and stealth photography and video recording by strangers and clients have arisen as seriously as new possibilities in grassroots activism, immediate responses to emergencies and possible skill-building.[33] Experiences are therefore understandably mixed because mobile phone engagements of sex workers are on the users' own terms and in the context of specific social infrastructures.[34] Spaces of work have been transformed, especially for male sex workers, with mobile-phone internet blurring physical and digital boundaries and creating hybrid spaces.[35] For female sex workers, mobile phones have allowed secrecy from family and expansion of client networks, with the artefacts often themselves acting as payments in kind or gifts from clients and seen as targets of aspiration.[36] For interventions to assist and support sex work, mobile phones have been quite effective towards vulnerable, migrant and low-literate populations as their only personal communication device.[37] Mobile phones are therefore globally ubiquitous and synonymous with sex work even in the global south, though a great deal of the literature[38] has focused on issues of HIV and general public health, more than issues of socialty, solidarity, new platforms of monetary transaction and new hazards.[39]

In fact, the mobile phone itself has been constructed as an extension of the body. Even early research studies,[40] long before it became a universal human appendage, reported from observations that the mobile phone was perceived as a 'friend' or like 'part of one's anatomy'. With the steady global diffusion of the artefact, its role as an affective technology – that is, as one that mediated the expression, display, experience and communications of feelings and emotion – was soon commented upon in the academic literature.[41] The way in which the phone is held and touched (with its perennial proximity to the hand and body, even when not using it) made it strikingly different from other digital communication devices and allowed people to develop symbolic significance around it and emotional relationships with it.[42] First identified in studies among

[32] Nussbaum (2010); Maddocks (2018).
[33] See the detailed study by Panchanadeswaran et al. (2019).
[34] Sambasivan, Weber and Cutrell (2011).
[35] Ryan (2016, 2019).
[36] Stark (2013); Suryawanshi et al. (2013).
[37] Ibid.
[38] Such as the many works by Navani-Vazirani et al. (2015).
[39] Lowthers (2015).
[40] See Kiesler, Gant and Hinds (1994).
[41] Lasen (2004).
[42] Lasen (2004); Campbell (2008).

Finnish adolescents, the mobile phone was seen as an 'extension of the hand' with respect to the fact that the hand was the most important part of the body that manipulated the physical environment around it.[43] And beyond just the hand, the body itself was said to 'wear' this communication technology like a second skin, thereby humanising it, and allowing it to radiate a consciousness and display of the self, a sense of style and an aesthetic.[44] Naturally, therefore, the mobile phone has been adopted, conceptualised and embraced practically as a prosthetic,[45] not simply because of its communicative abilities but because it fundamentally transformed people's perception (and construction) of themselves and the world.[46] While there are context-specific social constructions of the usage of the mobile phone,[47] a sizeable number of consistencies remain. So much so, there has even been a term – 'apparatgeist' – attached to the spirit behind the effects and uses of mobile phones that are considered universal and consistent even across disparate cultures,[48] from Finnish teenagers right up until street-based sex workers in the alleys and parks of Bangalore city.

We know, through the workers' narrations, that in Bangalore (like in most other cities in the world), sex workers have adopted mobile phones and their digital platforms for solicitation, negotiation, advertising, solidarity, transaction, communication, and so on, and hence engage with the artefact as an extension of one's own body. Ubiquitous CCTV surveillance, media intrusions and broadcasting and even the deployment of phone cameras by police personnel, have been employed avowedly to control their bodies in the cityscape and 'decent' mainstream society. While these transition processes aggravate exclusion of certain unwanted groups and occupations, for street-based sex workers in general and for female workers in particular, their bodies get placed at the core of their position in the political order, placing them at the antipode of social power and privilege, and justifying subordination and oppression on them.[49] The social construction and colonisation of the sex worker's body are considered preconditions for the maintenance of social order, thereby valorising social and state practices of containment and control through new technologies, provoking sex workers' retaliatory contestation and negotiation of power (often, again, with new technologies) and assisting in the examination of privilege and marginalisation.[50] In fact, the structure and configuration of power itself can

---

[43] Oksman and Rautiainen (2003).
[44] Campbell (2008).
[45] McGuigan (2005).
[46] Campbell (2008); Townsend (2000, 2012).
[47] Kamath (2018).
[48] Katz and Aakhus (2002); Campbell (2008).
[49] Waylen et al. (2013).
[50] Brown and Gershon (2017).

be viewed in the entity of the body.[51] This need not always be from a macro or aggregate perspective alone. As Wendy Harcourt,[52] who has provided one of the most granular treatments of the theme of body politics, enlightened us, in the normative construction of gender and power, it is the everyday life or micro politics that shapes our knowledge and experience of the lived gendered body. And with the rise of digital media, the body has taken on further significance as a site of both self-representation and surveillance, with this tension underpinning particularly the female body because it is more subject to constant regulation through hegemonic femininity.[53] Digital life is lived through the body in one's engagement with the technologies around us, because digital sexual violence is very much an extension of sexual violence in everyday life and because technologies can easily help facilitate embodied harm.[54]

So, on the one hand, the politics of technology, experienced through externally enforced technologies or individually owned artefacts, are associated with the body and being of the street-based sex workers across gender and economic class. And, on the other hand, body politics is a natural experience for sex workers (particularly female and transgender) because the bodies and beings of these workers, in any case, have always been pinned up for sociopolitical contestation arising out of the deployment of their bodies (in its capacity for intimacy and sexual pleasure) for commerce, livelihood and survival. Hence, for street-based sex workers, if technological artefacts are either extensions of one's body or are weapons of reinforcing power over their bodies, at once, the politics of technology is absorbed into the domain of body politics, and body politics becomes a concern within the politics of technology. We, therefore, have an interesting reality, where (*a*) the body becomes a site for sociopolitical and technological experience and (*b*) the politics of technology reinforces body politics in novel dimensions. The body of the sex worker is therefore clamped with both body politics and the politics of technology, which mirror each other in a crucible that forces control over body and space. Sociopolitical experiences and technological experiences find the body as an arena to situate, providing within this site avenues for emancipation as well as avenues to unfurl their convolutedness.[55] At once, the public and private domains of existence of these workers are caught in one pincer grasp as a result of body politics and the politics of technology mirroring into one another in one clasp.

Let us now revisit the case of our workers in particular. The mobile phone provides a surrogate presence of the body of the worker in digital space, where

---

[51] Foucault (1980).

[52] Harcourt (2009).

[53] Baer (2016).

[54] Powell and Henry (2017).

[55] Adapting from Grosz (1994).

one is able to effectively solicit, negotiate and even offer limited forms of service and voyeurism to customers. The migration to and operation within digital spaces using mobile phones has gained especially significant validity during the time of writing this volume, when the COVID-19 pandemic is raging in India and sex workers have suffered disproportionately and with little state support. As a response to the prohibition of non-essential movement during the extraordinarily harsh lockdowns and seal-downs in India (grossly mismanaged, leading to mammoth humanitarian and labour crises, resulting in their eventual relative futility), street-based sex workers have resorted to even offering voyeuristic services through the phone. It has been observed and reported by sex worker unions in Karnataka and India that visually gratifying sexual services are now the main source of income for these workers, facilitated by digital payments in advance of the visual service offered. They now operate, quoting one worker in an earlier section, 'inside the phone'.

Hence, street-based sex workers feel some version of themselves replicated 'inside the phone', which is a boon in that it diminishes the threat of physical violence that is routinely encountered on the streets but also a bane in that one's bodily privacy is severely compromised, especially for our narrators who for long had been proud of much greater bodily agency compared to brothel-based workers in other cities. Privacy is again compromised when bodies are 'passed around' via the phone, which is exploited by the law enforcement, who virtually handcuff the worker and restrain her in the police station by holding hostage her phone, an extension of her body. Customers also hold the bodies of the workers hostage, threatening illicit circulation of images and videos until a ransom is paid. But sex workers have also narrated at length, as we have heard, how the phone is not only an extension of the hand but is also an extended ear, voice and heart. It appears, as we meditate more on these metaphors, that the phone is a proxy of the body itself, and hence the politics of the device mirrors and reflects the politics of the body.

However, an equally anthropomorphic casting of technological devices that exert control over the body in space and time is with respect to the CCTV in public spaces and private establishments. As evidenced by law-enforcement agents, this monitoring is to serve multiple purposes that not only include genuine crime and delinquency but also aid in the weeding out of immoral characters in public space. This, for all practical purposes, is the sifting and plucking out of undesirable bodies in the urban human landscape of the imagined city, which is motivated at its core by a reconstructed definition of the 'public' itself. This technology has elegantly continued the historical tradition of watching the immoral public woman. Nearly Orwellian in its experience, workers have narrated, as we heard, how they felt silently groped and harassed by these unreachable eyes. This was a battlefield in a silent picture. The outcome is an unwilling and helpless erosion of ownership of their bodies in space and across time, not in terms of the state or law enforcement dictating their choice of occupation, but (more horrifyingly) with respect to these agents possessing the knowledge and information about the bodily presence and movements of workers and exercising the power to draw from that knowledge to implement social control. This is in addition to ensuring that workers are fully aware of all this, with the strong backing and legitimisation of this bodily surveillance.

Television media as a techno-cultural actor has become a self-ordained guardian of social morality, whose self-assigned duty is to weed out dastardly elements such as street-based sex workers who threaten the purity of the female body by not only subjecting it to a commercial transaction but in the process also planting it on full view for hire in public spaces. Television media now bestows on itself the right and privilege of pre-emptive sting operations on these workers not only in order to wipe out this profession from the spectrum of urban informal work but also to control the bodily presence of these women in city spaces. This new emissary of social morality has given itself the full freedom to identify and victimise those bodies who are not in consonance with the larger social definition of legitimate public bodies (such as street vendors, recreational walkers, blue- and white-collar workers, families, shoppers, and so on). This new form of technological surveillance with sociocultural motives (that is, as a techno-cultural force) has emerged as a predatory actor that assists in urban human gentrification. With its intentions of scanning and scrutinisation of threats to morality and public health, it curtails the agency of the body in public and private spheres using invasive and public-humiliation tactics, and calls upon the public to comment upon and circulate these visuals, almost in the medieval manner of putting a person on stocks and pillories in the town centre. The patriarchal discourse around the definition and classification of the 'public woman' is regurgitated by this actor, inviting the gaze of the 'decent' citizen to reiterate and redevelop this definition and, therefore, redefine the legitimacy of her existence. The very question of bodily citizenship of street-based sex workers is raised by this actor since their existence and livelihood jars with cultural images and practices of the feminine body; this invites responses that result in what effectively is techno-cultural lynching.

When we understand technology as everyday experience and practice among the marginalised (and when 'equitable technological access' moves beyond merely redistributive issues of devices), oppressive power structures immediately stand tall before us, prompting us to evaluate the interaction between technology, citizenship and social justice.[56] Technological experience then becomes a site of struggle, and the visibly massive penetration of technology into everyday life

---

[56] Eubanks (2007).

provokes questions of social justice and sociocultural and political inequalities.[57] The need to ruminate over and include critical technological citizenship becomes a pronounced necessity, because technology is an actor itself on the shifting terrains of citizenship claims, and which can effortlessly erase socially just values as much as it can help build them.[58] Street-based sex workers can immediately testify to this with their technological experiences, which not only intersects with their bodily experiences but also with their urban citizenship and labour rights. Their ongoing struggles and movements seek to counter their technological status as 'implicated actors' – that is, those who may not be present in the development of technologies but who are certainly affected by the action by being discursively constructed and targeted by explicit political agendas embedded in the technologies they encounter.[59]

When Bangalore's sex workers face the wrath of neoliberal urban transition head-on, as they have over the last two decades, they have encountered new technological experiences both in the capacity of individually owned devices as well as externally enforced artefacts and platforms. While combating historical marginalisation, dispossession and violence, street-based sex workers have resorted to the phone as a new medium of response, but this very device has also led to new forms of virtual bodily violence and assault. Their experiences with CCTV cameras and television media has been overwhelmingly negative, with very little evidence that the former has 'protected' them (as law enforcement would like to assert) or the latter has reoriented the public discourse to assert their legitimacy as urban informal workers and citizens. As we have seen, the politics of these technologies have a unique fallout for this section of informal workers because it mirrors their body politics as well. If technological artefacts are extensions of the body or are weapons of reinforcing power over their bodies, the politics of technology and body politics effortlessly overlap in their case. The street-based sex worker's body becomes a site for sociopolitical and technological experience, simultaneously.

---

[57] Feenberg (1991); Shade (2011).
[58] Eubanks (2007).
[59] Oudshoorn and Pinch (2003).

7

Their City

We have been crawling all over their city. We have all been working, travelling, enjoying and living in their worksites and their recreational spaces. Our footprints overlap with theirs when we traverse through their world. We are actors in their theatre, as customers, adversaries, invisibles, accomplices, well-wishers and benefactors, adorning the garb of software engineers, factory workers, shopkeepers, food vendors, researchers, teachers, lawmakers, the police and other 'decent' people. Our structures sit as stage props in their cityscape, around which their material experiences are built, while our presence and our activities colour their individual and social experiences. The cartography of sex work is one of the shapes of this city, and the labour of sex workers contributes to running this glittering metropolis. However, they are cast as the unpleasant and the execrated, the threatening and the targeted, the invisible and the visible. They are one of the many non-blind people who stroke the surface of this elephant and, consequently, the beast needs to be redrawn, rewritten and reseen from their eyes, feet and minds. Their own unique experiences of the elephant's movements and transformations need to be understood. As a preparatory step towards this, we need to acknowledge that they too are some of the people associated with the elephant.

Old Bottle of Nostalgia, New Wine of Futurism

The elephant has been restless for a long while now, persistently striving to be something else. In the 1980s and early 1990s, Bangalore's planners wanted it to become India's Singapore. During the 1990s and after, for lack of originality in nomenclature (and abundant delusion), they wanted it to become India's Silicon Valley. Each of the Comprehensive Development Plans, the Bangalore Agenda Task Force, the Vision Group and other plans, charted out by the city's principal planning bodies, decade after decade, have had an undertone of image as a prime concern, with these bodies constituted by individuals from industry and commerce, by default, within their august panels. Plans have pushed for 'decongestion' of the inner city by removing slums and relocating dwellers (simultaneously, and contradictorily, wishing to protect them from eviction), replacement of huts, conversion of 'haphazard private shops' with 'fashionable'[1]

---

[1] The very word is seen in page 11 of the BDA Masterplan for 2001. In fact, a quick look at all Masterplans by the BDA seem to reflect similar language.

shopping complexes, beautification and residential development of existing, randomly inhabited areas, improvement of existing abutting villages, planned 'organised' commercial areas in the city core on 'modern lines'[2] to promote a central business district and Information Technology (IT) corridors along the periphery that would attract capital and enhance the image of the city as 'international', and the preservation of heritage architecture and landmarks with scant regard for preserving the informal economies around them.

During the 1950s and up until the 1980s, horizontal expansion pushed out the city's boundaries, creating new neighbourhoods and localities for upcoming middle- and upper-middle-class families, made possible by gobbling up villages (whose peasants migrated to the city to join the urban poor) and buying up productive agricultural tracts (whose owners became cash-rich overnight). Where horizontal growth of structures was not possible, such as in the city's core, vertical growth ensued. The sale and demolition of heritage residential buildings and their replacement with giant commercial and residential complexes became all too regular a sight. When both horizontal and vertical growth reached their limits, aggressive eviction and forced relocation of long-settled urban poor from their dense settlements to the city's outskirts was put into force. After the 1990s, the eastern and southern fringes of the city experienced explosive in-migration led by the swelling ITES sector, expediting the maniacal construction of apartment buildings in those areas, reprising the drama to gobble villages in the outskirts, erase agriculture, relocate people, add to urban poor, evict urban poor to outskirts, start all over. This wash–rinse–repeat cycle was spun over and over again, both within the city and at its fringes, and always against the urban poor and the marginalised. The city was cast as a locus of purely physical spaces that were defined economically, residentially or recreationally, and rarely as a conurbation of people and an assemblage of social groups that created an urban human ecology. Anything that was not decent enough, such as shanties in a slum or a row of street dwellers, was seen as a problem in the image trajectory of the city. The development plans of Bangalore served practically as blueprints for battle-plans to repeat the routine onslaughts against the poor and the marginalised; the eviction of thousands of families like in Ejipura in south-eastern Bangalore in repeated waves, and their relocation dozens of kilometres away, has become the stuff of legend.

The attitudes among the affluent emit a different chord, crooning a mourning hymn about the loss of a long 'golden era' of Bangalore, which they express eloquently in informal conversations with one another as well as on social media. Books such as TP Issar's *The City Beautiful*, luxuriously awash with glorious pictures

---

[2] It was striking to see, even as we write this, a report in *The Hindu* (29 June 2021) that a body called Bengaluru Smart City Limited had begun 'redevelopment' and 'improvement' works in KR Market to facilitate its 'smart makeover'.

of buildings and flowering trees, are drawn from in order to lend legitimacy to those conversations. While they are intended to be harmless reminiscences of a quieter, less-populated, less-polluted Bangalore and friendly recollections about localities and buildings, what is amusing is that these discussion fora are usually constituted by the very people who facilitated the damage they are complaining about. Other personal memoirs of Bangalore, such as Peter Colaco's popular *Bangalore: A Century of Tales from City and Cantonment*, swoon with slushy-sweet nostalgia effusing an anglicised privileged narration of what the city was until the 1990s, while sidestepping the trove of harsh realities manifestly visible in the days of yore. The lilt of writing and the illustrated caricatures in Colaco's memoir evoke an old Bangalore inhabited by genteel Citizens surrounded by a devoted army of the working class and how, by great misfortune, this snug paradise decomposed into a messy, chaotic scramble by immigrants whose harsh circumstances may be offered a token sympathy at best. Most of the conversations around urban transition in Bangalore, around nostalgia, appears to concern itself with the population boom caused by disagreeable immigration and the resultant explosion of traffic – with a hypocritical amnesia that the contributors to these conversations were themselves immigrants (or descendants of immigrants) at some point and that they too owned and drove vehicles in the city's open roads, but that it became inconvenient when everyone else, after them, immigrated and drove their vehicles too.

The dominant popular and policy discourses around urban transition in Bangalore, therefore, have revolved either around the nostalgic or the futuristic,[3] with models for further action that draw from either sentiment and little in the way of appreciating a wide spectrum of people, especially the pseudo-invisibles. Both models often battled inside the panelled rooms of planning and policy institutions, alternatively winning and losing, with the pseudo-invisibles perennially relegated to the lose–lose quadrant. Be it the nostalgia camp or the futuristic camp, being inclusive of large sections of the Populations and even a mention of the pseudo-invisibles would run the risk of transition plans becoming needlessly 'over-democratic', which was not only unnecessary but also dangerous since these groups were an aesthetic, moral and political threat to both the past and the future of this beautiful city.

In a full-frontal counter to all these, this book has explicated how pseudo-invisibles such as street-based sex workers have imaginaries and experiences of their own, too. Not only cosy neighbourhoods and their pensioners, but the sexscape of Bangalore also has experienced change, under the crushing weight of the neoliberal gentrified transition that rumbled above it. New spaces, new artefacts and new actors broke into their world, suddenly and gradually, and transformed the spatial and behavioural dynamic of their sector in this city – an

---

[3] A viewpoint also drawn from Janaki Nair's work, which we draw from across this paragraph.

occupation that is integral to the compass of informal labour and economy in this city. In their individual lives, these transitions have had jarring implications on their bodies and spirits, their families and livelihoods, and their very existence. Across the chapters, we have waded through the wrenching accounts of their transition experience, with them as a nucleus, across the spatial, the social and the technological. We hope to have, inspired by McQuiller Williams,[4] provided an extension to the sociology of urban sex space as well as the sociology of street-based sex work. And inspired by Leslie Kern,[5] we hope to have provided an intersectional analysis of urban transition woven through a combination of narratives, theory and popular culture. But more than anything else, probably more than even urban transition experiences, we hope to have reflected what J. Devika and Nalini Jameela had expressed so tellingly about the *ordinary-ness* of the sex worker and the unremarkable-ness of sex work in the lives of the poorest. The sex worker incontestably emerges as a subject with agency and power, who knows of one's rights and constraints, who exists outside the trafficked victim, who has family and friends and, above all, who has *aspirations*. There have been countless instances where they have proactively fought for their rights and around constraints, fully aware of their weapons and opponents, and by carefully studying the contours of the battlefields ahead. The saga of struggle continues for street-based sex workers in this city even as you read this, not only with regard to their traditional crusades of identity, individuality and citizenship and continuing health hazards but also in their battle to claim their right to their city.

Their Rights, Their City

The avowal of these pseudo-invisibles to reclaim their position of existence, movement, operation and political participation in the city is not only an assertion to re-appropriate spaces but to battle neoliberal urbanism itself, even if not articulated so by these individuals and their compatriots. It is a movement to cultivate the urban, more than simply for claiming more spaces.[6] As David Harvey[7] had persuaded while claiming the right to the city, derivative rights (such as the right to be treated with dignity) must become fundamental rights, and fundamental rights (in their contemporary and realised embodiment of the right to private property and profit) ought to become derivate rights.

The city must be individually and collectively 'made' through daily political, intellectual and economic engagements, as much as it 'makes' these individuals and collectives in turn.[8] Space, after all, is a social product with both built

---

[4] McQuiller-Williams (2014).
[5] Kern (2020).
[6] Purcell (2013).
[7] Harvey (1973, 2003).
[8] Ibid.

forms and embedded ideologies, that is, a social entity with particular, localised meanings.[9] Combining this with Henri Lefebvre's thought[10] on the right to the city, space (both lived and experienced) becomes primary due to its potency as a cauldron that melds together sociological and economic aspects of the complexity of human life; in this process, dismissing industrial capitalism's relegation of space into economic-reductionist terms which treat it simply as a marketable commodity.[11] Labour, in turn, actively produces space through its spatially embedded activities, making it crucial to study its everyday lived experiences and the manners in which it encounters representational space.[12] Extending these standpoints, the appropriation of spaces within the city becomes a 'right' (accompanied by de-alienation) and forces a transformation of our notions about who rightfully owns the city, that is, those who inhabit it and participate in it.[13] Naturally, these dynamics would lead to conflict among rights between the various social groups that are equally asserting them legally and morally, but this is a friction that must be faced and resolved.[14] The outcomes of this discord hold both the possibility of challenging marginalisation and oppression as well as the possibility of reinscribing new forms of domination.[15] This should not be surprising, as the city itself has never been a place of harmony, clarity or peace; it has been a site of creative destruction and a resilient, enduring and innovative social form.[16] The contours of the city, when choreographed through control and purification of urban space, provokes concerns about the expression of citizenship and social justice,[17] translated directly into concerns about the right to one's city.

Therefore, there is no choice. The battle for the city must be fought because it campaigns for the enfranchisement of people with respect to urban space, that is, those individuals who constitute the body of urban lived experience and lived space.[18] These individuals must take control of the conditions of their own existence and make the city their own again.[19] It is no wonder, therefore, that struggles for the right to the city come from the directly oppressed, and the thirst for aspiration comes from the alienated.[20] It is also no astonishment that movements over urban citizenship have spawned all over the global south and are

---

[9] Balshaw and Kennedy (2000).
[10] Lefebvre (2003 [1970], 1991 [1974], 1996).
[11] Purcell (2002).
[12] Chaudhary (2020).
[13] Purcell (2013).
[14] Marcuse (2009).
[15] Purcell (2002).
[16] Harvey (2003).
[17] MacLeod (2002).
[18] Purcell (2002).
[19] Purcell (2013).
[20] Marcuse (2009).

not restricted only to 'Occupy' movements in the West; even in India, ground-level dynamics of claiming rights to the city have long surpassed the legal sphere and graduated to the access, use, production, life and work in urban spaces.[21]

As we know by now, the struggles of street-based sex workers in Bangalore to reclaim their city spaces are not only around worker rights or gender rights alone, but *civil rights* in their holistic entirety, in the process rejecting the typecasting of their cohort (especially women workers) as 'fallen' or 'weak oppressed victims'. Their rights to their city draw their legacy from the basic civil, human and labour rights they have vociferously asserted. It speaks to the domains of the legal as well as the moral, existing rights as well as claimed rights and in an individual as well as a collective capacity.[22] Let us chart this departure away from 'sympathy' and towards rights, in the context of urban street-based sex workers.

Judith Walkowitz argued that the dynamics of urbanisation are married to cultural anxieties about working-class women (as derived from the distinction the state and society make between women); anxieties that can and must be controlled first of all by launching crusades against the body of the prostitute.[23] However, she continues, this need not be in the form of physical attacks – it can be achieved by casting sex workers (among working-class women) as objects of 'care and concern' and subsequently intensifying control on them so that their sexual and labour autonomy is severely compromised. Not only this, a fictitious homogeneity among workers and a singular truth about women is manufactured, by which the entire spectrum of subjectivity among sex workers is denied.[24] Hence, there is either the invocation of criminal law to address gender and worker rights (where the state enjoys powers of moral regulation) or an invocation of outdated conservative, protectionist attitudes that collapse (particularly female) workers as weak, vulnerable and helpless.[25] The Sex Workers' Forum has vehemently fought this for decades, arguing that rescue and rehabilitation is an erroneous strategy, first of all, since it is considered as the 'only solution' for (particularly female) sex workers; second, because it is a product of economic reductionism of sex work; and third, because it stems from morality and paternalism. This has to be challenged by asserting that sex workers have their own rights, by respecting their acknowledging the equivalence to other marginalised but politically successful groups and by demonstrating evidence of successes they have achieved so far.[26] This will lead the way to acknowledging the sex worker as a self-propelling, speaking subject capable of making economic choices and,

---

[21] Idiculla (2020).
[22] Zerah et al. (2011).
[23] Scoular (2004).
[24] Kapur (2005).
[25] Ibid.
[26] Cornish (2006).

in the process, claiming one's rights as a parent, worker and citizen, and blurring sexual, familial and cultural norms, creating the potential for more inclusive politics by opening the space for unaddressed issues in the rights of women, sexual minorities and cultural minorities.[27] These are not just legal demands but struggles that declare one's rights in a higher moral sense.[28] Interpreted in this manner, what street-based sex workers in Bangalore have stoutly advocated for in terms of human, civil and worker rights, and the rights to their city is, as Pratap Bhanu Mehta[29] has spelt out (with respect to distressed workers as a whole), not 'pity' or 'compassion' or 'care'. It is a demand for justice. Following Mehta, we understand that an approach on the basis of 'compassion' ends up actually reproducing power, inequality, othering, subjecthood and depoliticisation (which appeals to sentiment, individual discretion and mercy) while a *rights-based approach* on the grounds of justice – one that sex workers in Bangalore have adopted – demands state and institutional obligation, accountability, processes and, finally, citizenship. Their claim to urban citizenship has been as much about legitimacy as it has been about legality.[30]

Concurring with this approach, street-based sex workers have rejected the view of welfare based on rescue and instead advocated formidably for welfare based on citizenship, on labour rights and human rights; in this process, they have strived to reconfigure their relationship with the state as *citizens*.[31] They have neither begged for handouts that are typical during local election campaigns (besides the minimum government relief that all workers are entitled to) nor have they pursued state charity; instead, they have demanded for social and economic guarantees from the state to address their needs. Never budging from their claims for equal citizenship, they have employed their weapons of activism to work within structures and processes of local democracy and public intervention. They have rejected plans in terms of rehabilitation and zoned housing, and have instead worked for plans that seek greater access to systems of justice and citizenship rights and reclaiming agency. Seeking to exercise their capability, they have crusaded for development and rights in the same vein. They have worked for individual protection, but more so for protecting their rights, by not duplicating the self-entitlements of Citizens or even Populations, but in their *own space*, dismissing both derogatory and benevolence-based labels and categorisation by state and society. They have protested:

---

[27] Kapur (2005).

[28] Marcuse (2009).

[29] Mehta (2020).

[30] Zerah et al. (2011).

[31] This paragraph on recognising the rights-based approach that sex workers have followed draws from ideas in the series of talks broadcast online by J. Devika and Praveena Kodoth in June 2020 on rights-based welfare policy, based out of the Centre for Development Studies (CDS), Trivandrum.

The government has called us *damanitra mahila* ['oppressed women', see Chapter 5]. We are surely not that. By calling us that name, they have tried to make us decent women and have actually also encouraged us to quietly become ashamed of ourselves! Yes, we may be addressed as 'former sex workers' even if we move to another job. But so what? I may not proclaim it, but I don't feel guilty or embarrassed either.

All these groups and government people want us to feel bad about ourselves and come out of sex work to take up other jobs. But at the same time, they will never treat us as equals even in those other jobs. In fact, if you make someone feel bad for something she is or does, will you ever treat her as equal? They make our entire family feel bad too. Some people ask me who will marry my daughters. Those people will permanently stamp 'fallen woman', 'loose woman' or 'HIV spreader' on you, just like this tattoo is permanent on my wrist.

I have never heard them rescue high-class escorts. If they want to save oppressed people, why don't they rehabilitate garment workers, construction workers or even male sex workers? Why don't they liberate and rehabilitate oppressed wives? So many married women are less free than we are.

We are women who are oppressed in many ways. But we are not 'oppressed women'. If you see it that way, all women are 'oppressed women'. Why don't they go and save them all?

There are so many, many different types of sex workers on the street. But even though we all share many similar rights, no single solution from the government can ensure these common rights for all the different types of workers.

We are people who do sex work, and we want to be seen only that way. We are not crying out for someone to come and save us. This is not some movie where we are helplessly trapped, and some hero comes and saves us. Yes, we are trapped in poverty and violence, but we are not trapped in dishonour and shame. We want our rights, not your pity and your charity.

Adopting this spatial-, social- and labour-rights-based position, discarding the 'rescue and rehabilitate' position or a position of charitable sympathy, propels important claims that these workers and citizens are pushing ahead, not only for themselves but to initiate the reconfiguration of the urban imaginary as a whole. They are not damsels (or men or transgenders) in distress; they are citizens who have their own identities, their own unique rights as workers, their own contours and cartographies and their own imagination of their city. And not entirely incidentally or unconsciously, they will disrupt inequality in several spheres and layers in the process of advocating their right to exist and work in a neoliberal city.

Compatriots

The struggle to reclaim their rights ranges from concerns of health, workplace safety, violence from the police and mainstream society to even loftier missions for legitimacy of labour and existence. Sex worker unions, civil society organisations and other organisations that provide legal and medical assistance to street-based sex workers have created a strong presence of collectivisation in the sector in Bangalore. While the more significant and well-known movements and collectivisation strategies are in the sex work sectors of other cities (such as the Durbar Mahila Samanwaya Committee (DMSC) in Kolkata and Mumbai),[32] Bangalore city, too, has had its successful and ongoing strategies.

With the lacuna left by the state's general impassivity or fallacious typecasting of these workers, a whole range of civil society actors such as individuals and organisations have emerged over the last three decades, playing a significant role in empowering their rights and agency in negotiation. This support system has well-buttressed their struggles, which has emerged with a variety of actors coming on board. We can categorise them in three broad varieties: (*a*) organisations engaging in activism and intervention that are concerned specifically with the law (such as the ALF, Manthan Law or Reach Law), (*b*) civil society organisations concerned with human rights or rights of minorities (such as Sangama, SMS, Aneka, PUCL or Vimochana), and (*c*) individuals (including academics, lawyers, medical professionals and outreach workers who are either part of the aforementioned organisations or in their own capacities) and various mainstream and online media avenues. This support mechanism was not evolved overnight, but through a slow process that began with the struggle to build rapport with sex workers themselves, which was initiated by distributing pamphlets and instigating informal associations and meetings in their workspaces or other closed settings. This long saga drew from the fundamental legal and ideological basis that sex work by itself is not illegal and actually a form of informal work that is part of the labour-landscape of a city. Negotiations over the years were framed more in the form of working within the legal framework than employing combative or aggressive strategies. Improvement in legal literacy and legal guidance was the principal direction by which sex workers were trained to fight for their rights; this was along with the documentation of their struggle, a task that has been carried out meticulously under the guidance of organisations such as Sangama, the ALF and Reach Law for decades.

All these movements may not specifically target revanchist policies, but every agenda in these initiatives has attacked the spirit of revanchist urbanism and maintains as its core the reclamation of rights to the city. It was mentioned, an innumerable number of times by supporting civil society actors who we spoke to,

---

[32] See the extensive work of Prabha Kotiswaran and Nandini Gooptu on the collectivisation of sex workers in these cities.

that while sex workers certainly needed support, unlike in the past, these workers now were much more aware of their legal rights, did not need to be directly supported and certainly not rescued.

We know well that authorities such as the police have for long been using moral or normative grounds to arrest them, curtail their livelihoods and finally remove them from the mainstream city, which are for the most part arbitrary, parochial and well outside of the legal framework. Hence, negotiations on the legal front were usually intermeshed with contestations about the moral and cultural spheres around notions of sex work and the legality of their presence on the city streets. The supportive legal and civil society organisations in this regard were instrumental in facilitating open conversations on this, between the sex workers and the police. We were also told, by some of their compatriots in the legal sphere, that street-based sex workers have been even *demanding* more surveillance of public spaces to keep watch on the police for atrocity against them on the streets, turning the tables on the police.

Another effort has been in the direction of providing sensitisation programmes for male and female police personnel, members of the judiciary and other state emissaries, in formal and non-formal venues, through conversations, dialogues, theatre, writing, and so on. Modules and guidelines to deal with sex workers were documented for the police by these organisations, besides legal intervention. Also, as we have already seen in the earlier chapters, police detention and abuse were routine, partly due to the fact that there was generally no one to represent them or to negotiate with the police. Other sex workers defending them would also be detained, harassed or even arrested on various grounds. Aware of their vulnerability, supporting organisations provided capacity-building workshops and awareness programmes on guidelines on arrest and related legal formalities – including how to lodge formal complaints; how medical examinations and medical-legal certificates are to be demanded on the occasion of bodily violence by police; basic awareness on legal matters, including the question if women are detained in the police station after dusk; how the provision of *habeas corpus* is invoked; how complaints against abuse are to be brought up, demanding whether their rights were conveyed to them during arrest; and so on. On several occasions, these organisations and supportive individuals engaged in negotiations that went beyond the legal and into the blurred boundaries between the legal, moral and cultural. Another direction in which empowerment was built was by means of improving awareness among sex workers about various state departments and agencies and building rapport with them. This included familiarising with the Ministry of Women and Child Development or autonomous bodies such as the Human Rights Commission, various human rights initiatives, medical support staff, outreach workers, and so on, and also awareness about various state welfare programmes.

The slow and steady progress of such activities has started yielding fruit. During discussions with various supportive actors, it was often heard that while the rough edges of brutality still remain (even if worn out a bit), street-based sex workers in Bangalore now know 'how to take care of themselves' – a far cry from days gone by when sex workers would simply pay fines to the police or succumb to abuse and not contest their arrest or harassment. Prof. Rajendra of the PUCL even narrated how the looming blankness that they usually found themselves in the past has diminished:

They are no more in need of direct support and handholding as before.

In another conversation, Advocate BT Venkatesh of Reach Law stated:

When they get arrested now, we don't receive panic phone calls anymore, and over two decades of continuous training and awareness made them well equipped to stand up for their rights.

Two instances were quoted during the interviews with such organisations. In one recent case in 2017, when about a dozen sex workers were arrested at night, and the police threatened to call the media, sex workers did not succumb but instead questioned these arrests on the grounds of human rights, with the support of human rights activists, bringing this to media and public attention. In another instance in 2016, when there was severe physical abuse at the police station, sex workers took it up to the Karnataka High Court, which ruled in favour of the workers by ordering action against the accused police officers. In addition to these individual cases, sex workers have very successfully resisted moves to ghettoise them – echoing a trend by law enforcement all over the world – on the grounds that this was a means of spatial control over their livelihood as well as a denial of access to the city.

The establishment of formal and informal networks among these organisations and unions has been yet another direction by which empowerment is being built. These networks are among sex workers themselves at local, regional and national levels, and with the coalition of sexual minorities. The National Network of Sex Workers (NNSW) and the Karnataka Sex Workers Union (KSWU) are but two examples in this regard. While these two associations are unabashedly explicit in title and purpose – therefore offering a direct retort and confrontation to cultural and moral connotations of sex work from the state, society and media – other associations, which have been nonetheless proactive in this struggle, are more concealed and operate under the shelter of livelihood improvement organisations, community-based organisations or women's welfare organisations across the city.[33] As stated in the earlier chapter, networks among individual sex workers

---

[33] These organisations cannot be named here due to fears of hostility that they potentially face in their local regions and communities.

themselves, through digital platforms such as WhatsApp groups or disguised and camouflaged groups (or even open fora) on Facebook or other online venues, are also aplenty and have been very significant in addressing concerns at individual or local levels. At this point, we must also respect their right *not to* formalise, as much as *to* unionise or collectivise. This is driven mostly by a need for autonomy in their profession and their collective, as their cause is towards greater quality, security and dignity of work more than being listed in a formal registry of workers; the latter of which would compromise on their privacy and subject them to further moral judgement and 'reform' in their occupation. In this age of increasing demand from state and economy to conform to the tide of neoliberal capitalism (already concocted with caste), with greater digitalisation of commerce and state welfare, and with a push towards the reformulation of informal labour (towards precariatisation in the garb of formalisation), the strive of sex workers towards less formalisation seems to go pronouncedly against the grain.

We must also acknowledge the strides in justice offered by the Supreme Court of India across 2018, both in the decriminalisation of homosexuality as well as in the reinforcement of the rights of sex workers to refuse unwanted advances from any individual, thereby empowering them to seek justice against rape and assault – which the police mockingly termed 'natural' to these workers. In another development at the national level, in a move in July 2020, sex worker unions all over India collaborated to strongly protest against a study conducted under the banner of three illustrious institutions – Harvard Medical School, Massachusetts General Hospital and Yale School of Public Health – which recommended the indefinite shutting down of red-light areas to halt the transmission of COVID-19 in India. These were protested against not only because of the recommendation of indefinite closure (entirely insensitive to livelihood concerns) but also because of issues of methodology, transparency and misleading assumptions about sex work as such. The mainstream media covered this protest widely, demonstrating the power of collectivised sex workers to assert their identity and citizenship rights.

There is a locus of spaces and a menagerie of actors exclusive to street-based sex work in Bangalore city. The vertiginous transition of this metropolis, which rumbled over these spaces and cast its populace into a spell of neoliberal modernity and morality, ought to be understood through the voices of female, male and transgender street-based sex workers themselves. We need to hear more of these evocative narratives and build more granular counter-maps. The redrawing, rewriting and relooking at this libidinal city has certainly not ended with this book, and is a task that has to be iterated every few years using accounts from the eyes, feet and minds of this omnipresent workforce. Newer intersections that undergird their life and work will emerge, as will new spatial loci and agents, and undoubtedly new battles. New technological experiences will result with technological progress in the coming years, and, of course, new struggles to reclaim themselves, their rights and their city will have to be documented and analysed.

We have to rethink how we assume the easily misused term 'the public', as much as we need to rethink *who* the city is, what its layers are and as many facets as possible of the kaleidoscope of its transition process. These layers and their associated people are as much the city as anyone else. Bangalore is (and was) no Arcadia, but it is rightfully their city too, nonetheless, with all its welcoming and homely griminess. As a senior member of the KSWU declared, while agreeing to speak to us during our earliest conversations:

Take us seriously. We are humans, we are workers, we are citizens.

Appendix
More on Method

In this appendix, we elucidate further on oral histories and narrative enquiry methods used in our fieldwork and subsequent analysis.

The oral histories method has its basis in ethnography. To understand this, we borrow from Thomas Hylland Eriksen's exposition[1] on anthropological enquiry, which first prods us to understand the fundamental sociological difference between ascribed and achieved statuses in modern society. While an individual's achieved status is a function of merit and performance and may be acquired depending on the individual's access to a range of resources, one's ascribed status cannot be easily opted out of. Eriksen mentions a notion that modern societies are constituted of achieved statuses as opposed to traditional societies that are characterised mostly by ascribed statuses but argues that this may not necessarily reflect the reality about either society (if the two can even be compartmented in that manner). These ambiguities arise because there are well-rooted and substantially populated subaltern groups in modern societies that the more advantaged (or self-titled 'modern') locals may be embarrassed to present to researchers who seek narratives. The more privileged locals may direct and guide the researcher away from these subaltern groups, even if they do not harbour any animosity towards them. In fact, in our experience of seeking street-based sex workers, even those among the non-privileged Populations, such as street vendors, garbage collection workers and autorickshaw drivers, vehemently denied the existence of such people by a brushing hand gesture conveying denial. In some instances, they even chose to lie that they had never heard of these groups operating there, which we realised when sex workers, in separate conversations, reported being personally familiar to them. In situations such as these, where the subject group's very existence is denied or suppressed (let alone difficult to access), the ethnographic toolbox and the oral histories method emerge useful in extracting these sources of information by departing from expected mainstream methodological tools and going beyond what the researcher is guided and directed to by informants on the field-site. In general, too, ethnographies of such populations become important to examine the degree and operation of surveillance and exclusion.[2] Hence, this was an important basis on which we believed that the oral histories method was the ideal instrument to employ to collect narratives from street-based sex workers, as they heave a lifelong

---

[1] Eriksen (2014).
[2] Adapted from Norris (1997).

ascribed status as some of the most shamed cohorts of society, who would never be exhibited as legitimate people of the city, who would never be directed to by Citizens and Populations, and who have little access to the written word in order to claim their space in the contours of the urban imagination. The task was to understand, contextualise and reconstruct meaning from the point of view of these individuals who are routinely shoved to the 'other side' based on judgements of what is 'correct' or 'morally wanting', where the usual requirements of building trust and rapport must be extended much further, towards a goal of offering solidarity with them as well.[3]

Unstructured interviews are framed within a series of themes serving as guidelines to lead the discussion and stimulate the narrator to articulate one's experience. The themes of discussion range from basic descriptive to structural, paradigmatic, clarificatory, follow-up, comparison, contrast, and so on. A sampling of the number and type of respondents is not concerned with statistical representativeness. Respondents are usually sought out through theoretical or purposive sampling, never simple random sampling or any other sampling method that would serve quantitative methodologies. Naturally, this would mean that the number of respondents one ends up with as a 'sample' is quite limited.

Copious lengths of time are spent conversing with individuals, often repeatedly or even in groups akin to a focus-group discussion. The individuals that are sought after for oral histories usually inhabit rather bounded local environments, and they invariably know one another personally, which is usually the basis on which their social system is built and reproduced. Though their connections with specific individuals over the longer term are usually transitory in character due to modulations in power structures among themselves, their connection with these individuals is usually very robust during the short term, which is essential for survival, given their position in the social hierarchy. While the advantages of such connections are that snowball sampling becomes easier (as was our experience too), the downside is that it is next to impossible to speak to an individual who was significant in a narrator's life, say, a decade ago, as they would have now completely disappeared into the oceans of Populations or pseudo-invisibles.

While collecting their memories on a set of themes, personal stories are both corroborated and fitted alongside collective memory, political culture, shifts of power, and so on, by which an interplay is constructed between the individual longitudinal narrative and the historical trajectory of larger society. Social identity (perception of the self) is woven with agency (the circumstances of action), by which oral histories and conventionally documented archival accounts clarify, re-contextualise or even challenge one another, allowing us to triangulate and validate different (often divergent) perspectives of the same historical processes. Oral histories help us explicitly capture and lay out the stark differences between groups of varying privilege that overlap or are in close proximity in city spaces, yet who remain divorced from one another due to indifference, exclusion or protection of advantage.[4]

---

[3] Adapted from Norris (1997).
[4] Allen (1999).

This method complicates the historical narrative, broadens its width to include more voices in the larger picture and manufactures a rich and textured tapestry of social processes and intersections between personal narratives and social structures, all of which are filtered through the subjectivity of individuals.[5] Oral histories serve as potent material to provide the sociopolitical and even emotional contexts of the bigger picture, to gather a holistic understanding of the human condition.[6] It provides a more pixelated picture of the collective imaginary of the city, by weaving this imaginary using the wefts and warps of the unheard and the unseen.

We collected micro life-histories of twenty to thirty years.[7] Here, 'micro' does not imply a compromise in the quality and granularity of the narration, but only refers to a trimmed time period rather than an entire lifetime. Our collections of their narrations lasted around forty-five minutes to an hour for each worker or other actors associated with them. While there was no singular angle of enquiry in speaking to a spectrum of street-based sex workers across gender, age or caste, interesting common threads emerged when a collage of these narratives was put together. These threads, or guiding themes, included the nature of street-based sex work, everyday life on the streets and within city spaces, urban transition in Bangalore, violence and other repercussions, the police, other actors and agents and responses on the part of the street-based sex workers. Police atrocity and the status of the 'undesirable other' that these workers experience in the city was noticed as one of the reappearing themes throughout our conversations, even though the goal of the interactions with them was not exclusively about eliciting police-led aggression over and above other urban transition experiences. During our discussions with them, concerns regarding the shrinking of public spaces in the city also kept recurring since it had immediate and natural repercussions on the crumbling of operational areas of sex work in Bangalore, which, therefore, has aggravated the vulnerability of these informal workers with respect to their life and livelihood and, most importantly, their security in this city.

Collective temporality is important in narrative analysis[8] since individual and collective experiences and stories are placed on a continuum of people's lives, institutional lives and the lives of things, all across time. We probe into actions, happenings, feelings, moral dispositions, intimacies, aesthetic reactions and the existential conditions of the narrators, unearthing cultural stereotypes and attitudes that manifest in the language and tone of the narration. These may very likely be disparate and incoherent, but these subjectivities are what are actually sought. Narrations are usually in relation to an 'other', where the relationship with the 'other' is mediated and interpreted through the social locations and ascriptive identities attached to both the narrator as well as that 'other'. One has to always factor into the interpretation of these narrations how memories change and operate through time, and what aspects are focused upon and ingrained into memory at each time

---

[5] Ritchie (2003); Corrigall-Brown and Ho (2013); Porta (2014).

[6] Janesick (2014).

[7] Following Kamath (2018, 2020).

[8] We borrow from Clandinin and Connelly (2000) and Prakash (2015) in this section.

period that is narrated to the researcher. For this, it becomes critical to emphasise and record not only continuities but, importantly, the turning points or trajectory shifts in the narration as well. The shifting meaning attached to each of these vignettes of memory is probed into, along with the shifts in the roles and relations that the narrator acquires with every change of track in one's life.

At the end of the process, we collected not only the dimensions or aspects of an individual's (or cohort's) life, but also shifts of track and experience in the individual's life or in the environment around, and the strategies of adaptation by the individual (or cohort). In this process, we put spotlight on cultural shifts (in terms of new roles), social shifts (in terms of new interactions and relations) and psychosocial shifts (in terms of new self-conceptions) with each trajectory change. What we finally have is a collage of personal and social interactions, across space, and across past, present and future – therefore a metaphorical three-dimensional (interactive, spatial and temporal) narrative enquiry space. In this manner, we also departed from ethnography proper, though we did not dissociate entirely from it, by adopting its progeny – oral histories and narrative analysis (see Table A.1).

The journalistic narratives distilled from our secondary sources were followed chronologically and were appended by reports, press releases and booklets of various organisations mentioned earlier providing support to sex workers. This helped us to gain further clarity on the primary oral narratives we collected from sex workers in their different life cycles. The complementing of primary oral data with secondary archival information (instead of maintaining them separately as purely primary and purely secondary, respectively) were used together here to provide a richly textured

Table A.1 Oral histories and narrative analysis

Dimensions (Interactive and Spatial)	Shifts (Temporal)	Strategies (Retaliatory)
On the nature of life and work	On the nature of transition	On the nature of response
• Personal and social interactions	• Turning points	• Individual
• Social attitudes	• Trajectory shifts	• Collective
• Cultural stereotypes	• Paradigm shifts	• Collaborative
• Existential conditions	• Spatial aspects	• Legal
• Aesthetic reactions	• Social aspects	• Digital
• Moral dispositions	• Cultural aspects	
• Actions, feelings, happenings	• Psychosocial aspects	
• Intimacies		
• Idiosyncrasies		

Source: Authors' compilation from literature.

account of city imaginary and urban transition in its experience among these workers. As mentioned, we gained invaluable archival support from the organisation Sangama.

Certain fundamental principles of ethics were strictly followed, such as concerns of ethics and consent, rapport building with respondents, interview etiquette, thorough prior knowledge of research objective and guiding themes, and so on. While conducting conversations with street-based sex workers, special care was given to ethics around rapport building, data gathering and informant privacy. Verbal consent was sought before conducting our conversations, audio recordings were avoided, videos and photographs of individuals were taboo, and we took down handwritten notes as much as possible. No identifying information was collected, and workers were ensured anonymity throughout the study. Most of our conversations were indoors at venues and times decided by the narrators, within the sanctuaries of the civil society organisations that support them, to respect their safety and privacy.

References

Agustin, L. M. 1988. *Sex at the Margins: Migrations, Labour Markets, and the Rescue Industry*. London and New York: Zed Books.

Akrich, M. 1997. 'The De-Scription of Technical Objects'. In *Shaping Technology/ Building Society: Studies in Socio-Technical Change*, edited by W. E. Bijker and J. Law. London and Cambridge (MA): MIT Press.

ALF. 2014. *Police Violence against Sex Workers: An Interim Report*. Bangalore: Alternative Law Forum.

Allen, J. 1999. 'Worlds Within Cities'. In *City Worlds*, edited by Doreen Massey, John Allen and Steve Pike, 51–93. London and New York: Routledge and the Open University.

Amin, A., and N. Thrift. 2002. *Cities: Imagining the Urban*. Cambridge, UK, and Malden, MA: Polity Press.

Amster, R. 2003. 'Patterns of Exclusion: Sanitising Space, Criminalising Homelessness'. *Social Justice* 30, no. 1: 195–221.

Anderson, E. 1990. *Code of the Street: Decency, Violence, and Moral Life of the Inner City*. New York and London: WW Norton.

———. 2013. *Streetwise: Race, Class, and Change in an Urban Community*. Chicago: University of Chicago Press.

Anjaria, J. S., and C. McFarlane. 2011. 'Introduction: Conceptualising the City in South Asia'. In *Urban Navigations: Politics, Space, and the City in South Asia*, edited by J. S. Anjaria and C. McFarlane, 15–34. New Delhi: Routledge.

Atkinson, R. 2003. 'Domestication by Cappuccino or a Revenge on Urban Space? Control and Empowerment in the Management of Public Spaces'. *Urban Studies* 40, no. 9: 1829–1843.

Baer, H. 2016. 'Redoing Feminism: Digital Activism, Body Politics, and Neoliberalism'. *Feminist Media Studies* 16, no. 1: 17–34.

Balshaw, M., and L. Kennedy. 2000. 'Introduction'. In *Urban Space and Representation*, edited by M. Balshaw and L. Kennedy. London: Pluto Press.

Banerjee-Guha, S. 2010. *Accumulation by Dispossession: Transformative Cities in the New Global Order*. New Delhi: SAGE Publications.

Banerjee, S. 1998. *Dangerous Outcast: The Prostitute in Nineteenth-Century Bengal*. Calcutta: Seagull Books.

Belina, B. 2007. 'From Discipline to Dislocation: Area Bans in Recent Urban Policing in Germany'. *European Urban and Regional Studies* 14, no. 4: 321–336.

Bell, D., and G. Valentine. 1995. *Mapping Desires*. London: Psychology Press.

Bender, T. 2007. 'Conclusion: Reflections on the Culture of Urban Modernity'. In *Urban Imaginaries: Locating the Modern City*, edited by A. Cinar and T. Bender, 167–179. Minneapolis: University of Minnesota Press.

Benjamin, S. 2010. 'Manufacturing Neoliberalism: Lifestyling Indian Urbanity'. In *Accumulation by Dispossession: Transformative Cities in the New Global Order*, edited by S. Banerjee-Guha, 92–124. New Delhi: SAGE Publications.

Bernstein, E. 2007. *Temporarily Yours: Intimacy, Authenticity, and the Commerce of Sex*. Chicago and London: University of Chicago Press.

Binnie, J. 2000. 'Cosmopolitanism and the Sexed City'. In *City Visions*, edited by D. Bell and A. Haddour, 178–190. London and New York: Routledge.

Boris, E., S. Gilmore and R. Parrenas. 2010. 'Sexual Labours: Interdisciplinary Perspectives towards Sex as Work'. *Sexualities* 13, no. 2: 131–137.

Bose, P. S. 2015. *Urban Development in India: Global Indians in the Remaking of Kolkata*. New Delhi: Routledge.

Bosi, L., and H. Reiter. 2014. 'Historical Methodologies: Archival Research and Oral History Social Movement Research'. In *Methodological Practices in Social Movement Research*, edited by D. D. Porta. Oxford: Oxford University Press.

Brenner, N., and N. Theodore. 2002. 'Cities and Geographies of Actually Existing Neoliberalism'. *Antipode* 34, no. 3: 349–379.

Brown, W. 1992. 'Finding the Man in the State.' *Feminist Studies* 18, no. 1: 7–34.

Browne, K., J. Lim and G. Brown. 2009. *Geographies of Sexualities: Theory, Practices and Politics*. Surrey: Ashgate.

Brown, N., and S. A. Gershon. 2017. 'Body Politics'. *Politics, Groups, and Identities* 5, no. 1: 1–3.

Büdenbender, M., and D. Zupan. 2017. 'The Evolution of Neoliberal Urbanism in Moscow: 1992–2015'. *Antipode* 49, no. 2: 294–313.

Burte, H., and L. Kamath. 2017. 'Violence of Worlding: Producing Space in Neoliberal Durban, Mumbai, and Rio de Janeiro'. *Economic and Political Weekly* 52, no. 7: 66–74.

Burton, A. 1994. *Burdens of History: British Feminists, Indian Women and Imperial Culture: 1865–1915*. Chapel Hill: University of North Carolina Press.

Busza, J. 2006. 'For Love or Money: The Role of Exchange in Young People's Sexual Relationships'. In *In Promoting Young People's Sexual Health*, edited by R. Ingham and P. Aggleton, 146–164. London: Routledge.

Buzdugan, R., A. Copas, S. Moses, J. Blanchard, S. Isac, B. M. Ramesh, R. Washington, S. S. Halli and F. M. Cowan. 2010. 'Devising a Female Sex Work Typology Using Data from Karnataka, India'. *International Journal of Epidemiology* 39, no. 2: 439–448.

Campbell, S. 2008. 'Mobile Technology and the Body: Apparatgeist, Fashion, and Function'. In *Handbook of Mobile Communication Studies*, edited by J. Katz, 153–165. MIT Press.

CASSUM. 2007. 'The Bangalore Metro: For?' Collaborative for the Advancement of the Study of Urbanism through Mixed Media, Bangalore. https://casumm. wordpress.com. Accessed on 1 December 2019.

Chacko, S., S. Panchanadeswaran and G. Vijayakmar. 2016. 'Sex Work as Livelihood: Women, Men and Transgender Sex Workers in Karnataka'. In *Land, Labour and Livelihood: Indian Women's Perspectives*, edited by B. Fernandez, M. Gopal and O. Ruthven, 133–153. Cham: Palgrave Macmillan.

Chatterjee, P. 2004. *The Politics of the Governed: Reflections on Popular Politics in Most of the World*. New York: Columbia University Press.

Chaudhary, T. 2020. 'From "Spaces of Work" to "Spaces of Struggle"'. In *City, Culture, and Society* 20. https://doi.org/10.1016/j.ccs.2019.100324.

Chava, J., P. Newman and R. Tiwari. 2018. 'Gentrification of Station Areas and Its Impact on Transit Eidership'. *Case Studies on Transport Policy* 6, no. 1: 1–10.

Cinar, A., and T. Bender. 2007. 'Introduction – The City: Experience, Imagination, and Place'. In *Urban Imaginaries: Locating the Modern City*, edited by A. Cinar and T. Bender, xi–xxvi. Minneapolis: University of Minnesota Press.

Clandinin, D. J., and F. M. Connelly. 2000. *Narrative Inquiry: Experience and Story in Qualitative Research*. San Francisco: Jossey-Bass.

Clavell, G. G. 2011. 'The Political Economy of Surveillance in the (Wannabe) Global City'. *Surveillance and Society*, 8, no. 4: 523–526.

Cockburn, C., and S. Ormrod. 1993. *Gender and Technology in the Making*. London: SAGE Publications.

Cohn, B. S. 1996. *Colonialism and Its Forms of Knowledge: The British in India*. Princeton: Princeton University Press.

Coleman, R., and J. Sim. 2000. 'You'll Never Walk Alone: CCTV Surveillance, Order, and Neo-liberal Rule in Liverpool City Centre'. *British Journal of Sociology* 51, no. 4: 623–639.

Cornish, F. 2006. 'Challenging the Stigma of Sex Work in India: Material Context and Symbolic Change'. *Journal of Community and Applied Social Psychology* 16, no. 6: 462–471.

Corrigall-Brown, C., and M. Ho. 2013. 'Life History Research and Social Movements'. In *The Wiley-Blackwell Encyclopedia of Social and Political Movements*, edited by D. della Porta, D. Snow, B. Klandermans and D. McAdam. Oxford: Blackwell.

Crehan, K. 2016. *Gramsci's Common Sense: Inequality and its Narratives*. Durham: Duke University Press.

Crush, J. 1992. 'Power and Surveillance on the South African Gold Mines'. *Journal of Southern African Studies* 18, no. 4: 825–844.

Cunningham, S., and T. D. Kendall. 2011. 'Prostitution 2.0: The Changing Face of Sex Work'. *Journal of Urban Economics* 69, no. 3: 273–287.

D'Cunha, J. 1991. *The Legalisation of Prostitution: A Sociological Inquiry into the Laws Relating to Prostitution in India and the West*. Bangalore: Wordmakers.

D'Souza, and H. Nagendra. 2011. 'Changes in Public Commons as a Consequence of Urbanisation: The Agara Lake in Bangalore, India'. *Environmental Management* 47, no. 5: 840–850.

Dalla, R. L. 2000. 'Exposing the "Pretty Woman" Myth: A Qualitative Examination of the Lives of Female Streetwalking Prostitutes'. *Journal of Sex Research* 37, no. 4: 344–353.

Damodaran, A., and T. Haldar. 2016. 'Peri-Urban Villages of Bangalore, India'. In *Designing Sustainable Urban Futures*, edited by M. Albiez, G. Banse, K. Lindeman and A. Quint, 85–93. Karlsruhe: KIT Scientific Publishing.

Davidson, M. 2007. 'Gentrification as Global Habitat: A Process of Class Formation or Corporate Creation?' *Transactions of the Institute of British Geographers* 32, no. 4: 490–506.

Davis, M. 1990. *City of Quartz: Excavating the Future in Los Angeles*. London: Verso.

De Neve, G., and H. Donner. 2006. *The Meaning of the Local: Politics of Place in Urban India*. London and New York: Routledge.

Derkzen, M. L., H. Nagendra, A. J. Van Teeffelen, A. Purushotham and P. H. Verburg. 2017. 'Shifts in Ecosystem Services in Deprived Urban Areas: Understanding People's Responses and Consequences for Well-being'. *Ecology and Society* 22, no. 1: 51.

Desai, R., and R. Sanyal. 2012. 'Introduction'. In *Urbanising Citizenship: Contested Spaces in Indian Cities*, edited by R. Desai and R. Sanyal. New Delhi: SAGE Publications.

Ditmore, M. H., A. Levy and A. Willman. 2010 *Sex Work Matters: Exploring Money, Power and Intimacy in the Sex Industry*. London and New York: Zed Books.

Doshi, S. 2015. 'Rethinking Gentrification in India: Displacement, Dispossession and the Spectre of Development'. In *Global Gentrifications: Uneven Development and Displacement*, edited by L. Lees, H. B. Shin and E. López Morales, 101–120. Bristol: Policy Press.

Drèze, J., and A. Sen. 2013. *An Uncertain Glory: India and its Contradictions*. Princeton: Princeton University Press.

Duncan, N. 1996. *Body Space: Destabilising Geographies of Gender and Sexuality*. London and New York: Routledge.

ECL. 2019. *The Sacred and the Public*. Bangalore: Everyday City Lab.

Eriksen, T. H. 2014. *An Introduction to Social and Cultural Anthropology: Small Places, Large Issues*. New Delhi: Rawat.

Eubanks, V. 2007. *Digital Dead End: Fighting for Social Justice in the Information Age*. Cambridge (MA) and London: MIT Press.

Feenberg, A. 1991. *Critical Theory of Technology*. New York: Oxford University Press.

Ferguson, J., and A. Gupta. 2002. 'Spatialising States: towards an Ethnography of Neoliberal Governmentality'. *American Ethnologist* 29, no. 4: 981–1002.

Fey, M. 2017. 'Serve and Protect: Also Those at the Margins? Three Essays on Police, Prostitution, and Policy'. PhD dissertation. Graduate Institute of International and Development Studies, Geneva.

Flusty, S. 2004. *De-coca-colonization: Making the Globe from the Inside Out*. London and New York: Routledge.

Foucault, M. 1980. *Power/Knowledge: Selected Interviews and Other Writings 1972–1977*. New York: Pantheon.

Froystad, K. 2006. 'Anonymous Encounters: Class Categorisation and Social Distancing in Public Places'. In *The Meaning of the Local: Politics of Place in Urban India*, edited by G. De Neve and H. Donner, 159–182. London and New York: Routledge.

Fyfe, N. 1991. 'The Police, Space and Society: The Geography of Policing'. *Progress in Human Geography* 15, no. 3: 249–267.

Fyfe, N., and J. Bannister. 1996. 'City Watching: Closed Circuit Television Surveillance in Public Spaces.' *Area* 28, no. 1: 37–46.

Ghertner, D. A. 2014. 'India's Urban Revolution: Geographies of Displacement beyond Gentrification'. *Environment and Planning A: Economy and Space* 46, no. 7: 1554–1571.

Ghosh, S. 2005. 'Surveillance in Decolonised Social Space: The Case of Sex Workers in Bengal'. *Social Text* 2, no. 83: 55–69.

———. 2008. 'Elusive Choice and Agency: A Feminist Re-Reading of the Sex Workers' Manifesto'. In *Prostitution and Beyond: An Analysis of Sex Work in India*, edited by R. Sahni, K. Shankar and H. Apte, 54–73. New Delhi: SAGE Publications.

Goldman, M. 2008. 'Inside the "Bangalore Model" of World-city Making: Excitement, Inter-urban Accumulations, and Large-scale Dispossession'. Paper presented at the Social Science Research Council Conference on Inter-Asian Connections, Dubai.

———. 2010. 'Speculative Urbanism and the Making of the Next World City'. *International Journal of Urban and Regional Research* 35, no. 3: 555–581.

Gooptu, N. 2000. 'Sex Workers in Calcutta, and the Dynamics of Collective Action'. UNU-WIDER Working Paper 185, United Nations University World Institute for Development Economics Research, Helsinki.

———. 2002. 'Sex Workers in Calcutta and the Dynamics of Collective Action: Political Activism, Community Identity, and Group Behaviour'. In *Group Behaviour and Development: Is the Market Destroying Cooperation?*, edited by J. Heyer, F. Stewart and R. Thorp, 227–253. Oxford: Oxford University Press.

Gooptu, N., and N. Bandyopadhyay. 2007. 'Rights to Stop the Wrong: Cultural Change and Collective Mobilisation, the Case of Kolkata Sex Workers'. *Oxford Development Studies* 35, no. 3: 251–272.

Gothoskar, S., and A. Kaiwar. 2014. 'Who Says We Do Not Work? Looking at Sex Work'. *Economic and Political Weekly* 44, no. 46: 54–61.

Grosz, E. 1994. *Volatile Bodies: Toward a Corporeal Feminism*. London: Routledge.

Gupta, D. 2000. *Culture, Space, and the Nation State: From Sentiment to Structure*. New Delhi: SAGE Publications.

Hackworth, J. 2011. *The Neoliberal City*. Ithaca and London: Cornell University Press.

Harcourt, C., and B. Donovan. 2005. 'The Many Faces of Sex Work'. *Sexually Transmitted Infections* 81, no. 3: 201–206.

Harcourt, W. 2009. *Body Politics in Development*. London and New York: Zed Books.

Harvey, D. 1973. *Social Justice and the City*. Oxford: Basil Blackwell.

———. 1989. 'From Managerialism to Entrepreneurialism: The Transformation in Urban Governance in Late Capitalism'. *Geografiska Annaler* 71, no. 1: 3–17.

———. 2003. 'The Right to the City'. *International Journal of Urban and Regional Research* 27, no. 4: 939–941.

Heitzman, J. 2004. *Network City: Planning the Information Society in Bangalore*. New Delhi: Oxford University Press.

Herbert, S. 1996. 'The Geopolitics of the Police: Foucault, Disciplinary Power and the Tactics of the Los Angeles Police Department'. *Political Geography* 15, no. 1: 47–59.

Hoang, K. K. 2011. 'She's Not a Low Class Dirty Girl!: Sex Work in Ho Chi Minh City, Vietnam'. *Journal of Contemporary Ethnography* 40, no. 4: 367–396.

———. 2015. *Dealing in Desire*. Berkeley and Los Angeles: University of California Press.

Holst, T. 2015. 'Touring the Demolished Slum? Slum Tourism in the Face of Delhi's Gentrification'. *Tourism Review International* 18, no. 4: 283–294.

Hubbard, P. 1998. 'Community Action and the Displacement of Street Prostitution: Evidence from British Cities'. *Geoforum* 29, no. 3: 269–286.

———. 1999. *Sex and the City: Geographies of Prostitution in the Urban West*. Oxon and New York: Ashgate.

———. 2001. 'Sex Zones: Intimacy, Citizenship, and Public Space'. *Sexuality* 4, no. 1: 51–71.

———. 2004a. 'Revenge and Injustice in the Neoliberal City: Uncovering Masculinist Agendas'. *Antipode* 36, no. 4: 665–686.

———. 2004b. 'Cleansing the Metropolis: Sex Work and the Politics of Zero Tolerance'. *Urban Studies* 41, no. 9: 1687–1702.

Hudalah, D., and N. Adharina. 2019. 'Toward a Global View on Suburban Gentrification: From Redevelopment to Development'. *Indonesian Journal of Geography* 51, no. 1: 97–105.

Idiculla, M. 2020. 'A Right to the Indian City? Legal and Political Claims over Housing and Urban Space in India'. *Socio-Legal Review* 16: 1.

Jacobs, J. 1964. *The Death and Life of Great American Cities: The Failure of Town Planning*. Harmondsworth: Penguin.

Jameela, N. 2007. *The Autobiography of a Sex Worker*, translated by J. Devika. New Delhi: Westland.

Janesick, V. J. 2014. 'Oral History Interviewing: Issues and Possibilities'. In *The Oxford Handbook of Qualitative Research*, edited by P. Leavy, 300–315. Oxford and New York: Oxford University Press.

Jeffreys, E., A. Autonomy, J. Green and C. Vega. 2011. 'Listen to Sex Workers: Support Decriminalisation Anti-Discrimination Protection'. *Interface* 3, no. 2: 271–287.

Jeffreys, S. 2009. 'Prostitution, Trafficking, and Feminism: An Update on the Debate.' *Women's Studies International Forum* 32, no. 4: 316–320.

Johnsen, S., and S. Fitzpatrick. 2010. 'Revanchist Sanitization or Coercive Care? The Use of Enforcement to Combat Begging, Street Drinking and Rough Sleeping in England'. *Urban Studies* 47, no. 8: 1703–1723.

Jolin, A. 1994. 'On the Backs of Working Prostitutes: Feminist Theory and Prostitution Policy'. *Crime and Delinquency* 40, no. 1: 69–83.

Kaliyanda, K. M. 2016. 'Gendered Cityscape: Neoliberal Urban Restructuring and the Everyday Lives of Street Based Workers in Bangalore, India'. Master's dissertation. Department of Gender Studies, Central European University, Budapest.

Kamath, A. 2020. *The Social Context of Technological Experiences: Three Studies from India*. London and New York: Routledge.

———. 2018. '"Untouchable" Cell Phones? Old Class Exclusions and New Digital Divides in Peri-urban Bangalore'. *Critical Asian Studies* 50, no. 3: 375–394.

Kamath, A., and Neethi, P. 2021b. 'Disappearing Spaces and Betraying Allies: Urban Transition and Street-Based Sex Workers in Bangalore'. *Globalizations*. DOI: 10.1080/14747731.2021.1984796.

Kamath, A., and Neethi, P. 2021a. 'Body Politics and the Politics of Technology: Technological Experiences among Street-Based Sex Workers in Bangalore'. *Gender, Technology, and Development* 25, no. 3: 294–310.

Kapur, R. 2005. *Erotic Justice Law and the New Politics of Postcolonialism*. London: Routledge.

Katz, J. E., and M. A. Aakhus. 2002. *Perpetual Contact: Mobile Communication, Private Talk, Public Performance*. Cambridge, UK: Cambridge University Press.

Kaur, R. 2020. *Brand New Nation: Capitalist Dreams and Nationalist Designs in Twenty-First Century India*. Stanford: Stanford University Press.

Kelly, P. 2008. *Lydia's Open Door: Inside Mexico's Most Modern Brothel*. Berkeley, Los Angeles, and London: University of California Press.

Kempadoo, K. 1999. 'Slavery or Work? Reconceptualising Third World Prostitution'. *Positions* 7, no. 1: 225–237.

Kerkin, K. 2003. 'Re-placing Difference: Planning and Street Sex Work in a Gentrifying Area'. *Urban Policy and Research* 21, no. 2: 137–149.

Kern, L. 2020. *Feminist City: Claiming Space in a Man-Made World*. Toronto: Verso.

Keswani, K. 2019. 'The Logic of Design: Its Role in Understanding the Antecedents of Urban Informality'. *Journal of Urban Design* 24, no. 4: 656–675.

Keswani, K., and S. Bhagavatula. 2015. 'Territoriality in Urban Space: The Case of a Periodic Marketplace in Bangalore'. In *Informal Urban Street Markets: International Perspectives*, edited by C. Evers and K. Seale, 136–149. London and New York: Routledge.

———. 2020. 'The Ordinary City and the Extraordinary City: The Challenges of Planning for the Everyday'. Working paper 15. Azim Premji University, Bangalore.

Kiesler, S., D. Gant and P. Hinds. 1994. 'The Allure of the Wireless, Technical Report TR 1994-2'. Information Networking Institute, Carnegie Mellon University, Pittsburg, Pennsylvania.

Kinnell, H. 2002. 'Why Feminists Should Rethink on Sex Workers' Rights.' UK Network of Sex Work Projects, Edinburgh, UK.

Kissil, K., and M. Davey. 2010 'The Prostitution Debate in Feminism: Current Trends, Policy and Clinical Issues Facing an Invisible Population'. *Journal of Feminist Family Therapy* 22, no. 1: 1–21.

Klauser, F. R. 2007. 'Difficulties in Revitalising Public Space by CCTV: Street Prostitution Surveillance in the Swiss City of Olten'. *European Urban and Regional Studies* 14, no. 4: 337–348.

Kong, T. S. 2006. 'What It Feels Like for a Whore: The Body Politics of Women Performing Erotic Labour in Hong Kong'. *Gender, Work and Organization* 13, no. 5: 409–434.

Kotiswaran, P. 2008. 'Born unto Brothels: Toward a Legal Ethnography of Sex Work in an Indian Red-Light Area'. *Law and Social Inquiry* 33, no. 3: 579–629.

———. 2011. *Sex Work*. New Delhi: Women Unlimited.

———. 2012. *Dangerous Sex, Invisible Labour: Sex Work and the Law in India*. New Delhi: Oxford University Press.

———. 2019. 'Has the Dial Moved on the Indian Sex Worker Debate?' *Economic and Political Weekly* 56, no. 22: 10–12.

Kovacs, A. 2020. 'When Our Bodies Become Data, Where Does That Leave Us?' Medium, 28 May. https://deepdives.in/when-our-bodies-become-data-where-does-that-leave-us-906674f6a969. Accessed on 21 July 2020.

Kunkel, J. 2016. 'Gentrification and the Flexibilization of Spatial Control: Policing Sex Work in Germany'. *Urban Studies* 54, no. 3: 730–746.

Lasen, A. 2004. 'Affective Technologies: Emotion and Mobile Phones'. Receiver, Digital World Research Centre, Surrey, UK. https://www.academia.edu/472410/Affective_Technologies_Emotions_and_Mobile_Phones. Accessed on 14 November 2019.

Law, L. 2000. *Sex Work in Southeast Asia: The Place of Desire in a Time of AIDS*. London: Routledge.

Lefebvre, H. 1991 [1974]. *The Production of Space*, translated by D. Nicholson-Smith. Oxford: Blackwell.

———. 1996. *Writings on Cities*. Cambridge (MA): Blackwell.

———. 2003 [1970]. *The Urban Revolution*, translated by R. Bononno. Minneapolis: University of Minnesota Press.

Leitner, H., E. Sheppard, K. Sziarto and A. Maringanti. 2007. 'Contesting Urban Futures: Decentering Neoliberalism'. In *Contesting Neoliberalism: Urban Frontiers*, edited by H. Leitner, J. Peck and E. Sheppard, 1–26. New York: Guildford Press.

Lerum, K. 1998. 'Twelve-step Feminism Makes Sex Workers Sick: How the State and the Recovery Movement Turn Radical Women into "Useless Citizens"'. *Sexuality and Culture* 2: 7–36.

Lipsky, M. 1969. *Street-level Bureaucracy: Dilemmas of the Individual in Public Service*. New York: Russell Sage Foundation.

Lorway, R., S. Reza-Paul and A. Pasha. 2009. 'On Becoming a Male Sex Worker in Mysore: Sexual Subjectivity, "Empowerment", and Community Based HIV Prevention Research'. *Medical Anthropology Quarterly* 23, no. 2: 142–160.

Lowthers, M. 2015. 'Sexual-Economic Entanglement: A Feminist Ethnography of Migrant Sex Work Spaces in Kenya'. PhD thesis. Electronic Thesis and Dissertation Repository 3423, University of Western Ontario, Canada.

Lupton, D. 2015. *Digital Sociology*. London and New York: Routledge.

Lyon, D. 2009. *Identifying Citizens: ID Cards as Surveillance*. Cambridge: Polity Press.

Macki, P., R. Bromley and A. Brown. 2014. 'Informal Traders and the Battlegrounds of Revanchism in Cusco, Peru'. *International Journal of Urban and Regional Research* 38, no. 5: 1884–1903.

MacLeod, G. 2002. 'From Urban Entrepreneurialism to a Revanchist City? On the Spatial Injustices of Glasgow's Renaissance'. *Antipode* 34, no. 3: 602–624.

MacPhail, C., J. Scott and V. Minichiello. 2015. 'Technology, Normalisation, and Male Sex Work'. *Culture, Health, and Sexuality* 17, no. 4: 483–495.

Maddocks, S. 2018. 'From Non-consensual Pornography to Image-based Sexual Abuse: Charting the Course of a Problem with Many Names'. *Australian Feminist Studies* 33, no. 97: 345–361.

Mandelbaum, D. G. 1973. 'The Study of Life History: Gandhi'. *Current Anthropology* 14, no. 3: 177–206.

Marcuse, P. 2009. 'From Critical Urban Theory to the Right to the City'. *City* 13, no. 2–3: 185–197.

Martin, N. K. 2007. 'Porn Empowerment: Negotiating Sex Work and Third Wave Feminism'. *Atlantis* 31, no. 2: 31–41.

Massey, D. 2011. 'Landscape/Space/Politics: An Essay'. Future of Landscape. https://www.thefutureoflandscape.wordpress.com/landscapespacepolitics-anessay. Accessed on 8 May 2018.

Massey, D., J. Allen and S. Pile. 1999. *City Worlds*. London and New York: Routledge.

McDowell, L. 1995. 'Body Work: Heterosexual Gender Performances in City Workplaces'. In *Mapping Desires*, edited by D. Bell and G. Valentine, 67–88. London: Psychology Press.

McGuigan, J. 2005. 'Towards a Sociology of the Mobile Phone'. *Human Technology* 1, no. 1: 45–57.

McQuiller Williams, L. 2014. 'Sex in the City: Why and How Street Workers Select Their Locations for Business'. *Journal of Contemporary Ethnography* 43, no. 6: 659–694.

Mehta, P. B. 2020. 'Beyond Solidarity: The Migrant Labour and the Unemployed Will Be Demanding Their Rights, Not Our Mercy'. *New Indian Express*, Opinion, 18 April.

Mitchell, D. 1997. 'The Annihilation of Space by Law: The Roots and Implications of Anti-Homeless Laws in the United States'. *Antipode* 29, no. 3: 303–335.

———. 2003. *The Right to the City: Social Justice and the Fight for Public Space*. New York and London: Guildford Press.

Mohan, S. 2017. 'Politics of Urban Space: Rethinking Urban Inclusion and the Right to the City'. In *Women, Urbanization, and Sustainability*, edited by A. Lacey, 157–177. London: Palgrave Macmillan.

Mokkil, N. 2013. 'Remembering the Prostitute: Unsettling Imaginations of Sexuality'. *Tapasam* 7, nos. 1–4: 113.

Monahan, T. 2008. 'Editorial: Surveillance and Inequality'. *Surveillance and Society* 5, no. 3: 217–226.

Monroe, J. 2005. 'Women in Street Prostitution: The Result of Poverty and Brunt of Inequity'. *Journal of Poverty* 9, no. 3, 69–88.

Mundoli, S., B. Manjunatha and H. Nagendra. 2017. 'Commons that Provide: The Importance of Bengaluru's Wooded Groves for Urban Resilience'. *International Journal of Urban Sustainable Development* 9, no. 2: 184–206.

Murphy, A. K., and S. A. Venkatesh. 2006. 'Vice Careers: The Changing Contours of Sex Work in New York City'. *Qualitative Sociology* 9, no. 2: 129–154.

Murray, S. B. 2003. 'A Spy, a Shill, a Go-2Between, or a Sociology: Unveiling the "Observer" in Participant Observer'. *Qualitative Research* 3, no. 3: 377–395.

Nagendra, H. 2016. *Nature in the City*. New Delhi: Oxford University Press.

Nagendra, H., and D. Gopal. 2010. 'Street Trees in Bangalore: Density, Diversity, Composition and Distribution'. *Urban Forestry and Urban Greening* 9, no. 2: 129–137.

Nair, J. 2005. *The Promise of the Metropolis: Bangalore's Twentieth Century*. New Delhi: Oxford University Press.

————. 2012. 'In Other Words: The Indian City and the Promise of Citizenship'. In *Urbanising Citizenship: Contested Spaces in Indian Cities*, edited by R. Desai and R. Sanyal. New Delhi: SAGE Publications.

Natrajan, B. 2012. *The Culturisation of Caste in India*. London: Routledge.

Navani-Vazirani, S., D. Solomon, Gopalakrishnan, E. Heylen, A. K. Srikrishnan, C. K. Vasudevan and M. L. Ekstrand. 2015. 'Mobile Phones and Sex Work in South India: The Emerging Role of Mobile Phones in Condom Use by Female Sex Workers in Two Indian States'. *Culture, Health, and Sexuality* 17, no. 2: 252–265.

Nayar, P. 2015. *Citizenship and Identity in the Age of Surveillance*. New Delhi: Cambridge University Press.

Neethi, P. 2016. *Globalization Lived Locally: A Labour Geography Perspective*. New Delhi: Oxford University Press.

————. 2020. 'New Revanchism and the Urban Undesirables: Street-Based Sex Workers of Bangalore'. *City* 24, 5–6: 759–777.

Norris, C. 1997. *Surveillance, Order and Social Control*. Hull, UK: Economic and Social Research Council.

Nussbaum, M. C. 2010. 'Objectification and Internet Misogyny'. In *The Offensive Internet: Speech, Privacy, and Reputation*, edited by S. Levmore and M. Nussbaum, 68–91. Cambridge, MA: Harvard University Press.

Oksman, V., and P. Rautiainen. 2003. 'Perhaps It Is a Body Part: How the Mobile Phone Became an Organic Part of the Everyday Lives of Finnish Children and Teenagers'. In *Machines That Become Us: The Social Context of Personal Communication Technology*, edited by J. Katz, 293–311. London and New York: Routledge.

Oudshoorn, N., and T. Pinch. 2003. 'Introduction: How Users and Non-Users Matter'. In *How Users Matter*, edited by N. Oudshoorn and T. Pinch, 1–29. Cambridge, MA: MIT Press.

Overall, C. 1992. 'What's Wrong with Prostitution? Evaluating Sex Work' *Signs* 17, no. 4: 705–724.

Pai, A., M. S. Seshu and L. Murthy. 2018. 'In Its Haste to Rescue Sex Workers, "Anti-Trafficking" Is Increasing Their Vulnerability'. *Economic and Political Weekly* 53, no. 28. https://www.epw.in/engage/article/raid-and-rescue-how-anti-trafficking-strategies-increase-sex-workers-vulnerability-to-exploitative-practices. Accessed on 1 April 2022.

Panchanadeswaran, S., A. M. Unnithan, S. Chacko, M. Brazda, N. B. Wilson and S. Kuruppu. 2019. 'Female Sex Workers' Use of Mobile Phones in India: Lessons in Effective Engagement'. *Human Technology* 15, no. 1: 79–99.

Peck, J., and A. Tickell. 2002. 'Neoliberalising Space'. *Antipode* 34, no. 3: 380–404.

Pheterson, G. 1996. *The Prostitution Prism*. Amsterdam: Amsterdam University Press.

Pitman, B. 2002. 'Re-mediating the Spaces of Reality Television: America's Most Wanted and the Case of Vancouver's Missing Women'. *Environment and Planning A* 34, no. 1: 167–184.

Porta, D. D. 2014. 'Life Histories'. In *Methodological Practices in Social Movement Research*, edited by D. D. Porta, 262–289. Oxford: Oxford University Press.

Powell, A., and N. Henry. 2017. *Sexual Violence in a Digital Age*, London: Palgrave Macmillan.

Prakash, A. 2015. *Dalit Capital: State, Markets and Civil Society in Urban India*. New Delhi: Routledge.

Prasad-Aleyamma, M. 2018. 'Cards and Carriers: Migration, Identification and Surveillance in Kerala, South India'. *Contemporary South Asia* 26, no. 2: 191–205.

Prins, G. 2001. 'Oral History'. In *New Perspectives on Historical Writing*, edited by P. Burke, 120–157. Cambridge: Pennsylvania State University Press.

Purcell, M. 2002. 'Excavating Lefebvre: The Right to the City and Its Urban Politics of the Inhabitant'. *Geojournal* 58, no. 2: 99–108.

———. 2013. 'Possible Worlds: Henri Lefebvre and the Right to the City'. *Journal of Urban Affairs* 36, no. 1: 141–154.

Rajan, R. S. 2003. *The Scandal of the State: Women, Law, and Citizenship in Postcolonial India*. Durham and London: Duke University Press.

Ranganathan, M. 2011. 'The Embeddedness of Cost Recovery: Water Reforms and Associationism at Bangalore's Fringes'. In *Urban Navigations: Politics, Space, and the City in South Asia*, edited by J. S. Anjaria and C. McFarlane, 165–191. New Delhi: Routledge.

Rao, U. 2016. 'Urban Negotiations and Small-Scale Gentrification in a Delhi Resettlement Colony'. In *Space, Planning, and Everyday Contestations in Delhi*, edited by S. Chakravarty and R. Negi, 77–89. New Delhi: Springer.

Richter, M. 2012. 'Sex Work as a Test Case for African Feminism'. *Buwa! Sex and Health* 2, no. 1: 62–70.

Rishbeth, C., and B. Rogaly. 2018. 'Sitting Outside: Conviviality, Self-care and the Design of Benches in Urban Public Space'. *Transactions of the Institute of British Geographers* 43, no. 2: 284–298.

Ritchie, D. A. 2003. *Doing Oral History: A Practical Guide*, 2nd Edition. New York: Oxford University Press.

Robotham, D. 2005. *Culture, Society, and Economy*. London: SAGE Publications.

Rogaly, B. 2016. 'Contesting Neoliberal Common Sense: Bottom-up History and the Struggle over Urban Space'. In *Re:development: Voices, Cyanotypes and Writings from the Green Backyard*, edited by J. Brennan, 51–54. London: Silent Grid.

Roy, A. 2009. 'Why India Cannot Plan Its Cities: Informality, Insurgence and the Idiom of Urbanization'. *Planning Theory* 8, no. 1: 76–87.

Ruti, M. 2016. *Feminist Film Theory and Pretty Woman*. New York: Bloomsbury Academic.

Ryan, P. 2016. 'Follow: Exploring the Role of Social Media in the Online Construction of Male Sex Worker Lives in Dublin, Ireland'. *Gender, Place, and Culture* 23, no. 12: 1713–1724.

———. 2019. *Male Sex Work in the Digital Age: Curating Lives*. London: Palgrave Macmillan.

Sahni, R., and V. K. Shankar. 2008. 'Market, Histories, and Grassroots Evidence: Economics of Sex Work in India'. In *Prostitution and Beyond: An Analysis of Sex Work in India*, edited by R. Sahni, K. Shankar and H. Apte, 169–195. New Delhi: SAGE Publications.

Sambasivan, N., J. S. Weber and E. Cutrell. 2011. 'Designing a Phone Broadcasting System for Urban Sex Workers in India'. *Proceedings of the SIGCHI Conference on Human Factors in Computing Systems,* May 2011, Vancouver, Canada.

Sanath, G. S. 2018. 'Everyday Life versus "World-class" Aspirations: The Re-Imagined Roads of Bangalore City'. South Asia @LSE Blog, 19 June. http://eprints.lse.ac.uk/id/eprint/90671. Accessed on 1 October 2019.

Sanders, T. 2004. 'The Risk of Street Prostitution: Punters, Police, and Protester'. *Urban Studies* 41, no. 1: 1703–1717.

Sariola, S. 2010. *Gender and Sexuality in India: Selling Sex in Chennai*. London and New York: Routledge.

Sassen, S. 2002. 'Global Cities and Survival Circuits'. In *Global Woman: Nannies, Maids, and Sex Workers in the New Economy*, edited by B. Ehrenreich and A. R. Hochschild, 254–275. New York: Henry Holt and Co.

Schultz, V. 2006. 'Sex and Work'. *Yale Journal of Law and Feminism* 18, no. 1: 223–234.

Scoular, J. 2004. 'The "Subject" of Prostitution: Interpreting the Discursive, Symbolic, and Material Position of Sex/Work in Feminist Theory'. *Feminist Theory* 5, no. 3: 343–355.

Shade, L. 2011. 'Review of Digital Dead End: Fighting for Social Justice in the Information Age by Virginia Eubanks'. *Journal of Information Policy* 1: 182–184.

Shah, S. P. 2014. *Street Corner Secrets: Sex Work and Migration in the City of Mumbai*. Durham and London: Duke University Press.

Shapiro, S. 2000. '"Whose Fucking Park? Our Fucking Park!": Bohemian Brumaires (Paris 1848/East Village 1988), Gentrification, and the Representation of Aids'. In *Urban Space and Representation*, edited by M. Balshaw and L. Kennedy, 146–161. London: Pluto Press.

Short, J. R. 2014. *Urban Theory: A Critical Assessment*. London: Palgrave.

Shourie, S., and E. Fernandes. 2017. 'Mobile Phone Solicitations and HIV Risk among Sex Workers in India'. *MRIMS Journal of Health Sciences* 5, no. 4: 157–158.

Simmons, M. 1998. 'Theorizing Prostitution: The Question of Agency'. *Sexuality and Culture* 2: 125–148.

Simone, A. M. 2004. 'People as Infrastructure: Intersecting Fragments in Johannesburg'. *Public Culture* 16, no. 3: 407–429.

Smith, N. 1996. *The New Urban Frontier: Gentrification and the Revanchist City*. New York: Routledge.

———. 2002. 'New Globalism, New Urbanism: Gentrification as Global Urban Strategy'. *Antipode* 34, no. 3: 427–450.

SMS. 2013. *Violence against People in Sex Work in India*. Submitted to the Special Rapporteur on Violence Against Women, Sadhana Mahila Sangha, Bangalore.

Snyder-Hall, R. C. 2010. 'Third Wave Feminism and the Defence of "Choice"'. *Perspectives on Politics* 8, no. 1: 255–261.

Sparke, M. 1996. 'Displacing the Field in Fieldwork: Masculinity, Metaphor, and Space'. In *Body Space: Destabilising Geographies of Gender and Sexuality*, edited by N. Duncan, 212–233. London and New York: Routledge.

Srinivas, L. 2002. 'The Active Audience: Spectatorship, Social Relations, and the Experience of Cinema in India'. *Media, Culture, and Society* 24, no. 2: 155–173.

———. 2005. 'Imaging the Audience'. *South Asian Popular Culture* 3, no. 2: 101–116.

———. 2010a. 'Cinema Halls, Locality, and Urban Life'. *Ethnography* 11, no. 1: 189–205.

———. 2010b. 'Ladies Queues, "Roadside Romeos," and Balcony Seating: Ethnographic Observations on Women's Cinema-going Experiences'. *South Asian Popular Culture* 8, no. 3: 391–307.

Srinivas, S. 2001. *Landscapes Of Urban Memory: The Sacred and the Civic in India's High-Tech City*. Hyderabad: Orient Longman.

Stark, L. 2013. 'Transactional Sex and Mobile Phones in a Tanzanian Slum'. *Suomen Antropologie: Journal of the Finnish Anthropological Society* 38, no. 1: 12–36.

Suryawanshi, D., T. Bhatnagar, S. Deshpande, W. Zhou, P. Singh and M. Collumbien. 2013. 'Diversity among Clients of Female Sex Workers in India: Comparing Risk Profiles and Intervention Impact by Site of Solicitation. Implications for the Vulnerability of Less Visible Female Sex Workers'. *PLoS One* 8, no. 9: e73470.

Sutherland, K. 2004. 'Work, Sex, and Sex-Work: Competing Feminist Discourses on the International Sex Trade'. *Osgood Hall Law Journal* 42, no. 1: 139–167.

Svenonius, O. 2018. 'The Body Politics of the Urban Age: Reflections on Surveillance and Affect'. *Palgrave Communications* 4, no. 1: 1–10.

Swanson, K. 2007. 'The Regulation of Indigenous Beggars and Street Vendors in Ecuador'. *Antipode* 39, no. 4: 708–728.

Tambe, A. 2008. 'Different Issues/Different Voices: Organisation of Women in Prostitution in India'. In *Prostitution and Beyond: An Analysis of Sex Work in India*, edited by R. Sahni, K. Shankar and H. Apte, 73–101. New Delhi: SAGE Publications.

Tani, S. 2002. 'Whose Place Is This Space? Life in the Street Prostitution Area of Helsinki, Finland'. *International Journal of Urban and Regional Research* 26, no. 2: 343–359.

Tonkiss, F. 2005. *Space, the City, and Social Theory: Social Relations and Urban Forms*. Cambridge, UK: Polity Press.

Townsend, A. M. 2000. 'Life in the Realtime City: Mobile Telephones and Urban Metabolism'. *Journal of Urban Technology* 7, no. 2: 85–104.

———. 2012. 'Mobile Communications in the Twenty-First Century City'. In *Wireless World: Social and Interactional Aspects of the Mobile Age*, edited by B. Brown, N. Green and R. Harper, 62–79. Berlin and Heidelberg: Springer Science and Business Media.

Tripathi, P., and C. Das. 2020. 'Social Distancing and Sex Work in India'. *Economic and Political Weekly* 55, no. 31 (1 August): 21–23.

Upadhya, C. 2007. 'Employment, Exclusion, and Merit in the Indian IT Industry'. *Economic and Political Weekly*, 42, no. 20: 1863–1868.

Upadhya, C., and A. R. Vasavi. 2006. 'Work, Culture, and Sociality in the Indian IT Industry: A Sociological Study'. Report submitted to the Indo-Dutch Programme for Alternatives in Development. National Institute of Advanced Study (NIAS), Bangalore.

Vanka, S. P. 2014. 'Public Space and Life in an Indian City'. PhD thesis. University of Michigan.

Vijayakumar, G., S. Chacko and S. Panchanadeswaran. 2015. 'As Human Beings and as Workers: Sex Worker Unionisation in Karnataka, India'. *Global Labour Journal* 6, no. 1: 79–96.

Voicu, I. 2018. 'Book Review of "Feminist Film Theory and Pretty Woman" by Mari Ruti'. *Close Up: Film and Media Studies* 2, no. 1: 101–103.

Wacquant, L. 1996. 'The Rise of Advanced Marginality: Notes on its Nature and Implications'. *Acta Sociologica* 39, no. 2: 121–139.

———. 1999. 'Urban Marginality in the Coming Millennium'. *Urban Studies* 36, no. 10: 1639–1647.

———. 2008. *Urban Outcasts: A Comparative Sociology of Advanced Marginality*. Cambridge, UK: Polity Press.

Wahab, S. 2006. 'Evaluating the Usefulness of a Prostitution Diversion Project'. *Qualitative Social Work* 5, no. 1: 67–92.

Wajcman, J. 2004. *Techno Feminism*. Cambridge: Polity Press.

————. 2007. 'From Women and Technology to Gendered Technoscience'. *Information, Community, and Society* 10, no. 3: 287–298.

Walkowitz, J. R. 1980. *Prostitution and Victorian Society: Women, Class, and the State.* Cambridge, UK: Cambridge University Press.

Walks, R. A. 2006. 'Aestheticization and the Cultural Contradictions of Neoliberal (Sub)urbanism'. *Cultural Geographies* 13, no. 3: 466–475.

Waylen, G., K. Celis, J. Kantola and S. L. Weldon. 2013. *The Oxford Handbook of Gender and Politics.* Oxford and New York: Oxford University Press.

Weatherall, A., and A. Priestly. 2001. 'A Feminist Discourse Analysis of "Sex Work"'. *Feminism and Psychology* 11, no. 3: 323–340.

Weber, R. 2002. 'Extracting Value from the City: Neoliberalism and Urban Redevelopment'. *Antipode* 34, no. 3: 519–540.

Weitzer, R. 2009. 'Sociology of Sex Work'. *Annual Review of Sociology* 35: 213–234.

————. 2010. 'The Ethnography of Prostitution: New International Perspectives'. *Current Sociology* 39, no. 3: 262–269.

Whitehead, J., and N. More. 2007. 'Revanchism in Mumbai? Political Economy of Rent Gaps and Urban Restructuring in a Global City'. *Economic and Political Weekly* 42, no. 25: 2428–2434.

WHO. 1988. *STD Control in Prostitution: Guidelines for Policy.* Geneva: World Health Organisation.

Williams, E. L. 2014. 'Sex Work and Exclusion in the Tourist Districts of Salvador, Brazil'. *Gender, Place and Culture* 21, no. 4, 453–470.

Yang, Q., and M. Zhou. 2018. 'Interpreting Gentrification in Chengdu in the Post-Socialist Transition of China: A Socio-Cultural Perspective'. *Geoforum* 93: 120–132.

Zatz, N. D. 1997. 'Sex Work/Sex Act: Law, Labor, and Desire in Constructions of Prostitution'. *Signs: Journal of Women in Culture and Society* 22, no. 2: 277–308.

Zerah, M. H., S. T. Lama-Rewal, V. Dupont and B. Chaudhuri. 2011. 'Introduction: Right to the City and Urban Citizenship in the Indian Context'. In *Urban Policies and the Right to the City in India,* edited by M. H. Zerah, S. T. Lama-Rewal, V. Dupont and M. Faetanini, 1–12. New Delhi: Social and Human Sciences Sector, UNESCO.

Index